WARRING GENEALOGIES

In the series *Critical Race, Indigeneity, and Relationality*,
edited by Antonio T. Tiongson Jr., Danika Medak-Saltzman,
Iyko Day, and Shanté Paradigm Smalls

ALSO IN THIS SERIES:

Maryam S. Griffin, *Vehicles of Decolonization: Public Transit
in the Palestinian West Bank*

Erin Suzuki, *Ocean Passages: Navigating Pacific Islander
and Asian American Literatures*

Quynh Nhu Le, *Unsettled Solidarities: Asian and Indigenous
Cross-Representations in the Américas*

WARRING GENEALOGIES

Race, Kinship, and the Korean War

Joo Ok Kim

TEMPLE UNIVERSITY PRESS
Philadelphia • *Rome* • *Tokyo*

TEMPLE UNIVERSITY PRESS
Philadelphia, Pennsylvania 19122
tupress.temple.edu

Library of Congress Cataloging-in-Publication Data

Names: Kim, Joo Ok, 1982– author.
Title: Warring genealogies : race, kinship, and the Korean War / Joo Ok
Kim.
Other titles: Critical race, indigeneity, and relationality.
Description: Philadelphia : Temple University Press, 2022. | Series:
Critical race, indigeneity, and relationality | Includes bibliographical
references and index. | Summary: "Warring Genealogies examines the
racial legacies of the Korean War through Chicano/a cultural production
and U.S. archives of white supremacy"—Provided by publisher.
Identifiers: LCCN 2021059259 (print) | LCCN 2021059260 (ebook) | ISBN
9781439920572 (cloth) | ISBN 9781439920589 (paperback) | ISBN
9781439920596 (pdf)
Subjects: LCSH: Mexican Americans—Social conditions—20th century. |
Korean War, 1950–1953—Social aspects—United States. | Korean War,
1950–1953—Participation, Mexican American. | Discrimination in the
military—United States—History—20th century. | Literature and
transnationalism—United States. | White nationalism—United States.
Classification: LCC E184.M5 K53 2022 (print) | LCC E184.M5 (ebook) | DDC
951.904/21—dc23/eng/20220324
LC record available at https://lccn.loc.gov/2021059259
LC ebook record available at https://lccn.loc.gov/2021059260

Printed in the United States of America

9 8 7 6 5 4 3 2 1

CONTENTS

ACKNOWLEDGMENTS

I am deeply grateful to the people and collectives who inspired and sustained me in writing this book. The research began as a dissertation project at the University of California, San Diego, guided by an incomparable committee. I thank Lisa Lowe, Shelley Streeby, Dennis Childs, Jin-kyung Lee, and Curtis Marez for their extraordinary care, brilliance, and courage. Engaging with each of you—your ferocious intelligence and profound compassion—has been transformative. I've written versions of this in my heart and it sounds better in there; out here, I say thank you.

At the University of Kansas (KU), the energy and good cheer of Cécile Accilien, Giselle Anatol, Anna Balmilero, Ignacio Carvajal, Angela Gist-Mackey, Shantel Martinez, Robert McDonald, Ashley Muddiman, and Magalí Rabasa kept me going. To this day, Jari Peters, Maryemma Graham, Cécile, and Giselle keep me breathing. I thank current and former members of the American Studies department at KU who offered support throughout my time there as assistant professor: Ben Chappell, Betsy Esch, Jennifer Hamer, Nicole Hodges Persley, Randal Jelks, Margaret Kelley, Clarence Lang, Cheryl Lester, Ray Mizumura-Pence, Terri Rockhold, Dave Roediger, Sherrie Tucker, and Robert Warrior. I admire the KU undergraduate and graduate students I was fortunate enough to learn from, including members of the Latinx Research Working Group. I also thank the directors and staff members at the Center for East Asian Studies, in particular for their support for Megan Spurgeon, who was a wonderful undergraduate research assistant. This book project was a recipient of KU's New Faculty General Research Award and the College of Liberal Arts and

Sciences Research Excellence Initiative Grants, which provided support for writing and book production.

At UCSD, I'm delighted to be part of the faculty in the Department of Literature, to continue my work alongside those who sparked my research, and to build with new colleagues. The final stages of book production were completed in shared virtual space with Andrea Mendoza, Sal Nicolazzo, Erin Suzuki, and Ameeth Vijay. UCSD's Institute of Arts and Humanities provided support for book production. The University of California's President's Postdoctoral Fellowship provided time to begin the manuscript process, and I thank my postdoctoral mentor, James Kyung-Jin Lee, as well as the Department of Asian American Studies at UC Irvine. Additional institutional support that made the writing of this book possible include the Ford Foundation Dissertation Fellowship, the Library of Congress Florence Tan Moeson Fellowship, and the American Philosophical Society's Franklin Research Grant.

I'm in awe of the teams at Temple University Press who navigated working through the COVID-19 pandemic with such grace and care. Sara Jo Cohen and Sarah Munroe worked with this book in its earliest stages, and Shaun Vigil sustained its development with good humor, a great deal of patience, and impeccable professional attention. My thanks to the TUP team, including Ann-Marie Anderson, Gary Kramer, Kate Nichols, and Ashley Petrucci. I carry so much appreciation for Danika Medak-Saltzman, who supported the publication of this book in the Critical Race, Indigeneity, and Relationality series. Danika and the anonymous reviewers advanced this book with their generous, sensitive, and utterly illuminating feedback. I'm grateful to Jamie Armstrong for copyediting, and to Hannah Bailey for indexing. I must acknowledge Arte Público Press for use of "New Battery," "Fit for Duty," "Old Friend," "Nagoya Station," "Brief Encounter," and "A Matter of Supplies," from Rolando Hinojosa, *From Klail City to Korea with Love: Two Master Works* (Houston: Arte Público Press, University of Houston, 2017). And a huge thanks to Thao Nguyen for use of lyrics and for the best sonic company. "Fool Forever" by Thao Nguyen / © 2016 Thanks for Playing (ASCAP) administered by Wixen Music Publishing, Inc. / All Rights Reserved. Used by Permission. Portions of Chapter 3 were previously published as "Sleuth Cities: East L.A., Seoul, and Military Mysteries in Martin Limón's *Slicky Boys* and *The Wandering Ghost*," *Journal of Asian American Studies* 17, no. 2 (2014): 199–228. Copyright © Johns Hopkins University Press.

Much gratitude to those who've read drafts and shared insightful feedback over the years. Mike Baccam, Crystal Baik, Gabriela Cázares, Juliana Choi, Josen Masangkay Diaz, Takashi Fujitani, Aneeka Henderson, Ashvin Kini, Jim Lee, Surbhi Malik, Yumi Pak, Chris Perreira, Laura Reizman, Rosaura Sánchez and Beatrice Pita, Amanda Solomon Amorao, Thea Quiray Tagle, Ma Vang, and Robert Warrior have improved this book in immeasurable ways. I also thank Seungsook Moon, Suzy Kim, and participants of the SSRC Korean Studies Workshop for Junior Faculty. Being part of the First Book Institute at Penn State, directed by Sean X. Goudie and Priscilla Wald, was such an extraordinary experience, and I thank them and our cohort. In addition to Sean and Priscilla's perceptive guidance, I'm especially thankful for Tina Chen's incredible mentorship during both the institute and the Association for Asian American Studies Junior Faculty Workshop. The fantastic writing group that formed from the institute has shaped this book, and I'm grateful always to Jessica Hurley, Sunny Yang, Meina Yates-Richard, and Abby Goode for years of the smartest feedback and bighearted encouragement.

For their generous engagement throughout the stages of this work, my warmest gratitude goes to Luis Alvarez, Jody Blanco, Erica R. Edwards, Fatima El-Tayeb, Cheryl Higashida, Sharon P. Holland, Grace Kyungwon Hong, Helen Heran Jun, Jodi Kim, Mariam Lam, Crystal Parikh, Dylan Rodríguez, Erin Suzuki, Lisa Yoneyama, and especially Cathy Schlund-Vials, who is an amazing mentor. I'm deeply humbled by the spirit and verve of Minju Bae, Crystal Baik, Patrick Chung, Christine Hong, Monica Kim, and Ji-Yeon Yuh, whose activist and scholarly work has sharpened my political actions, teaching, and writing. I thank the members of the Ending the Korean War Teaching Collective for their unceasing political commitment to a decolonizing peace and formal end to the Korean War.

When I think about the lovely, convivial, and furiously clever people who opened their homes, shared advice and, just as important, shared delicious meals, and kept company along the way, I suddenly feel shy. My love and respect for Victor Betts, Josen Diaz, Ash Kini, Chien-ting Lin, Lisa Lowe, Yumi Pak, and Chris Perreira: I cherish you, and us, wherever we may be. Much gratitude for Aimee Bahng, Benjamin Balthaser, Angie Chau, Kimberly Chung, Jason Farr, Stephanie Gomez Menzies, Kyung Hee Ha, Ren Heintz, Bernadine Hernández, Anita Huizar-Hernández and Joaquin Rios, Becky Kinney, Yumi Lee, Maurice Rafael Magaña and Susy Chavez, Sara Mameni, Kit Myers, Tom X. Sarmiento, John Tran, and Ma Vang. Ashon Crawley's gorgeous writing and artwork quickens one's pulse, and I thank him for "thy word have i hidden in my heart . . . (number 4)," which graces the cover. And what a true pleasure to return to Southern California, in proximity to the dazzling Crystal Baik, Julie Burelle, José Hector Cadena, Dennis and Saranella Josen, José Fusté, the extended Kim family, Jim Lee, Jin-kyung Lee, Curtis Marez, Meli and Esteban Martínez, Yumi Pak, Jade Power-Sotomayor, John Rieder, Davorn Sisavath, Amanda and Drew, Shelley Streeby, Niall and

Lianne Twohig, Katie Walkiewicz, and Sal Zárate. Davorn, I'm ready for outdoor happy hour whenever you are!

The Kim and Perreira families deserve their own whole book of acknowledgments. Time and space do curious things: several of us returned to Kansas from all over, an unexpected lease of time spent together, a blessing. And while in Kansas, I also had time with Grandpa, and time after his death to reflect on the shape of his life, the stunning forces that convened for us to sit together, half watching *M*A*S*H* like it was the most ordinary thing in the world. But then, time and space do curious things: Chris and I returned to San Diego, where the Perreiras had been all along. I'm grateful for the cousins, Susie, Di, Anne, and Jenny Kim. And so thankful to be close once again to Sylvia, Mike, Eddie, Hector, Dominic, and Bella Perreira (and Mia). Chris is my constant through time and space, the one I rely on to find my way home. I dedicate this book to my umma and appa, who grow good things from the ground, who take seriously blooms and blossoms, who both live lives of fierce integrity. I love you.

NOTE ON TERMINOLOGY

Korean words follow the Revised Romanization or the McCune-Reischauer system. For English-language publications, Korean names follow the Western convention of the surname following the given name. Korean historical actors follow the Korean convention of the surname prior to the given name. For current legibility of usage, I use *South Korea* to refer to the Republic of Korea and *North Korea* to refer to the Democratic People's Republic of Korea.

For most of the Chicano/a literary works I examine, I retain the use of *Chicana*, *Chicano*, and *Chicana/o*, rather than using *Chicanx*, for both the historical significance and specificity of the Korean War and Cold War era, as well as the authors' self-identifications. I also retain the use of *Mexican American*, *Mexican*, and *Latino/a* if used in self-identification in the U.S. context. For broader institutional, identificatory, and collective contexts, I use *Latinx*. I briefly take up this discussion in chapter 2.

WARRING GENEALOGIES

INTRODUCTION

Warring Genealogies

Oh mighty man of war
How we tether
together
I know you make a fool of me forever

—THAO & THE GET DOWN STAY DOWN

On July 25, 1950—just a month into the Korean War—Ezekiel Gandara of Lincoln, Nebraska, arrived in Pusan, Korea. The young Mexican American army engineer, like many after the Incheon landing in September 1950, was eager to return home, back to his family for Christmas: "You take a 17-year-old kid and tell him that and that's the best thing that's going to happen to him. It didn't happen." He was instead posted on burial detail, not to return home until 1952. While on burial detail, he encountered an elderly couple in a run-down hut who had frozen to death. "We called them mamasan and papasan," he narrates. Gandara dug their grave, difficult in that frozen ground, and buried them. "I've often thought to myself," Gandara recalls, "they're somebody's mother, father, grandma, grandpa, brother, sister. Did they ever find them? . . . Did anyone ever find them?"[1] As far as Gandara knows, his recitation of their imagined kin is what remains of their family story. While strangers, his burial and half-century-long mourning of the elders, and his 2001 interview ruminating on whether they were ever found, routes complex transnational kinship affiliations.

The following spring, on April 27, 1951, an Associated Press photographer captured a Confederate flag waving from the tent of SFC Eugene Bursi, of Memphis, Tennessee (fig. I.1). For those who could claim *blood descent*, the United Daughters of the Confederacy would confer the Korean Conflict Cross of Military Service, itself fashioned after that flag. The Daughters, pedigreed in the Confederacy, thus sought to secure a settler genealogy of "a nation that rose so pure and white."[2] All the while, U.S. military personnel such as PFC

Figure I.1 In Korea on
April 27, 1951.
(Courtesy of AP Images)

Gandara and others—Latino, Black, Indigenous, and Asian—would encounter the sharp, familiar paradox of risking their lives for democracy abroad, even
as by "a special act of Congress, the Fifth Maryland Regiment flies the Confederate flag" in Korea.[3] How do we understand these racialized narratives
and racializing events emerging from the Korean War? And in what ways
does this war, and knowledge production about it, impact how the United
States leveraged race and kinship for Cold War expansion? Navigating the
contradictions of a nominally integrated U.S. military, Mexican American
soldiers like Gandara identified considerations of kinship that questioned the
violence implicit in maintaining and reproducing the white nuclear family.

These stories—which I provisionally frame here as family stories of the
Korean War, unorthodox as they may appear—only become stranger in the
following years, making unfamiliar the presumed logics of kinship. In the summer of 1954, the year following a ceasefire that ended combat but not the
war, prisoners of Leavenworth Federal Penitentiary in Kansas adopted by
proxy a Korean boy named Bok Nam Om and documented their mail-order

adoption in Leavenworth's prison magazine, *The New Era*. The prisoners' efforts to claim kinship with Bok Nam Om, however, are underwritten by their attempts in 1950 to leverage the Korean War for their release from the penitentiary, to send "Americans, your own flesh and blood," to the war, in place of racially suspect "Asiatics: Japanese, Chinese, and Filipinoes [*sic*]."⁴ And the prisoners did mean blood, quite literally, as they participated—voluntarily or not—in Red Cross blood drives throughout the Korean War, blood that both the Red Cross and U.S. military segregated by race. Even as the white prisoners mobilized the Korean War to access conditional belonging to the national family, Chicano veterans negotiated the return to a racially segregated United States by writing literature that imagined Asia as an alternative space for building kinships. Both the white prisoners' carceral participation in the Cold War U.S. phenomenon of proxy adoptions and the formation of transpacific kinships in Chicana/o literature devise unlikely kinships from the Korean War.

Such narratives, as family stories, compose subterranean archives of Korean War knowledge productions that reshape our understanding of the war's profound, and often underacknowledged, impact. The Korean War has interrupted our senses of kinship, crafting it into a series of proxies: familial, epistemological, spatial. I argue in *Warring Genealogies* that proxy kinships, emerging from literary, cultural, and archival texts, critically recast hegemonic formulations of kinship in the wake of the war. While the memorialization of the war in archives, monuments, and dominant historiography asserts exclusive imperatives of who constitutes the national family, Chicano veterans and Korean diasporic writers refashion kinship through critiques and queer mobilizations of knowledge production. Especially within the context of the military as renewing itself toward progress rather than dismantling the U.S. military as an apparatus engineered for imperial outputs, understanding the extant queer imaginaries of the Korean War offers a challenge against discourses of homonationalist incorporations of the war. How might the configuration of the Korean War as a queer formation unsettle the war's conscription into familiar nationalist rehearsals?

Within Chicano cultural production, for instance, I deliberate on the figuration of East Asia as spatial proxy for kin making. Reconsidering Ramón Saldívar's 1990 reading of Rolando Hinojosa's work, which situates Korea and Japan as proxies for South Texas, I trace the multiple proxies emerging from Chicano/a cultural production about the Korean War. In doing so, the theoretical implications for Chicana/o studies and the Cold War become apparent: Chicano subjects in the Korean War are themselves selectively figured by the state as a proxy for racial inclusion in the U.S. military, which necessitates tactics of refusal to be *known*, culminating in racial and national disaffiliations. Such refusals to sanction U.S. Cold War imperatives in the Chicano/a works, operating in direct contrast to comprehensive knowledge claims, offer critical affiliations and distinctly nonlinear temporalities of the Korean War. Among the affiliations, one of the most significant includes historical imaginings of kinship that glimpse transformations of cultural and epistemological possibility beyond Cold War limitations.

Warring Genealogies examines the elaboration of kinships between Chicano/a and Asian American cultural production, between white penitentiary prisoners and the Korean proxy adoptee, and between the United Daughters of the Confederacy and their acts of memorializing Confederate veterans of the Korean War. By considering white supremacist expressions of kinship—in prison magazines, memorials, U.S. military songbooks—to critiques of such expressions in Chicana/o and Korean diasporic works about the war through poetry, plays, and novels, this book conceptualizes racialized formations of kinship emerging from the Korean War as a problem of knowledge. The cultural texts' reflections on kinship theorize entwined formations of genealogy and knowledge production as central preoccupations of the unended Korean War. Attempts to manage the violence of hegemonic familial relationships obscure the possibilities of understanding the Korean War as integral to ongoing anxieties about race and kinship. Indeed, the contemporary resurgence of explicitly white supremacist imperatives of kinship coalesces through transnational relationships with militarized empire, even as alternative kinships challenging white supremacy emerge through such U.S. imperial actions.

Decolonization, Racial Intelligence, and Cold War Politics of Knowledge

A normative Cold War politics of knowledge, disciplined into area studies and history in the U.S. academy, scripts not only a singular understanding of the Cold War but also the very questions that could be posed to confront the limits of Western liberal governance. In this dominant emplotment, rehearsals on the Korean War go like this, with the marginalized undercurrents of the war parenthetically responding to the normative U.S. Cold War script:

The United States liberated Korea from Japanese colonialism in August 1945

(even as the terms of the 1905 Taft-Katsura agreement negotiated Japanese control of Korea in exchange for U.S. access to the Philippines.)

The United States established military governance in September 1945
to help Koreans learn democracy
*(a contradictory "decolonization through military occupation"[5] un-
dercutting a transitional People's Republic of Korea, which by September 1945 had "drafted a radically democratic constitution."[6])*

The North Koreans made war on an innocent South Korea on June
25, 1950, inaugurating the Korean War
*(covering over guerilla warfare and U.S.-sanctioned anticommunist
massacres as early as 1948, when war had already begun.)*

And the heroic efforts of U.S. and UN forces brought an end to the
Korean War on July 27, 1953.
(The war remains unended.)

The continuance of this emplotment, echoed in U.S. national memory through
an indefinable yet unequivocal defense of South Korea from communism,
suggests an epistemological forfeit. This emplotment requires diminishing
the multivalent complexities of race wars, from the "heterogeneity of the
Asia-Pacific War(s)"[7] to the Cold War representational deployment of U.S. racial equality. This emplotment requires an unquestioned conviction in linear
progression, an orderly timeline that has been "securitized, with the risks
unevenly distributed" on the deferred decolonization of the peninsula.[8] More
broadly, it requires an unwavering fidelity to the nation's monopoly on historical authenticity.

The Korean War itself, as a problem of knowledge, contends with unsanc-
tioned memories yielding incompatible genealogies. The origin story of the
war in U.S. historiography opens with a conflict—the North Korean attack
on South Korea on the hot, hot day of June 25, 1950. This origin story unfolds in the hardships endured by GIs, the tedious gains and losses of territory
for three years, the firm belief that the boys, as they say, will be home in time
for Christmas.[9] This origin story is insistently cycled in dominant U.S. discourse, if noted at all, as a war that saved South Korea from the perils of communism. This origin story unequivocally locates the beginnings of the war in
the North Korean attack on South Korea on June 25, 1950. This origin story
simultaneously reifies and erases the U.S. Army Military Government in
Korea, from 1945 to 1948—reifies, because the United States capitalized on
the symbolic value of "liberating" Korea from Japanese colonialism in 1945,
and erases, because of the military government's status as yet another occupying force in the peninsula, despite the demonstrated predictability of the U.S.

disavowal as itself an imperial power. This origin story represses the long history of anticolonial resistance against Japan, evacuates the complex struggles by Korean peoples to determine their own governance, underplays global decolonization movements, and selectively memorializes June 25, 1950, as the day North Korea attacked. This selective, temporal memorialization, rather like an image, excludes anything exceeding its frame—other dates, other times, other possibilities for explaining who, when.

Scholars working at the interdisciplinary intersections of ethnic studies, gender and sexuality studies, and transpacific critique have established the Korean peninsula's suspended decolonial condition as provisioning the durability of the global Cold War's afterlives.[10] Such scholarship composes a growing body of vital critique on the Korean War, challenging continual reproductions of nationalized knowledge formations that are governed by Cold War ideological and disciplinary logics. U.S. Cold War historiography situates the United States as architects of democracy, equality, and freedom, positioned to accommodate difference and inaugurate official antiracism, the very necessity for which emerged as a condition for post–World War II U.S. global ascendency.[11] Jodi Melamed observes the epistemic continuity of white supremacy in the state's transition to a nonredistributive antiracism, "making the constitution of modernity as much a knowledge-based racial project as it was an economically and politically based one."[12] I present below two related instances of the Korean War as a project of racial intelligence, codified within nationalist Cold War frameworks to "achieve white supremacist outcomes."[13]

The first is Melinda Pash's *In the Shadow of the Greatest Generation: The Americans Who Fought the Korean War* (2012), a narrative history in which she writes, "Americans today still grapple to make sense of this abbreviated, limited, half-won conflict that became the first hot war of the Cold War."[14] For whom is this war *half won*? For the millions of Korean refugees, civilian casualties, and diasporic subjects, in what temporality is the war *abbreviated*? And in whose sensibility is the war *limited*, when as early as 1948, the U.S. Army Military Government "encouraged scorched-earth policy" in its anticommunist suppression of the April 4 Cheju Uprising?[15] To be sure, Pash identifies important white supremacist perspectives—such as Corporal Clyde Queen's exclamation in September 1950, "Those Gooks! They're not even part human!"—yet continues on to explain that "South Korean civilians looked so much like North Korean adversaries that it could be difficult to tell the difference."[16]

Contextualized within the U.S. Air Force's indiscriminate carpet-bombing of the peninsula, "it could be difficult to tell the difference" offers multiple readings. The immediate reading absolves the mass killing of Korean civilians by aerial warfare, implicitly sanctioning a militarized genealogy of U.S. aerial warfare from the Korean War through the wars in Iraq and Afghanistan.[17] Another reading evokes the U.S. orientalist history of racial knowing, from William Elliot Griffis's *Corea, the Hermit Nation* (1882), to the 1941 *Life* article "How to Tell Japs from Chinese," to the Korean body's "capacity for veracity," for truth telling and self-governance as measured by U.S. military lie-detector experiments,[18] by turns classifying the knowability or inscrutability of "Oriental" bodies. The white supremacist difficulty of grasping complex difference is telling indeed. At issue is not whether white supremacist structures can index with more precision but rather the accepted narratives generated to obscure and absolve culpability while ensuring white supremacy's continuance, a protraction of the Western liberal epistemic violence anchoring what Lisa Lowe observes as an "economy of affirmation and forgetting."[19]

Likewise, the knowledge-based racial project of the Center for the Study of the Korean War, located in Independence, Missouri, coordinates epistemic reinforcements of Cold War modernity. The center was founded by Paul Edwards, a Korean War veteran and prolific author on the subject of the war. While my chapter 4 considers the center itself in more detail, I examine here Edwards's 2018 book, *The Mistaken History of the Korean War: What We Got Wrong Then and Now.* As the title suggests, the book's focus is provisioning a corrective to the mistaken and the wrong. One of the infrastructural challenges Edwards identifies for getting it right occurs in the educational system, which has fallen "under the influence of publicly accepted social sciences, ethnic studies, [and] sensitive history."[20] Offering no understanding of ethnic studies as a field of knowledge, Edwards attributes the problem of the Korean War's mistaken history to the "emergence of gender consciousness, labor studies, racial and ethnic considerations . . . and a whole range of 'specialists' [that] have left little time and less money for considerations of the military."[21] This pedagogical parallel universe, in which critical intellectual thought centering gender, labor, and race is very well funded at the expense of the military, repeats logics of the late twentieth-century culture wars and indicates their rehearsals in moments of crises.

Edwards recommends a solution to this grievance, a recourse to the educational victimhood of military history posed by critiques from gender, labor, and ethnic studies: "If we are not going to teach military history in our educational system, then it may well be time to reinstate the draft, to reenact a selective service agency that organizes conscription and the reintroduction of the citizen soldier. There are a lot of good reasons for reconsidering this."[22] The corrective to the mistaken history of the Korean War is not critical inquiry but the institutional resurrection of the militarized logics and procedures that themselves organized the conditions for the Korean War. My intent here is not a simple dismissal of such claims, bewildering as they may appear. Rather, by elaborating on two recent scholarly texts on the Korean War, I seek to contextualize the epistemological tenor established by liberal nationalist frameworks. The Cold War politics of knowledge generate *racial anxieties* about the war, preoccupied with sustaining an unmarked whiteness in U.S. liberal knowledge production and in treating Korean War discourse as the nation's property.[23]

Pash's unintentionally suggestive phrase excusing the U.S. military's bombing of Korean civilians ("it could be difficult to tell the difference") offers another perspective with broader epistemic possibility for Korean War knowledge production as a project of racial formation. Telling the difference, in the mode of distinguishing, is a racial project. The difficulty in telling the difference, in the mode of historical recounting, is a racial project. And not being told at all, to live burdened by what Grace Cho has described as the "process of nurturing a ghost through shame and secrecy," is a racial project.[24] In the context of empirical and evidentiary methodologies, Avery Gordon asks: "How can we *tell* the difference between one story and another's? It will all hinge, as we shall see, on that double modality of telling—to recount and to distinguish."[25] So how telling is this observation from Edwards? "A significant number of Korean [War] veterans did not tell their wives or children that they had been in Korea. Of the populations that visit the Center for the Study of the Korean War over a year's time, much of it is made up of older women and teenage children who, on their husbands' and fathers' deaths, had just learned they served in Korea."[26] The possibility for radical Korean War knowledge production, conscious of, *critical* of its tethering to U.S. Cold War politics of knowledge, dwells at the thresholds of epistemology, genealogy, and kinship.

Epistemological Proxemics: Studying Queer Proximities

Warring Genealogies considers the historically specific and culturally articulated interplays among race, kinship, and genealogy during the Korean War as epistemological concerns. The Korean War, obscured within academic and popular discourses, continues to function as epistemological proxy "in language nonidentical with itself": as a precursor to the Vietnam War in occasional U.S. history classes, as an antecedent to the buildup of the U.S. security and counterintelligence apparatus, as an unended war to endless wars, and perhaps most visibly in the peninsular manifestation of a Cold War binary—capitalist, communist.[27] Such epistemological adjacencies further obscure the disciplinary quandaries constructed around the Korean War. Critical scholarship has theorized an apparent inscrutable quality of the Korean War, described by Jodi

Kim as an epistemological conundrum, by Daniel Kim as a kind of translation, by Roderick Ferguson as inhabiting a ghostly nature, and by Crystal Parikh as presenting an "*incommensurability* of any analogizing."[28] Attending to such epistemological tension about the war brushes up against area studies imperatives to perpetuate bifurcated Cold War logics. Critical memory practices and cultural studies methods pose a continual defiance to the Cold War narrative affixed to U.S. security rationales. This book takes as a central concern the preoccupation with controlling knowledge production and traces the history of U.S. knowledge production about Korea, as well as the material sites of archival knowledge production about the Korean War. In particular, the book contends with disciplinary limits that isolate and assert singular histories presented as neutral arbiters rather than as situated in political particularities. This contention, at heart, questions disciplined epistemologies that obstruct thinking across the boundaries of what can be known.

The epistemological conundrum of the Korean War composes Cold War anxieties about knowledge production, which convene empiricist modalities as ideologically untouched. A rearticulation of epistemology, then, departs from the Cold War paradox concerning the simultaneously replete and empty characterization of usable knowledge against racialized enemies of the state and moves toward what José Esteban Muñoz conceptualizes as an "*epistemologically and ontologically humble*" queer hermeneutic.[29] Such a queer hermeneutic defamiliarizes privileged sites of Cold War inquiry and attends to the ephemeral, which "does not rest on epistemological foundations but is instead interested in following traces, glimmers, residues, and specks of things" otherwise made incomprehensible, whether in a state archive, a static methodology, or an inventory of nationalist history.[30] In upending Cold War historiography's gravitational will toward the possessive corrective of the Korean War, queer critique's intervention animates the war's multiplicities and "permits the tracing of U.S. militarism's racially queer genealogy in Asia and the Pacific."[31] How might the Korean War be considered otherwise, if configured through a queer of color critique? And how might the Korean War as queer formation extricate from the homonationalist reproduction of gay incorporation and selective endowment of cultural citizenship into the state's liberal regime?[32]

An assimilationist project of Cold War historiography's possessive corrective could be demonstrated in Pash's book, which presents the inclusion of gay men to the narrative history of the Korean War:

> In addition to cigarettes and liquor, some men in the war theater found love or something like it. Especially for gay men, who faced persecution and suspicion back in the States, Korea and Japan provided the

opportunity for both openness and fulfillment. . . . Indeed, most homosexuals found commanders more than willing to look the other way so long as they performed well on the job. In the zone, one "could be as open as you wanted to be" and there existed little pressure to act straight. Gay men stationed in Japan frequented gay bars there, but willing partners turned up elsewhere as well. Straight men in Korea, Japan, and aboard ship courted homosexuals when women were in short supply or likely to be infected with venereal diseases and when they needed sex but could not endure the thought of being unfaithful to their wives with another woman. In general, gays found serving overseas a refreshing experience, free of some of the fear and repression they suffered at home.[33]

The presentation of this narrative history functions in remarkable tandem to bolster "homonationalism"—structures constituted of juridical, legislative, political, and other entities that strategically enlist and selectively endow homosexual cultural citizenship in service of U.S. national security interests.[34] The scenic violence of nostalgia scripted above, colored with cigarettes, liquor, and "love or something like it," storyboards an egalitarian promise of (presumably white) sexual fulfillment without its liberal contradictions. At issue is not the narratives themselves but rather their representational deployment of sexual freedom that obscures contextual materiality: the profound destruction of the Korean War, as well as the conditions that ensure homophobic "fear and repression" back home.

What disallows this Korean War historical narrative from inquiring "what kinds of emancipation are being generated in and through sexuality?"[35] The emphasis on the "openness and fulfillment" of deracinated gay inclusion in racialized systems of destruction operates to exclude radical queer visions to dismantle such structures of militarized violence. Rather than cruising utopia, a war of profound destructive magnitude is scripted into "a refreshing experience," an occasion for "aboard ship" cruising. It serves as liberal narrative precursor to the U.S. military's inclusion of gays and lesbians prior to "Don't Ask, Don't Tell" and its repeal and anticipates the U.S. military's weaponization of homophobia as rationale for military intervention in postsocialist regions and across the Middle East.[36] Enlisting "homosexuals" as proxy, "when women were in short supply," for both wives and "another woman," disengages from the misogynist operations of the U.S. military, which furthermore understands women as vectors "likely to be infected with venereal diseases."

Such Cold War narrative histories place in unlikely proximity the Korean War "liberation" of both Koreans and gay U.S. military personnel. And perhaps what it reveals in this Korean War context is an accidental acknowledgment that, despite how the U.S. nuclear family is posited as a normative aspiration, its very engineering and social reproduction has always been "queer." Returning to Muñoz's *queer hermeneutic*, this book asks: How do these proximities upend reproductions of patriarchal kinship structures and Cold War knowledge formations? In what ways do such warring genealogies affiliate with queer genealogies? What might facilitate the destabilizing of structures that render unthinkable queer knowledge productions of the Korean War? And what entanglements produce the queerness of the Korean War? I suggest that Chicano/a literature, in its engagements with race and kinship in the Korean War, theorizes queer temporalities of the war.

Scholarship in critical fields of inquiry has traced the Cold War and neoliberal university's incorporation of the radical political desires of differentially positioned social movements into such disciplines and fields as ethnic studies to manage, order, integrate, secure, and rule subjects marked as unruly. Tethered through Cold War militarization in Southeast Asia, Asian American studies and Chicana/o studies function as familiar strangers that share historical moments of formation. Activating a convergence of the fields reveals insights about forgetting, incorporation, and coalition. The Chicano/a cultural production I examine in chapters 2 and 3, which includes works by Rolando Hinojosa, Luis Valdez, Rosaura Sánchez, and Tomás Rivera, compellingly theorizes the paradoxical problem of the forgotten Korean War, presenting the war in a series of absences, unknowns, and proxies. The importance of working through unknowns in Chicano/a cultural production operates partially in the refusal of empiricist Cold War logics. Also significant, however, are the discourses animating Chicano/a studies as a field, in particular the vulnerabilities presented in the perception of the field as being forgotten. Rather than insist upon a definitive conclusion, the Chicano/a cultural texts I examine instead meditate, through representations of kinships, queer temporalities that refuse to anticipate closure, remarkably mirroring the unended status of the Korean War itself.

Chicana/o literary scholars, from Rosaura Sánchez to Ramón Saldívar to José Limón, have argued how Chicano/a cultural production about the Korean War has particularized the contradictions undergirding Cold War racial operations. Inspired by their debates, I suggest that Chicano/a cultural production refuses to authorize nationalist impulses that seek to affix the Korean War within Cold War area studies logics. In distinct contrast to area studies imperatives to master knowledge about racialized subjectivities, the formally diverse and genealogically subversive Chicano/a cultural works I examine cast the Korean War as a series of *unknowns*—family members missing in action, the possibility of children fathered by GIs, the deeply unsettling uncertainty about why the war is happening and so relentlessly impacting Chicana/o communities. The conceptualization of an *"epistemologically and ontologically humble"* queer hermeneutic, in relation to Chicano/a writings about kinship in Korea, destabilizes Cold War knowledge production. Queer, multiracial kinships offer gorgeously disruptive modes for undoing normative parameters of family, expanding ideas for *not knowing* who is kin, gesturing toward a relatedness and sociality that requires interdependent material care. In his study of the family in Chicano/a cultural politics, Richard T. Rodríguez theorizes the uneven and at times contradictory mobilizations of family, reflecting a "desire to conjoin sources that fall outside traditional disciplinary locations or historical mappings—illustrat[ing] la familia as a genealogical tradition that entails successive shifts contingent upon changing kinship discourses and formations."[37] I consider a Chicana/o literary genealogy from this framework, which theorizes Cold War anxieties—not least of which include racially disproportionate military participation—specifically in relation to Chicana/o literature's preoccupation with the Korean War.

Thinking across disciplinary divisions and logics on the Korean War's unended legacies yields critical, seditious knowledge. The context of the Korean War opens up adjacencies of familial thematics alongside the concern with knowledge production. Imperative to articulating "that which breaks through social narratives to permit a bleeding, meanings unanchored and moving away from their traditional moorings" within the Korean War context is a method of bringing together the familiar strangers of official documents and disciplined histories, in relation to cultural works and memories gone rogue.[38] Such a reflection charts the distance of what is knowable or within sight: a range of perception, which mediates thresholds of perception, of that which is within archival grasp or evading disciplinary recognition. Knowledge, after all, hinges on the edge between what is familiar and what is beyond one's ken.

Disciplined Genealogies and the Production of the Forgotten War

In the United States, the Korean War earned the designation of the "forgotten war" prior to ceasefire in 1953, a designation that persists even as mainstream discourse frames North Korea as an ontological threat, while obscuring its embeddedness in that war.[39] The Korean War is selectively and unevenly remembered in the United States: by those directly affected, by a slim column of academic texts (in contrast to World War II and the Vietnam War), by the stone and mortar of its memorials and those who visit them. U.S. nationalist discourses enclose the complexities of the Korean War, preserved in U.S. history as an event that liberated South Korea from communism. Given such a construction, it is important to discern how the Korean War is remembered, in particular how it serves to both reinforce and disrupt memories of racial terror, normative kinship, and imperial expansion. The passive construction of the forgotten war linguistically removes the agent of memory from the equation, leaving in its wake the idea that there remain only the inculpable inheritors of an unknowable history.

Indeed, scholars theorize the production of forgetting as central to practices of selective remembrance, theorizations that are pivotal for apprehending the epistemological aporia of the Korean War. On the intertwined imperial investments between Japan and the United States, Lisa Yoneyama asserts that they "in fact mutually coproduce amnesia about their histories of colonialism and military expansion in the Asia-Pacific."[40] On the Korean War more specifically, Monica Kim writes "the Korean War seems to confound the usual elements of historical narrative. The difficult contradictions one comes across when attempting to give shape to this war seem to multiply with every attempt. The Korean War is a war that is 'forgotten' in the annals of United States history but that has been in plain sight of the world continuously through the latter half of the twentieth century into the second millennium in the form of the hypermilitarized Demilitarized Zone (DMZ) on the Korean peninsula," in the midst of which are the psychic implications of "enforced forgetting," as Grace Cho articulates by both U.S. nationalist processes and "families like mine where someone survived the horrors of war to bring us here."[41] Tracing discourses of genealogy disorders the powerful, continual exercises of nationalist and disciplinary obfuscations.

While genealogy is commonly understood as family history—a positivist charting of kin, a practice of simultaneous excision and incorporation—the concern with genealogy as method animates how we might come to "establish a historical knowledge of struggles and to make use of this knowledge tactically today," with acute attention to how "genealogy as a method thematizes the body, power, and social institutions where fictive truths and values are enacted upon the body," as Emma Pérez offers in *The Decolonial Imaginary*.[42] This book considers both family genealogy—whether articulated as supremacy for white nationalists, discordantly truncated for Korean children orphaned by war, or queerly fashioned within Asian-Latinx imaginings—as well as the conceptual elaboration of genealogy at the thresholds of knowledge production. Definitional anxieties about genealogy, on the violent fictions sedimented in U.S. nationalist origin stories, underpin the Korean War's epistemological parameters. Disciplinary preoccupations with ordered singularities, via the evacuation of complex narratives out of state-sanctioned history, do more than preclude connections across multiple fields of study. They also function as secretary, as a keeper of secrets, on the emergence and unfolding of the Korean War. Genealogical disclosures therefore inhabit politicized terrains of knowledge production, explicitly attentive to shifting matrices of power.

Genealogy bears specific meanings within critiques of colonialism and empire in relation to gender, race, and sexuality. Indigenous studies in particular makes acute inquiries into the colonialist logics of biological parsing, and Black studies has long theorized the paradoxical derivative logic of the one-drop rule, in critical dialogue with kinship.[43] While genealogy as method invites "lineal associations, amalgamated intimacies, the speculative horizons of kinship, and insinuated exclusions, inclusions, and indifferences," a fidelity to U.S. nationalist genealogical interests represents "the potentially dangerous and reactionary practice of what we can call settler genealogy," as David A. Chang states in his study of moʻokūʻauhau (genealogy) and expansive Kanaka kinship as transgressive decolonial methodology.[44] For Kanaka Maoli scholar kuʻualoha hoʻomanawanui, considering "one's disciplinary or academic genealogy" is of equal importance, as Erin Suzuki observes in *Ocean Passages*, which foregrounds "engaging more directly with Indigenous Pacific concepts of relationality [as] a necessary step in decolonizing transpacific critique."[45] Yoneyama's vital call to continue interrogating the transpacific, especially in relation to Native Pacific critique, animates what she calls, inspired by Keith Camacho's work, a decolonial genealogy of the transpacific.[46] Each of these studies shares the concern with how knowledge production has been organized and disciplined, indeed how "the institutional division of knowledge into discrete academic disciplines is itself a legacy and effect" of U.S. racial governance.[47] Against the foundational limitations of discrete disciplines, Camacho considers how we "understand Pacific Islander interventions across the U.S. empire need not be limited to any one field of study, nor to any single genealogy or territory."[48] Finally, Danika Medak-Saltzman theorizes that the very condition and structure of periodization in academic disciplines function to elide and naturalize disengagements with Indigeneity.[49]

Given the disciplinary elisions noted above, a tension laced throughout *Warring Genealogies* is the reckoning with genealogy as epistemological emergence and an inquiry into genealogy's queer refusal of reproductive logics, in particular at the level of disciplines. The state-sanctioned origin story of the Korean War itself is tethered to the production of Cold War area studies. Even as the U.S. Army Military Government occupied the Korean peninsula during 1945–1948, area studies in U.S. universities proliferated and used social scientific methodologies that "not only privileged Western modernity, but also produced evidence that non-Western or nonmodern societies needed industrial development and social modernization."[50] The concomitant genealogical suturing of Cold War area studies to the provisional prehistory of the Korean War offers a metacritical framework from which to analyze knowledge production. Such an attention to genealogy, to the way it is conceptually affiliated to knowledge and to kinship in Korean War epistemology, reorders another alternative genealogy—that of the United States itself. It foregrounds the violent fictions and contradictions constituting white nationalist U.S. genealogies, the perversely avoidant family stories—framed here as U.S. Cold War historiography, perceived more broadly elsewise as the state's history— devised to continually reconstruct the national family.

The Korean War has been characterized in popular culture and history through metaphors of masculine kinships: as a fratricidal war, as brothers at war, as the brotherhood of war. Two of the most profound, ongoing legacies of the unended war are the division of families following the division of Korea and the inauguration of transracial adoption from the peninsula. Within U.S. history, dominant understandings of family operate as fundamental discourses determining power and privilege. The common applications of family in nationalist discourses reveal their roots in the settler conception and biopatriarchal extension of U.S. nationhood, from Founding Fathers and Republican Motherhood to the ongoing weaponization of "family values" used to demarcate rigid parameters of normative sociality. Family delimits access to property and inheritance and, through the mid-twentieth century, defines which gendered and racialized subjects were themselves constructed *as* property. Patriarchal authority self-naturalizes family hierarchies. Such definitions symbolize the nation, reproducing and stabilizing meanings of family and justifying uneven power relations within the state and between the United States and Korea.

In the U.S. context, those who live beyond the state's approved boundaries of kinship are not only marginalized but constructed as deviant threats to the social order, a construction that strives to perpetuate a consistently normalized reinforcement and obfuscation of a manufactured, fluctuating, and unstable metric of kinship. Those whose lives exceed the state's definitions of family also continually disrupt the naturalized conceptions of kinship to expose the selectively inclusive and exploitative functions of dominant notions of family. Expanded further, such a queer understanding of kinship intimates possibilities for alternative formations of relationships that can reconfigure dominant notions of family.[51] As constructions that are always in process and continually being made and unmade, family and kinship are evolving dynamics. While the nationalist metaphor of kinship is not unique to the Korean War, applying scrutiny to how the metaphor is wielded allows us to disrupt normalized representations and envision alternative socialities otherwise obscured by permitted uses of kinship.[52]

Kinship is central to Korean adoption studies, with scholars identifying critical interventions that destabilize transnational adoption as a naturalized outcome of the Korean War by illuminating its role "in fortifying militarized humanitarianism and white heteronormative constructions of family and nation."[53] This body of scholarship also indexes the lived materiality of Korean adoption, locating the entangled policy practices that sanction states' rehearsals of normativity, from the "domestic Korean social welfare policy" to how U.S. immigration policy "works simultaneously to encourage transnational adoption."[54] Furthermore, Korean adoption studies scholars have critiqued the erasure of infants and children from the parameters of Korean family registry and broader genealogical frameworks, identifying transnational adoption as "one of the Korean modernity project's most long-lived mechanisms of power, used to cleanse the country of 'impure' and 'disposable' outcasts in the name of social engineering and eugenics."[55] If akin can also mean analogous and affiliated, the Korean War era yields reactionary discourses that attempt to consolidate the assimilation into hegemonic formations: to enforce narrow definitions of family, to tether the experiences of nonwhite peoples' socialities to that of the white nuclear family model, and to politically compel the building of a South Korean state that functions in analog with U.S. imperial mandates.

Nested within the absenting of the Korean War is a genealogy underscoring the anticommunism of the U.S. public's mundane vernacular, such that uses of the term *communism* could be experienced as what Crystal Baik identifies as *reencounters* "of return and remembering that denaturalize naturalized temporalities, solidified presumptions, and historical knowledges."[56] And as scholars and cultural producers have observed, the extreme violence of anticommunist surveillance and punishment by the South Korean state has exploited Korean kinship structures, by politically targeting family members of those suspected of affiliating with communism.[57] Traces of anticommunist violence can be found in the absence, the *excision* of, family members from South Korean genealogies and reflects how the Korean War is so commonly censored out of family histories across the Korean diaspora. What transnational relationalities and kinships might emerge from such transpacific anticommunist surveillances of kinship? And more specifically attending to the Korean War's impact on U.S. racial formations, what conditions of Cold War erasure, knowledge, and memory contributed to the difficulty of contending with the Korean War in Chicano/a studies?

Another Cold War proxy, the U.S. war in Vietnam, is perhaps the clearest catalyst for what we understand as antiwar activism in the Chicano Movement—an ethnic nationalist movement met with vital critique by Chicana feminists, who challenged its internal hierarchies to work toward collective, redistributive liberation. The impact of Chicana antiwar actions, as Grace Kyungwon Hong and Belinda Rincón have observed, identified transnational enactments of grief, an echo of Ezekiel Gandara's mourning for the elderly Korean couple he buried during the Korean War. The U.S. state's FBI surveillance of organizations (including the American Indian Movement, Black Panthers, and Brown Berets) and individuals within the Chicano Movement and its rhetorical equation of antiwar protests with communism represent another convergence of kinship, knowledge production, and Cold War anticommunism: "Chicana/o antiwar activists also posed a threat to the nationas-family as the state became increasingly preoccupied with quieting antiwar protestors. . . . The state justified its probe into these groups by labeling them as subversive Communist organizations and therefore threats to national security."[58] Not only did such antiwar activism disrupt the U.S. framework of *nation-as-family*; it also theorized a form of transpacific affinities through explicit uses of kinship, whether in embodied public performances of grief as Chicana mothers, siblings, and other relations or in conceptualizations that "Chicanas/os and the Vietnamese were engaged in parallel anticolonial struggles for autonomy from U.S. imperialism. This inspired many Chicana/o activists to identify the Vietnamese as 'kindred spirits' in battle against U.S. imperialism rather than as enemies of the state."[59] The significant scholarly corpus on Chicana/o studies and the Vietnam War invites working against linear historical progression to trace the Korean War's impact in the field, suggesting the epistemological affinities that might emerge from broader Cold War anticommunism.

Critical feminist scholarship in Chicana/o Studies theorized essential conceptualizations of erasure, memory, loss, and recovery, challenging the very frameworks by which Chicana subjectivities are, as Emma Pérez observes, written out of history or, as Catherine Ramírez states, "simply did not exist" in both dominant historiography and "'their textbooks,'" as well as within Chicano histories.[60] Maylei Blackwell offers "retrofitted memory" as a framework with the dexterity to confront hegemonic projects that are also incomplete and, as with the Korean War, unended.[61] Returning to my earlier concern with the disciplinary conditions of Cold War erasure that disallow theorizing the Korean War in Chicano/a studies, and attentive to Chicana feminist critiques of epistemic violence, I follow Sandra K. Soto's argument that "the quest for

Chicana visibility can only take us so far. We need more broad-based, substantive, and innovative techniques and methods in order to interrupt the inherently limiting" divergences that uphold "our reliance on *mastery*" to instead read like a queer.[62] The Korean War's manifestations through the Chicano/a cultural production I examine as a series of unknowns, Muñoz's "*epistemologically and ontologically humble*" queer hermeneutic, and Soto's invitation to *demaster* "epistemological disciplining" inform the methods of this book.[63]

On Methods

Warring Genealogies examines the conflicting strategies employed by white nationalist archives and Chicano cultural productions to argue that contradictions of U.S. racial citizenship and kinship are routed through U.S. militarization in Asia. Indeed, examples such as Leavenworth prisoners' reframing of racial discourse for the purposes of proxy adoption and military enlistment during the Korean War suggest the necessity of examining how such discourses are refined in the practices of U.S. imperial war in Asia. Even as white prisoners in Leavenworth used the Korean War as an occasion to petition for their release, Chicano cultural production reveals the extent to which Mexican American subjects were disproportionately recruited for the war, often facing incarceration if they refused enlistment. Critical studies of whiteness and critical race studies scholars have observed that whiteness maintains power and perpetuity through its naturalization as unmarked. Such critiques have inspired me to consider that in the context of the Korean War, it in fact served as an occasion to entrench whiteness by explicit and intentional discourses of kinship, such as proxy adoption, segregated blood donation, and the efforts of the United Daughters of the Confederacy. While the mobilization of kinship as metaphor and material condition in the service of securing white supremacy is itself fundamental to establishing the United States as a settler formation, I am interested too in how Chicana/o cultural production theorizes horizons of kinship that strive toward dismantling such structures. The book thus broadens comparative studies of race, kinship, and empire through the war. It does so by examining how the Korean War was leveraged to refashion U.S. articulations of race and kinship, which persist in unexpected formations to the contemporary moment.

Recent U.S. scholarship has enhanced historical and literary considerations of the war.[64] However, not only are Latino/a and Korean relationships emerging from the Korean War underexamined; the condition of forgetting emerges in unanticipated forms of Chicano studies in particular. Yet discourses about the highly visible anxieties on the Korean peninsula selectively obscure the emergence of such tensions in the Korean War, which continue to reverberate throughout U.S. national and foreign policy. This study advances conversations about the Korean War in transnational American cultural studies and theorizes the limitations and possibilities of disciplinary conditions binding Asian American and Latinx studies. This interdisciplinary project charts the undertheorized racial and kinship formation of the Korean War, through literary frameworks and informed by methods from cultural studies and feminist and queer of color critique. Rather than excavating the empirical data of the Korean War and enclosing it within an authoritative historical record, I look to official histories, archives and archival materials, and literature and oral histories to examine the different operations by which race and kinship in the war are disclosed and forgotten. The untold stories of the Korean War through these sources, often partially expressed and imperfectly narrated, allow for more nuanced understandings of race and kinship along and against the grains of U.S. nationalism.

I therefore bring together a set of texts, archives, and populations that may appear counterintuitive but, taken together, collectively theorize cultural memories of the Korean War as a site of knowledge production through which understandings of race and kinship are renovated. *Warring Genealogies* centers archives as generative sites of contradictions embedded in theorizing kinships. Lisa Yoneyama and Lisa Lowe have posited the critical importance of reading across archives to consider previously disaggregated imperial histories as essential for perceiving the unfolding violence of liberalism.[65] Continuous with the Benjaminian critique of universal history's method, which lacks "theoretical armature," this book declines an additive "mass of data to fill [an] homogeneous, empty time."[66] *Warring Genealogies* looks to unlikely archives of the war to illuminate other epistemologies that yield comparative critiques of U.S. empire. The archival densities and diversities relocate understandings of how Korean War knowledge is produced and destabilize hegemonic conceptualizations of knowledge production. Indeed, in addition to deliberating on why these legacies should be considered in relation to each other, this book takes as its concern how they have been epistemologically disciplined into being kept apart. The affiliations I chart in the chapters are often terrible white supremacist narratives and unlikely stories of transpacific yearning, tethered in discomfiting formations. Yet tracing such warring genealogies produces ways of bypassing binary understandings and instead conjures alternative possibilities nuancing how race and kinship are configured through the Korean War. Cultural memory is therefore an important analytic in this project, as both a critical terrain on which knowledge production about the Korean War is diverted from prevailing narratives and an ambivalent terrain that can be as nationalist as official, linear history. Within this intensely contested site of struggle, the production of the Korean War as a benevolent intervention is shaped in such a way that replicates nostalgic nationalism and obscures stories that embody critiques of U.S. wars in Asia. Such stories, partially expressed and imperfectly narrated, unsettle the fictions of totality that attempt to project narratives, fully formed, from nationalist archives and libraries.

Outline of the Book

The Cold War has registered historically through proxy engagements in geopolitical terrain both distant from and intimate to the United States and the Soviet Union. To consider the Cold War's military actions as manifested through proxy wars is understood as foregone. Yet the term *proxy* registers an enduring afterlife of the Cold War, during which "'proxy' became inseparable from 'war,' and while proxy states were inflamed, the superpowers unleashed a proliferation of geopolitical calculations. Indeed, once proximity gave way to proxy, material conditions gave way to figuration. Every war is fought with figures of speech, but proxy war launched a new logic of substitution."[67] Such a "logic of substitution" aligns proxy in a set of discourses derived from and more robustly conceptualized than the Korean War as proxy war. More specifically, I consider the significance of proxy in relation to adoption, as in the first chapter's focus on the proxy adoption of a Korean boy by Leavenworth penitentiary prisoners, and to queer kinship, especially in the Asian-Latino proxy kinships elaborated by Chicano/a cultural works.

The book, in chapter 1, opens with a close reading of a letter from a Korean adoption sponsor agency, reprinted by the prisoners of U.S. Penitentiary (USP) Leavenworth in the penitentiary's prison magazine, *The New Era*. The letter thanking the prisoners for their sponsorship is radically misunderstood, operating as an allegory for Cold War knowledge production. This chapter focuses on the 1954 proxy adoption of a Korean boy, Bok Nam Om, by USP Leavenworth prisoners. I examine the logics undergirding the kinship between USP Leavenworth prisoners and Bok Nam Om, arguing that Cold War ideologies allowed prisoners to situate their claims of national belonging against the use of Asian American GIs in the Korean War. I suggest that the same ideologies also justify, rather than contradict, their proxy adoption as "rightful fathers" of Bok Nam Om. By adopting Bok Nam Om, the prisoners participated in the burgeoning post–World War II U.S. phenomenon of sponsoring orphans abroad, particularly in the East Asian nations destroyed by war. Through analyses of *The New Era*, this chapter constructs an argument elaborating the proxy kinships engendered during a proxy war, building on the theoretical foundation for the book.

Chapter 2 builds on the notion of proxy to consider the triangulation of Asian-Latino kinships that contest the structure of racially inclusive liberal discourse during the Korean War. In chapter 1, I argue that white Leavenworth penitentiary prisoners asserted their stake in racially configuring the national family through their engagement with proxy adoption. While the white prisoners mobilized kinship discourses to consolidate their affiliation with white patriarchal nationalism, Chicano veterans of the Korean War negotiated complex challenges of returning to a racially segregated United States and began to write literature that constructed Asia as an alternative, proxy space for building kinships. And even as white prisoners in Leavenworth used the Korean War as an occasion to petition for their release from the penitentiary, Chicano cultural production reveals the extent to which Mexican American subjects were disproportionately recruited for the war, often facing incarceration if they refused enlistment. Chicano cultural production about the Korean War further particularizes such contradictions undergirding Cold War racial operations. Theories of Asian-Latino proxies, and the continued discussion of the proxy, elaborated through forms, wars, and kinships, guide this chapter. While the previous chapter focuses on the Leavenworth prisoners' reframing of racial discourse occasioned by the proxy adoption and military enlistment during the Korean War, this chapter considers the proxy of the Korean War in Chicano literary discourse, as both a site of alternative kinship as well as a queer temporal and spatial disruption for theorizing the war and Chicano literature.

Chapter 2 examines the cultural works of Rolando Hinojosa (*Korean Love Songs* and *The Useless Servants*) and Luis Valdez (*I Don't Have to Show You No Stinking Badges* and *Zoot Suit*), which constitute complex counterrepresentations of the Korean War and critique U.S. racialization—in particular the narrative of the United States as a benevolent savior—that structure mainstream histories of the war. The narratives offer unique theorizations of Asian-Latino kinship emerging from the war, devising new intimacies that exceed state-sanctioned formations of marriage, family, and inheritance. In particular, they rescript the white nationalist imperatives of the U.S. military in military songbooks. An examination of their works, while addressing the lacuna of scholarship on Latinos and the Korean War, aims beyond the inclusion of recovering veterans' narratives. It also advances possibilities for capacious theorizing among multiple fields of knowledge production as disciplinary interlocuters in the context of the Korean War.

In chapter 3, I take up what Raymond Chandler characterizes in his 1950 essay "The Simple Art of Murder" as "the coolie labor" of writing detective stories to frame the hierarchies of "racial hatred and an inflated sense of pride" in Martin Limón's novels *Slicky Boys* and *The Wandering Ghost*. The date of publication for Chandler's 1950 essay also marks the official beginning of the Korean War, a war that was critical for shaping the urban spaces of East LA and the U.S. military districts of Itaewon and Tongduchon. I examine Limón's portrayals of an impoverished East LA as a gritty California counterpart to the desperate, sexually violent, and racist military districts in Itaewon and Tongduchon. This chapter builds on the Asian-Latino and proxy kinships of the prior chapters, considering the Chicano protagonist's own status as a former foster child who as U.S. military police adopts Korea—via proxy—as home and family. I argue that Limón's military police procedural genre functions as an aperture into sexual labor and the twinned militarized expansion of U.S. bases from Southern California to Korea. The novels' relationship to notions of home, domesticity, and "coolie labor" suggests operations of power via circuits of empire, including how militarized white womanhood is leveraged as a savior figure of Korean women.

Explicitly leading from the figure of militarized liberal white womanhood in the third chapter, the final chapter analyzes the role of white supremacist women's organizations and the politics of funding Korean War archives that frame the war within a rubric of white nationalist kinship. This chapter traces the genealogy of U.S. histories about Korea to Korean War archives and memorials sanctioned and supported by the United Daughters of the Confederacy. Throughout this chapter, I analyze Susan Choi's *The Foreign Student* as a novel that proposes alternative temporalities to dominant Korean War narratives, ultimately disrupting the orientalist moves of the United Daughters of the Confederacy. Building on the United Daughters as a counterpart to the "rightful fathers" of USP Leavenworth in the first chapter, this chapter brings the discussion of kinship in the context of the Korean War to an uneasy fruition. Returning to the Korean War vignettes presented in the introduction, and working in continuity from the final chapter, the coda takes up the dismantling of Confederate memorialization amid the contemporary visibility of white supremacist demonstrations in relation to knowledge production about and memories of the Korean War.

Although the book is structured at the thematic axes of white nationalism and Asian-Latino kinship, I do not suggest an easy opposition between the two in its organization. This book takes as its concern continuing debates on the stubborn yet sophisticated templates of racialization, in particular those conversations that center deep-rooted legacies of colonialism, exclusion, and assimilation. As a central critical apparatus, this book foregrounds the occupation of Indigenous lands, racial slavery, and gendered racial labor exploitation as undergirding the development of the modern U.S. state. It examines such ongoing and historical violence at the intersections of U.S. imperial war in Korea. While the chapter arrangements begin and end with white nationalist narratives, with Asian-Latino kinship chapters constituting the middle, each chapter negotiates the complex workings of white supremacy, a preoccupation with white purity that manifests its will through an exclusionary kinship. Therefore, chapter 1 examines the settler colonial logics that echo logics of white possession enabling Leavenworth prisoners to claim proxy adoption of a Korean child in the wake of the Korean War; chapter 2 focuses on U.S. military ballads that craft long histories of military empire and Chicano literary defiance to such forms; chapter 3 considers the strange reappearance of liberal white womanhood in a Chicano military police procedural in Korea; and the final chapter examines the liminal status modulating the apparently contradictory inclusiveness of white supremacy and the lethal rigidity of anti-Blackness, buttressed by the Korean War.

Fictive Kin

As a consequence of this confluence, thinking through Korean War legacies across sites structured to be siloed, other voices insisted upon their presence. The accidental witness to Rolando Hinojosa's useless servants, the desire to inhabit the trajectory of a letter addressed to USP Leavenworth, to punctuate terrible family histories and intervene in the forms of war—these moments are bound to be both strange and familiar. Genealogical rifts, speculative kin torn asunder, imperfectly convened by dint of genre and form in Chicano/a cultural production, are all forged through how we understand the war. The Korean boy, proxy adopted by prisoners, dwells alongside the cinematic deaths and proxy resurrections of the Chicano GIs who may have known him, who themselves speculate on their own unknown Korean Chicano sons and daughters, left behind in 1953. Twenty years after this phantom sibling, a Chicano foster kid from LA enlists in the U.S. Army and for the first time finds kinship in his adopted homeland of the Korean peninsula. All the while, and never thinking they would meet, in fact grounded in the surety of disciplined knowledge production to ensure that they do not meet, archives rooted in Confederate impulses draw on much longer settler genealogies of violence to capture the stories.

But elsewhere, otherwise, are those who long for complex iterations of kinship.

"AMERICANS, YOUR OWN
FLESH AND BLOOD"

Carceral Kinships of the Korean War

The letter arrives in the post. Penned in elegant writing in postwar insecurity, its journey was long, but the aim was true: traveling across oceans and continents, the letter arrives to the penitentiary bearing the imprint of a newly formed nation-state. Its mailing label may have read "1300 Metropolitan. Leavenworth, Kansas," authored by a hand more accustomed to writing in Korean than in English. Having reached its destination, the letter passes through more hands, these hands practiced in the order of chronicling and the art of newspapering. Such hands, after all, labored to produce the award-winning prison magazine, *The New Era*. At the press, housed in the penitentiary, the letter is turned, turned again, turned once more, bearing witness to the hesitation occasioned by the unfamiliar script. But it is time, and the winter 1954 issue must not be delayed. The letter slips in, the machine begins rolling, the ink exploring the capillaries opened up by the foreign font. The heartfelt message is rendered upside down.

This image in figure 1.1, from U.S. Penitentiary (USP) Leavenworth's prison magazine *The New Era*, tells the story of a Korean boy named Bok Nam Om, adopted via proxy by the prisoners in 1954. The article documenting the adoption begins with this letter from Bok Nam Om's sponsor agency, encapsulating the tensions mediating the relationship between the agency and the prisoners. The letter is reprinted upside down, with a translation of one fragment in English at the bottom of the page, reading, "Our country was much damaged." This misprint suggests more than misrecognition, the singular phrase selected for translation obscuring the conditions for the "much dam-

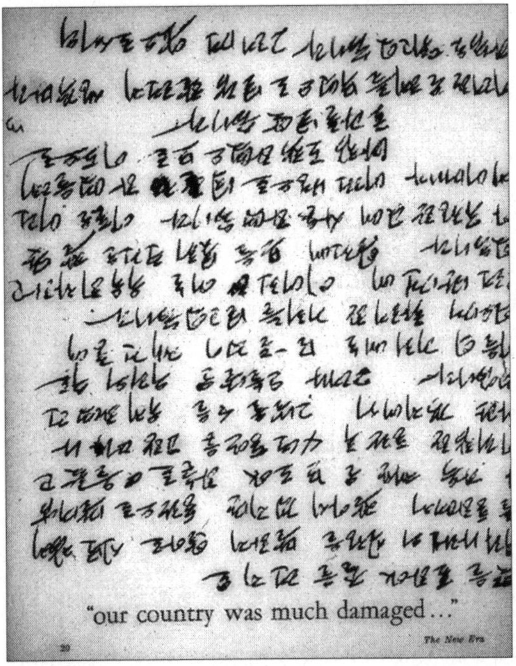

"our country was much damaged..."

Figure 1.1 "Bok Nam Om," *The New Era*, Winter 1954, 20. (Courtesy of the National Archives at Kansas City)

aged" country—the devastation created by the Korean War. Discursively, the translated fragment justifies Bok Nam Om's long-distance salvation by the prisoners, whom I argue become peculiarly positioned as rightful "fathers" sanctioned through their claims to liberal white personhood, white carceral subjecthood, and their leveraging of citizenship.

This image also tells the story of the burgeoning post–World War II U.S. phenomenon of sponsoring orphans abroad, particularly from Korea, flattened by war. Many of these proxy adoptions were enacted by sending money through established organizations and by exchanging letters and photographs. A previous issue of *The New Era*, published in the summer of 1954, introduces Bok Nam Om as the sponsored baby, narrating his birth in a UN refugee camp on September 17, 1953, in which he "spent the days in a cold hovel without heat."[1] Describing the "confusion, disorder, disease, and filthiness" of the refugee camp, the article addresses the prisoners, stating, "Your sponsorship may well be the difference between life and death for this child. He will receive two shipments in your name during the sponsorship year. They will contain a good supply of evaporated milk, cereal, and other essential food."[2] A reprinted letter, dated March 29, 1954, from John Mace—executive director of the Save the Children Federation—notes, "with great satisfaction, that

$146.20 was collected in the recent campaign," promising that the prisoners "will be sent full information regarding the child with not only its name and history but its picture."[3] The issue reprints another letter from the organization, dated April 28, 1954, from Lucille Hutchinson of the Baby Sponsor Relations division: "We are today assigning a baby sponsorship in their behalf, for Bok Nam Om, a very needy baby in Seoul, Korea. Enclosed you will find the case history, sponsorship certificate and other information. I hope your men will be pleased with their Korean baby and I hope that they will enjoy a correspondence with the family."[4]

Taken together, this correspondence from the summer 1954 issue of *The New Era* constructs a double-edged context for the proxy adoption of Bok Nam Om. Secured in the diction of concern, the "cold hovel" in which Bok Nam Om was born, replete with "disorder, disease, and filthiness," employs a blunt, untroubled humanitarian logic that drives the proxy adoption. The transactional tone of the Save the Children Federation correspondence embodies a telling dehumanization, from the executive director's "great satisfaction" with the money collected in exchange for "not only its name and history but its picture" to the Baby Sponsor Relations division's wish that the prisoners "will be pleased with their Korean baby." The humanitarian tension structuring the motivations of the prisoners and the federation aligns with the Cold War mandate to establish global supremacy by proxy, imposing a kinship by the proxy adoption of a baby born in the wake of a proxy war.

And so the misprinted letter from the sponsor agency, after journeying so far, heralds more than the effort to forge kinship. In this practice of kinship, the prisoners symbolically occupy roles as fathers of a weak and defenseless "Oriental" child. Within a normative framework of kinship, defined by patriarchal authority and protection, this symbolic relationship becomes naturalized as benevolent and necessary. Yet the practice of discursively adopting Bok Nam Om functions also to obscure the rhetoric of family that saturates such genealogies of power: the violent U.S. intervention in Korea that poses as a benevolent paternalistic action and the state's systematic stripping of civil life from prisoners that itself acts as an exercise in parental discipline. The prisoners are confined, symbolically punished within the imagined national family, deprived of their own families as well as parental authority, and subject to the paternal administration of the state.

Yet the very fact that the prisoners could imagine adopting via proxy from the confines of the penitentiary, and documenting and circulating the adoption through their access to print capital, is tethered to racialized structures defining gradations of personhood. Prior to the adoption of Bok Nam Om, *The New Era* also published an editorial on the racialized unfitness of Asian subjects as GIs, against which the white prisoners of USP Leavenworth were positioned as rightful, deserving, and voluntary participants in the Korean War. The 1950 July–September issue documents prisoner William Jones's open letter, signed by the inmates and addressed "To Whom It May Concern." The open letter articulates the need for additional troops "to send our fighting forces into Korea to combat communism and to check its spread, [setting] a precedent that must be continued in many other critical points throughout the world." Jones imagines the white prisoners' belonging to the nation, evacuating or perhaps leveraging their carceral status in a federal penitentiary and their exclusion from civic life. Jones's identification with "our fighting forces" aligns his position unquestionably with the militarized state. As well, the letter enthusiastically supports the insistence on "combat[ting] communism," itself theorizing the Cold War narrative that cast Korea as a spectral domino that could potentially push the unchecked movement of communism into "many other critical points throughout the world."

Further, the prisoners' proxy adoption of Bok Nam Om engages an equation of substitute kinship, their careful self-positioning as rightful fathers operating in distinct tension with their discursive erasure of the history of Japanese American soldiers during World War II. Addressed "To Whom It May Concern," written by Jones, and signed "The Inmates," the letter is directed toward government authorities, expressing paternalistic concern about politically and militarily incapable Koreans, other "Asiatics," and U.S. troops involved in the war, which I excerpt here and discuss at length in following sections: "Rather than being in a position to help, both China and the Philippine Islands need help to save themselves from the fangs of communism. The Japanese, until a scant five years ago, were our dreaded enemy. Pearl Harbor was an example of their trustworthiness." The letter's argument for the extraction of prisoners-as-soldiers simultaneously echoes and erases the logics of Japanese internment camps, the letter proposing "volunteering" for carceral release even as it undoes the state's selective elevation of Japanese American participation in World War II. The letter's claims to political subjecthood thus hinges on rehearsing the enacted contradictions of the liberal state (Japanese American prisoners-as-soldiers) and the very disavowal of the specificities of Japanese American military participation. In distinction from the "Asiatics," who especially as citizens are racialized as communist threats, the letter argues that "inmates of our penal institutions . . . are Americans, your own flesh and blood," endowed with the self-sovereign necropolitical imperative to sacrifice their lives in service to the nation.

Such efforts, as I will demonstrate, augur resurrections from civil death—the legal mechanism for denuding persons of civic life, depriving persons of legal validity, and, in the case of Leavenworth prisoners, disciplinary subjection by the state—and betray the sharp, occult edge of claiming unadulterated white blood. And so, within the narrowly defined racial parameters of the "American family" in the Cold War U.S. imaginary, particularly given the discursive fungibility of family and nation during the period, perhaps such efforts are not unexpected at all. Rather, such efforts emerge as a logical contradiction: proxy adoption functions as an ideal solution for a white supremacist state that nonetheless must express "the relative inclusions of Asians and Pacific Islander peoples by postwar racial liberalism, which appeared to legitimize an official antiracism."[5] The U.S. Cold War execution of democracy and benevolence in response to global decolonization movements represents not only the management of white supremacy but in fact constitutes the very strategies that sustain it—as Lisa Yoneyama has observed, "In the global Cold War rivalry the disavowal of formal colonialism and white supremacy became a U.S. foreign policy concern of utmost urgency because of the need to mobilize the Third World countries, many of which were then emerging as new nation-states."[6] Within the larger concerns mediating the Cold War, the prisoners of USP Leavenworth participate in a discursive incorporation of Asian bodies into the national family. The proxy adoption of Bok Nam Om by USP Leavenworth prisoners offers an unlikely animation of adoption writ large during a period of Asian exclusion from the United States, tethering the legacies of transnational adoption and racially engineered immigration restriction to the prisoners' negotiations with carceral personhood and belonging. This story discloses the burdened genealogies of U.S. military empire in Korea, and the proxy adoption casts into sharp relief the fraught contingencies shaping normative liberal definitions of family.

While the prisoners' proxy adoption of Bok Nam Om attempts to reconcile the contradictions of their expulsion from the national family by remodeling a racial and gendered hierarchy that positions the prisoners as capable of exercising biopolitical imperatives of family making, the adoption also itself fractures such a hierarchical conception of kinship. Two occasions, both documented in *The New Era*, demonstrate the reworking of kinship narratives: the discursive blood ties created with the adoption of Bok Nam Om and the prisoners' blood donations for U.S. soldiers in Korea, both of which enabled the prisoners to argue for—however tenuous—their belonging to the nation. The prisoners and their adoption, their claims to liberal white personhood within the Cold War, and their attempts to articulate, both figuratively and literally, their blood as fit for fighting in the Korean War where "Asiatics: Japanese, Chinese and Filipinoes [*sic*]"[7] are not, function as a significant lens revealing contesting discourses of race and kinship. The warring genealogies of proxy adoption, white nationhood, and the differential racial matrix forged through the U.S. intervention in the Korean War emerge in *The New Era*. The catalyzing crucible of the war produced unanticipated and strange manifestations of white nationalist kinship. The prisoners' access to what Cheryl Harris theorizes as "whiteness as property" enables such claims, in particular against "Asiatic" GIs rendered as treacherous and untrustworthy of a place in the white American family. Just as the prisoners petition for release against the othered bodies of "Asiatic" GIs, they also further their blood claim to the white nationalist family by donating blood to support white GIs in the Korean War. The prisoners' efforts for inclusion in the Korean War, their segregated blood donation drives, and the proxy adoption facilitate their reentry into civil society, relieving them of their status as civilly dead and reinstating their place as rightful fighters and fathers in the exclusive American family.

The New Era of USP Leavenworth

The humidity weighed oppressively on the foreman's body, the air made thick with the 1898 Kansas sun and the dust drifting off bricks. Brick by brick, prisoners labored, twelve hours a day, constructing the penitentiary that would house those rendered criminal by the state. The foreman's eyes had to be all, unyielding—and he wasn't shy about discipline. Just yesterday he sentenced a prisoner to "carry the baby," chaining him to the twenty-five-pound metal ball that would hinder his movements for weeks—this for the audacity of grumbling about rations, saying it was both too little and too disgusting. He'd gotten extra rations now, the foreman thought grimly, twenty-five pounds of them. It was a big job, to oversee the convict laborers building the first federal prison, authorized by Congress after state and county jails crowded beyond capacity, beyond the fees Congress would pay to them to house federal prisoners. And the foreman resolved again that he would see the construction through, not dropping out like the cowards who went by the title "guard" only to quit, sometimes days after signing on. He didn't understand the scope of the sentence he gave himself, because it would be twenty-eight years before the building was complete, in 1926.

Almost a century earlier, in 1827, Colonel Henry H. Leavenworth of the U.S. Army occupied the place that would become Fort Leavenworth, serving as both a destination and stopping point for settlers in westward expansion. USP Leavenworth's origins and operations are intimately tied to U.S. acts of war, racial slavery, and empire. Kenneth LaMaster, former institutional historian at USP Leavenworth, tellingly states that the site "provided protection for fur traders from the incursions of Native Americans."[8] The fort's estab-

lishment hinged on the forcible removals of members in the Kaw Nation and
the Osage Nation who inhabited the geographical region. Members of the
nations were pushed south to Indian Territory through a series of expansion
and Indian removal acts. LaMaster's phrase "incursions of Native Americans"
belies the relentless pace of settler colonialism, with the ostensible protection
of fur traders masking white desire to secure and protect a place systematically *made into* property, a process Aileen Moreton-Robinson has described
as "the possession of Indigenous lands as [the] proprietary anchor" underpinning white supremacy in capitalist economies.[9]

The Korean War is structured within a global scope of settler genealogies
as well: "In September 1950 *Collier's* magazine described the war in Korea as
tougher than Okinawa and reminiscent of 'Indian warfare,' evoking memories of the savagery associated with both racialized campaigns."[10] The Korean
War, histories of dispossession in Okinawa, and the long legacies of "Indian
warfare" that structure the United States as a nation become imbricated in
what Jodi Kim describes as settler modernity—"an ensemble of relations
significantly structured and continually reproduced through spatial exceptions taking shape in such forms as POW camps, refugee camps, military
bases and camptowns, unincorporated territories, and incorporated territories
admitted as U.S. states."[11] The origin story for USP Leavenworth, as well as
the prisoners' engagements with the Korean War, frames it specifically as an
integral part of global settler genealogies.

Fort Leavenworth continued to absorb the space, serving as the U.S.
Disciplinary Barracks in 1874, a military prison whose inmates built the
civilian penitentiary USP Leavenworth starting in 1897.[12] The architect who
designed Leavenworth intended the penitentiary to "be as impressive as other
national institutions," the outward qualities of the building erecting a perverse double of democratic statecraft.[13] Perhaps such materialization is not
so perverse but rather symbolizes an extension of prisoners impressed into
the hollow confines of liberal democracy. While Congress had previously
paid fees to state and county jails to house federal prisoners, the redoubled
acceleration of incarceration following the Civil War congested these carceral
spaces even further.[14] Congress's consequent ratification of the Thirteenth
Amendment is thus critical in the history of USP Leavenworth. The amendment, which Dennis Childs describes as "one of the most devastating documents of liberal legal sorcery ever produced under occidental modernity,"[15]
declares: "Neither slavery nor involuntary servitude, *except as a punishment for
crime whereof the party shall have been duly convicted*, shall exist in the United
States, or any place subject to their jurisdiction" (italics added). The "sur-
reptitiously terroristic utility of the emancipation amendment" emphasized

above inaugurates manifold acts of "legal sorcery," not least of which is the reconversion of people into government property.[16] USP Leavenworth therefore represents a dual elaboration of property—the land itself a "proprietary anchor"[17] and the criminalized subjects themselves converted into the state's property, subjects who are then forced to construct the penitentiary so that the state may continue warehousing those who "have been duly convicted."

As Joy James reminds us, following the ratification of the Thirteenth Amendment, "slavery would operate in a restricted fashion. Congress resurrected social death as a permanent legal category in U.S. life. . . . Law mandated the transition from chattel slavery to penal slavery, from personal property to 'public' property owned by the state (and leased to corporate interests)."[18] Congress's canonization of social death as legal category made possible the abstract and material infrastructure for USP Leavenworth, enabled the use of leased convict labor to construct the penitentiary, and augured—for certain, budgeted in—the aggressive horizon of U.S. expansion yet to come. Indeed, the phrase "any place subject to their jurisdiction" anticipates not just the construction of a federal penitentiary on occupied Indigenous lands but also the extraterritorial prisons to come at Guantanamo Bay and Abu Ghraib.

Federal statistics suggest that at the official beginning of the Korean War, Leavenworth was mostly populated with white prisoners. A 1991 Department of Justice report, *Race of Prisoners Admitted to State and Federal Institutions (1926–86)*, calculates that in Kansas, out of the 810 sentenced prisoners admitted to state and federal institutions in 1950, 671 people were categorized as white, and 137 people were categorized as Black. While the official records also report 2 prisoners of "other races" in 1950, they were included in the total count for Black prisoners. National Prisoner Statistics, a report from the Federal Bureau of Prisons recording the race of felony prisoners in state institutions in Kansas in 1950, reports 638 white male prisoners and 131 Black male prisoners. These numbers sit tensely, for the inherent instability of the state's recordkeeping, the shifting parameters of words like *justice, felon,* and *criminal,* along with the rigid boundaries regulating white and Black, suggest not only the contradictory mechanisms by which the state keeps track but, as itself an indictment of liberal modernity, as well as a mechanism for crafting unfree subjects. These data are also limited to the admissions in 1950 and reveal little about Leavenworth's demographics leading up to and after that year. Because numbers open up but do not in and of themselves craft narratives, a reading practice that brushes against official ledgers recording prisoner data and considered alongside historical urgencies of the moment yields more robust narratives.

USP Leavenworth is thus embedded within the histories of multiple and at times overlapping moments in U.S. empire. The penitentiary has incarcerated inmates who served or refused to serve in expansionist wars abroad and domestically—and in the case of the Civil War, one that precipitated the development of the federal penitentiary itself.[19] The intimate relationship between military and prison at USP Leavenworth is inextricably connected to U.S. imperial wars, warehousing those impressed into service both in continental U.S. expansion and expansion overseas: "Leavenworth housed military inmates, including veterans of the Civil War and the Frontier Army campaigns. Other troubled soldiers, sailors, marines and veterans arrived with subsequent conflicts: the Spanish American and Philippine Islands wars, the Mexican Border Campaign, the Great War."[20] With its military base origin, expanded to include military and civilian prisoners, as well as its role in the history of white settler expansion, USP Leavenworth represents the state's exercise of carceral power in its empire-building imperatives.

Such empire building was not limited to territorial expansion alone. For the inmates at USP Leavenworth, access to the print empire, to the imagined community afforded to prisoners, enabled them to discursively participate in the Korean War. As a reformatory mechanism founded in 1914, "as a part of a larger wave of progressive penal reforms that offered inmates recreational and educational privileges in exchange for better behavior," *The New Era* promised rewarding work to prisoners.[21] By 1949, *The New Era* was thriving and circulating in prison libraries throughout the United States. The *Southeast Missourian* reported in an article entitled "Prison Magazine Now on Display: Leavenworth Staff Has Excellent One," that *The New Era* was "listed among the best magazines of its kind and is therefore to be seen regularly in many libraries. It is edited by inmates, most of its articles and other material are written by the inmates, and the art work, printing and binding is a product of the industrial department of the prison. . . . Those who avail themselves of the privilege of perusing the *New Era* magazine will realize why the Leavenworth prison has such a high rating among penal institutions."[22] The following year, after the official beginning of the Korean War on June 25, William Jones—inmate at USP Leavenworth and editor of *The New Era*—mobilized the magazine to publish his argument for using prisoners to participate in the war in the July–September 1950 issue of *The New Era*.

Despite the benevolent reformist impulses structured into *The New Era*, this prison magazine also functions as a cultural text in tension with the circumstances of its production within a federal disciplinary institution. The content of the magazine is necessarily selective, produced under conditions of intense McCarthy-era scrutiny in the penitentiary. In the relationships *The New Era* records between two groups rendered excessive to state-sanctioned definitions of family—Korean War orphans and U.S. penitentiary inmates—

the prison magazine discloses inmates' claims of national belonging through their performance of embodying the ideals of kinship, in the role of fathers, in their proxy adoption of Bok Nam Om. For the prisoners, the proxy adoption of Bok Nam Om "created an avenue through which Americans excluded from other discourses of nationhood could find ways to identify with the nation as it undertook its world-ordering projects of containing communism and expanding American influence."[23] Underwriting this practice of kinship, however, are the liberal impossibilities of personhood, articulated through Indigenous dispossession, the sustained infrastructure of anti-Black violence, and the repudiation of Asian bodies, as evidenced by *The New Era*'s editorial pieces that petition for the participation of prisoners in the U.S. military during the Korean War, in response to the inclusion of "treacherous" Asian subjects in the U.S. military.[24] In their use of Bok Nam Om to represent the symbolic labor of democratic inclusion, the prisoners perform the habits of citizenship that would ostensibly resurrect their civil status.

To contextualize figure 1.1, the accompanying article for the letter from the sponsor agency, which was reprinted upside down, states:

> Inmates of prisons and reformatories in our country can be proud of their contributions to the fighting of wars. But they can be even more proud of their efforts to bring comfort to children who might otherwise perish. Leavenworth can be particularly proud of its part in this great undertaking. . . . [The sponsor agency's] gratitude is tremendous, as is evident in a portion of Bok Nam Om's letter: "Words cannot express the gratitude we feel in our hearts." These words show that we are helping to repair the "much damaged" areas of Korea. . . . Perhaps by aiding these children we have aided oudselves [*sic*] even more.[25]

The letter of gratitude from the sponsor agency, along with the article, suggests the writer's discursive occupation of the position of a paternal figure, who does not reflect on the necessary connection between "their contributions to the fighting of wars" and "their efforts to bring comfort to children who might otherwise perish." The article argues for the legitimacy of adopting a child who remains "over there" in Korea, a space seemingly demarcated from the United States by oceans and continental boundaries, and for the prisoners, contained by the cruel architecture of the penitentiary. Proxy adoption is thus rendered as ideal, demonstrating the abstract logic of helping Korean others without the others physically entering the boundaries of the United States. Indeed, the letter of gratitude from the sponsorship agency "show[s] that [inmates] are helping to repair" Korea, such that Bok Nam Om could, by virtue of the adoption, remain safely removed from the nation. And so "perhaps by aiding these children [inmates] have aided [themselves] even more," securing abstract paternity while imprisoned, which demonstrates the potential for white prisoners during the Korean War era to rehabilitate into the nation-state, without jeopardizing the normative parameters of the nation—from which the prisoners have also been removed.

Underpinning white supremacist ideology is the deployment of race as an instrument of social control, an instrument that replicates and wields its force through hierarchies. *The New Era*, during this moment, functions as a site of relative white racial access, engaging with and responding to the larger national circuit of print material, occasionally accessing spots in newspapers through the form of reprints, and addressing editorials to President Eisenhower.[26] Although mediated by the institutional strictures of the penitentiary, as well as the national constraints of anticommunism, white inmates nevertheless enjoyed a right of entry into print culture. During the Korean War period, *The New Era* registers the erasure of alternative imaginings[27] and demonstrates the degrees of differential racialized access to material and discursive sites of privilege, such as participating in national print culture, however limited, and claiming a stake in belonging to the idealized national family through the proxy adoption of Bok Nam Om.

Owning "Your Own Flesh and Blood": Whiteness as Property and the Pliability of Civil Death

The prisoners' visions of hegemonic kinship, which emerge through their support of the Korean War, begin years prior to the adoption in William Jones's 1950 editorial urging their release from the penitentiary so that they might join the U.S. military in Korea. In his discussion of scientific experiments on prisoners and the theory of consent in U.S. prisons and Nazi concentration camps, Giorgio Agamben states that "to speak of free will and consent in the case of a person sentenced to death or of a detained person who must pay serious penalties is, at the very least, questionable. . . . What the well-meaning emphasis on the free will of the individual refuses to recognize here is that the concept of 'voluntary consent' is simply meaningless."[28] William Jones's letter, however, suggests the nuanced ideologies operating on subjects with white supremacist access and reveals the logic of such a hierarchy replicating in USP Leavenworth during the Korean War. In other words, degrees of racialized differentiation and access to what Cheryl Harris calls "whiteness as property" modify "the concept of 'voluntary consent,'" such that even in an abject space of detention, prisoners racialized as possessing legitimate person-hood can "volunteer" to participate in the Korean War.[29]

While Jones reworks the narrative of voluntary conscription to fashion a narrative of choice and liberation from USP Leavenworth, for Black, Latinx, Indigenous, and Asian peoples, the ostensible choice is riddled with the con-tradictory violence of being racialized in a white supremacist state. Indeed, the white prisoners of USP Leavenworth can volunteer themselves for partici-pation in the Korean War because the white supremacist state equates white-ness with agency, action, and political will and legally reifies the property of white personhood, positioning whites as owners of their "own flesh and blood." Cheryl Harris defines white supremacy as

> privileging "white" as unadulterated, exclusive, and rare. Inherent in the concept of "being white" was the right to own or hold whiteness to the exclusion and subordination of Blacks. . . . In the commonly held popular view, the presence of Black "blood"—including the in-famous "one-drop"—consigned a person to being "Black". . . . Recog-nizing or identifying oneself as white is thus a claim of racial purity, an assertion that one is free of any taint of Black blood. The law has played a critical role in legitimating this claim.[30]

Jones identifies the white prisoners of USP Leavenworth as "Americans, your own flesh and blood," the ideology underpinning such a move defining the prisoners as "unadulterated, exclusive, and rare." In other words, in contrast to Asians characterized as deviant and treacherous, the white prisoners can exercise their *exclusive* and *rare* possession of *unquestionable* patriotism and citizenship, constructed through Black exclusion, the subordination of In-digenous peoples, and the robust volume of legalized restrictions of people of color. Lisa Cacho asserts that "those with social privilege often still interpret economic, social, political, and/or legal integration as a (conditional) 'gift.'"[31] While the white prisoners of USP Leavenworth clearly do not have access to broader social privilege, Cacho's statement nonetheless registers here. The let-ter suggests that Jones and other white prisoners negotiate these logics and, more significantly, engage with potential entitlement and access to the conditional gift of integration into the national family, political order, social possibility, and patriotic participation. The letter, then, crafts another fold into the discourse of white supremacy and whiteness as property: the racialized spectrum of differentiated access not just to whiteness but extending also to the question-able citizenship of Asians, in particular in the wake of Japanese internment.

U.S. nationalist ideology and the long series of legislation buttressing white supremacy imagines citizenship as exclusively white and masculine and instrumentally admits nonpropertied, noneducated white men and women and other racialized peoples into the realm of citizenship throughout centuries. Such an ideology underwrites Jones's anxiety that "President Truman has already signed a bill sponsored by Senator Lodge of Massachusetts to allow aliens to enlist in the U.S. Army. After five years they can quality for citizenship!" That "aliens . . . in the U.S. Army" could "qualify for citizenship" after only five years conflicts with U.S. citizenship's centuries-deep origins in white supremacist logic, as evidenced in the 1790 Naturalization Act. Such an audacious presumption to citizenship, coupled with the idea that incarcerated white citizens are rendered devoid of civil status and are thus unable to participate in the Korean War, forms the basis for the racialized anxiety in Jones's statement.[32]

Indeed, the letter rationalizes the racialized unfitness of "Asiatics: Japanese, Chinese and Filipinoes [sic]" as troops by naturalizing the teleological association of peoples with their assumed and undeveloped countries of origin: "Rather than being in a position to help, both China and the Philippine Islands need help to save themselves from the fangs of communism. The Japanese, until a scant five years ago, were our dreaded enemy. Pearl Harbor was an example of their trustworthiness." With this statement, Jones infantilizes China and the Philippines by charging that they require "help to save themselves from the fangs of communism." In contrast to the infantilized, helpless China and the Philippines, Jones builds urgency for the United States to intervene against "the fangs of communism," resonating with long-standing notions of the United States as a national paternal figure that takes up "the white man's burden."[33] The language "Americans, your own flesh and blood" situates "the fangs of communism" as particularly pernicious, poised to drain deserving citizens of their morally superior capitalist ideology. Indeed, the letter suggests larger tropes of a fully developed, masculine United States working to save the undeveloped, politically unsophisticated yellow and brown bodies from a fiendish economic system. The letter's rhetorical moves indicate that some prisoners aligned themselves with the narrative of national paternalism that constructs Asian nations as helpless, dreaded children, long before the prisoners' proxy adoption of Bok Nam Om.

In addition to their insistence on the racialized unfitness of "Asiatics," some prisoners also exercised the patriotic duty to contribute to the Korean War and adopted Bok Nam Om by proxy through the War Orphan Sponsorship program and Save the Children Federation. I suggest that the prisoners made use of virtual adoption to demonstrate their ability to conform to an abstract ideal of the model citizen, of a model member of the racially "pure" national family. However foreclosed the normative domestic sphere might be for the prisoners, the logic of national belonging extends to the hyper-controlled carceral space of the penitentiary. Ironically, the penitentiary represents what Dylan Rodríguez describes as "the production of a social logic essential to the current social order—a fabrication and criminalization of disorder for the sake of extracting and dramatizing order, compliance, authority."[34] Jones himself offers a passing reference to this militarized social order by way of explaining the presence of some prisoners in USP Leavenworth "who went through their formative years sans proper parental care. (Father in the Army—Mother in essential war industry.)" As persons differentially fabricated and criminalized into representing disorder, the prisoners of USP Leavenworth participating in the adoption draw on the same social logic, with the effect of replicating the national familial order and demonstrating charitable authority over such subjects as Bok Nam Om.

What does it mean for the prisoners and Bok Nam Om, both differently marked with civil death, to attempt to form ties of kinship forged in spaces of exception, in the spaces devastated by war and enclosed by domestic punishment? I suggest that *The New Era* articles function to remember this curious moment and to demonstrate, despite the articles' attempts to reclaim personhood for some of the prisoners, the white supremacist, heteropatriarchal, and capitalist state's imperatives of punishment. In *The New Era*, this punishment is embodied by the Korean civilian population (of which Bok Nam Om is one representative), the GIs drafted into the Korean War, and the prisoners negotiating white supremacist logic to seek liberation from one punitive enclosure to the putative freedom of the Korean War. Furthermore, not only do the articles trouble dominant understandings of kinship; they also make possible the distinctions between social death, as I argue above, and the discursive pliability built into the condition of civil death for prisoners racialized as white.

In distinction from the "Asiatics," William Jones's letter argues that "inmates of our penal institutions . . . are Americans, your own flesh and blood," thereby affirming white bodies as rightful members of the American family. The proxy adoption of Bok Nam Om by the prisoners of USP Leavenworth was legally circumscribed due to racially restrictive immigration policies, yet the same exclusionary practice enables participation from a segment of the population that otherwise would not be able to adopt.[35] *The New Era* articles rely on long-standing discourses of infantilized "Asiatics" to make white supremacist claims of legitimate national belonging by revaluing prisoners' criminalized statuses against others demarcated as subhuman. Yet the articles

Your Children's Progress:

Bok Nam Om

Four years ago in March when we became acquainted with Bok Nam he was a baby, less than one year old; he will be four on September seventeenth and is a sturdy little fellow as attested by his most recent photograph.

You men of Leavenworth befriended him when his need was the greatest, the urgency of that need has diminished, yet it is still there. Hunger is a still specter always at hand in Korea and the tense state of internal affairs makes living a reasonably normal life almost impossible.

Some advance have been made toward settling the displaced families of people like our little friend, Bok Nam, but the job is far from complete. Land must be reclaimed, the soil tilled, and crops planted. Two tired women and one little boy cannot survive without help.

Here is a paragraph from the last sponsorship status report. It shows plainly why Bok Nam needs our continued aid.

"The family still lives in a Refugee Camp on the outskirts of Seoul and numbers three: Bok Nam, his mother and a grandmother. No news has been heard of the missing father yet. (His) Mother does peddling and makes a little money. She has been greatly encouraged by the sponsorship and is firmly determined to do whatever is best for her son without her husband. She works hard from early morning till late at night and strives to improve their present circumstances.

BOK NAM still needs the help of his friends at Leavenworth.

Age one year

Brave Bok Nam

The retreat to Seoul was not in vain;
For dignity and purpose can arise from pain.
You, brave Bok Nam Om, have been the one
To make us know peace must be won.

Because we love you, because we care,
In our hearts we have made a prayer:
A prayer that you will laugh and play,
And each morning will begin a beautiful day.

A prayer you'll be happy, strong and free;
A prayer that some fine day you will see
How much you have helped us, why our thanks is due
For having the privilege of just knowing you.

R. P. DICKEY

Age three years six months

Figure 1.2 Reprint of Bok Nam Om's profile in *The New Era*. (Courtesy of the National Archives at Kansas City)

also complicate Christina Klein's question of transracial adoptions serving "as a means of social control," as the prisoners themselves delimit one boundary of national social control. While Klein's argument holds true for those who inhabit the political terrains of normative citizenship, the prisoners act in a field licensed with alternative workings of power. They are adopting to gain recognition as participants in the nation, the same nation that created the boundaries of exclusion for the prisoners in the first place. Proxy adoption enables the prisoners to negotiate the discourses of kinship required by the white supremacist state to navigate possibilities for ostensible liberation from the penitentiary. Yet as Eleana Kim shows in *Adopted Territory*, actual physical adoptions in the immediate aftermath of the Korean War were quite limited: four in 1953, eight in 1954, and then increasing to fifty-nine in 1955.[36] These numbers suggest that the possibility of adoption into the United States in 1953 was nearly always via proxy and, for the prisoners, in no material way altered relationships, either for Bok Nam Om or for themselves as incarcerated subjects. Thus the proxy adoption remains a dress rehearsal of reintegration for the white prisoners, an avenue to perform their possible reintegration into civil society, out of civil death. Nonetheless, such selective racialized access to the performance of national belonging highlights the impossibility for the nonwhite prisoner to demonstrate rehabilitation and reform and further perpetuates the nonwhite prisoner's ontological status as inherently criminalized.

Normative understandings of family and the national body are often defined in relation to legally constructed "outsiders," such as prisoners, a group that has been severed from social belonging throughout the history of the prison as an institution.[37] In his study of the penitentiary, Caleb Smith notes that "in the original American penitentiaries [of the late eighteenth century], the inmate was divested of rights, social connections, and identity, stripped down to a bare life no longer recognizable as human."[38] Through the disciplining and reforming mechanisms of the penitentiaries, white prisoners were then to be elevated back to the legal and social realms of citizenship and humanity, into the familial fold of the nation. Other scholars, such as Colin Dayan, theorize the prisoner as a figure marking the "legal fiction of 'civil death': the state of a person who though possessing *natural life* has lost all *civil rights*."[39] Reduced to bare life and subject to civil death,[40] prisoners are legally constructed to be excluded from affective and kinship possibilities, as "outside the boundary of human empathy: no longer recognized as a social, political, or individual entity."[41]

Within both formal, acknowledged systems of incarceration, such as prisons, and regimes of subjugation, such as Indigenous genocide and chattel slavery, white supremacy supplied "*a logic of social organization* that produces regimented, institutionalized, and militarized conceptions of hierarchized 'human' difference."[42] Within the prison system, which includes white and nonwhite prisoners, such a racially hierarchized logic operates, replicates, and intensifies this white supremacist social organization. Indeed, one way for USP Leavenworth prisoners to stake claims to the national family, in addition to adopting Bok Nam Om by proxy, was to donate blood to the UN forces in Korea, thereby materially sharing bloodlines with the defenders of the nation. The white supremacist social organization of the United States persisted stubbornly through its military occupation in Korea, as even the blood contribution and demonstration of belonging to the national family was segregated well into the Korean War.

In addition to the adoption of Bok Nam Om, the prisoners of USP Leavenworth imagined another avenue for constructing kinships during the Korean War by infusing blood into the U.S. and UN armed forces, to better defend against "the fangs of communism." The winter 1951 issue of *The New*

Era documents blood donations from inmates, followed by a list of donors, organized by the number of pints donated:

> Fighting blood for fighting men will have a little more meaning next month when blood bank time rolls around. Seventy-two hours after you have contributed, your blood will be reviving some United Nations warrior on the Korean battle front.
>
> . . .
>
> Approximately 250 volunteers will be called and the customary post-donation refreshments served. . . . Concerning the following listed donors, keep in mind that those credited with but one or two pints probably have not been here long enough to contribute more.

With the contributions of 250 "volunteers," the prisoners at USP Leavenworth perhaps literally enlivened "United Nations warrior[s]" during the Korean War. Yet the language of volunteerism within this carceral space, as well as the suggestion that those who have donated "but one or two pints" will have plenty of time to give more blood, suggests that the U.S. military is directly leeching blood from the inmates. In other words, veiled through the patriotic language of the article, the boundary between "voluntary" participation in the U.S. military and prison is increasingly blurred in the context of USP Leavenworth.

The same white supremacist ideology that enables both the notion of belonging to the U.S. nation and of self-possession—what Harris defines as "the act necessary to lay the basis for rights in property—was defined to include only the cultural practices of whites. This definition laid the foundation for the idea that whiteness—that which whites alone possess—is valuable and is property."[43] Despite the tense implication of consent residing in the statement "volunteers will be called" for blood donation, such an ideology again scripts white blood as valuable, as property that prisoners possess, notwithstanding their civilly dead status. Thus, the pliability of civil death for the white prisoners intersects with the impossibility of consent, forging a matrix of power through which differential avenues of license and punishment emerge. I do not mean to suggest that all prisoners were equally enmeshed in such exercises of power; nor do I mean to suggest that civil death does not carry severe consequences for the prisoners at USP Leavenworth. Rather, this instance of blood donation during the Korean War serves as a site for interrogating the workings of white supremacist ideology, articulated through attempts to forge kinship as well as possessing personhood.

Ultimately, the carceral population, through collective civil death, is made to reanimate state power, their blood donations fortifying the state's ability to kill with impunity, thereby laboring at the intersections of biopower and empire. In other words, a population rendered civilly dead is then resurrected through the potency of possessing white blood, which then provides transfusions for the U.S. military's killing of Korean and Chinese soldiers. Biopower—the state's interest in a "positive" logic engaging subjects in the preservation and reproduction of life—extends in this case to the management of prisoners as well as to the transfer of their blood donations to GIs, another population subject to total state authority, both cases instantiating "the break between what must live and what must die."[44] The state's absolute access to both GIs and prisoners during the Korean War, made kin through the alchemy of blood, delimits who must be detained and kept alive, for others to be conscripted and made to both kill and die.

The prisoners' blood donation indicates the compatibility of racism and biopower in both the abstract and material calculations of war—the enemy's death not only establishes the immediate personal safety of the self but guarantees into the future a "healthier and purer" life without the bad or inferior race (or the bad or inferior communist ideology).[45] I suggest that the example of blood donation demonstrates the compatibility of racism and biopower in both the abstract and material calculations of war—the enemy's death not only establishes the immediate personal safety of the self but guarantees into the future a speculative genealogy of purer white racial life. For instance, anxious about the consequences of nonsegregated blood donation, and clearly ascribing to a rather confounding pseudoscientific racism, the World War II veteran Pete Jarman asks, "How many white men, having a choice, would rather die there on the battlefield without plasma than run the chance of coming back to be the father, grandfather, or great grandfather of a brown, red, black, or yellow child?"[46] This speculative genealogy, the disavowal several generations into the future of a spectral "brown, red, black, or yellow child," operates in stark contrast to the prisoners' proxy adoption of Bok Nam Om. However, both cases of somewhat immaculate practices of kinship—proxy adoption and the notion that receiving blood transfusions from nonwhite donors would pollute the white man's reproductive blood—turn on the same contradictory axis that compels the imprisoned white man to proxy adoption and the impressed white GI to express fear about the power of nonwhite blood. Such an exercise of biopower intersects with the imperial interventions of the U.S. military on the Korean peninsula; the white supremacist logics that imbue the white prisoner with subjecthood; the ambivalent desire to both make live an "orphan" belonging to an inferior race while ensuring his physical distance from the nation; and the necessity of using prisoners, who are made to live within the strict purview of the state, to keep alive GIs, who are made to kill inferior others.

Ironically, it is not the "fangs of communism" that plague the prisoners of USP Leavenworth but rather the racial capitalist state that drains their blood. Despite U.S. federal penitentiaries' relatively "diverse" racial demographics, given that the Red Cross segregated donated blood, the penitentiary's blood collection efforts were likely segregated. Thus, the narrative of national belonging does not rescript racialization as the underlying plot, even if the details of the story shift to the collective confines of civil death. Yevette Richards notes that "although the American Red Cross eventually began to hire black employees, the organization continued to segregate blood during the Korean War until United Nations employees protested."[47] Catherine Ramírez documents a similar instance of blood segregation that *pachucas* faced during World War II: "To prove their patriotism, they offered to donate blood to the American Red Cross, but the organization rejected it on the grounds that they were Mexican."[48] The Red Cross's rejection registers the disqualification of the racialized and gendered pachuca subjects from national belonging and indexes a remove from the particular biopolitical project of enlivening U.S. imperial soldiers.

Such examples suggest that the ideology expressed in *The New Era*, that the prisoners are "Americans, your own flesh and blood," is shaped and constrained by racially exclusive and white supremacist boundaries in support of the national family fighting against communism in Korea. The prisoners' virtual blood ties with Bok Nam Om and giving blood to the U.S. soldiers fighting in Korea enable them to claim belonging in the nation. Yet these kinship ties are tangled with racial disquiet: the kinship ties with Bok Nam Om are proxy, and the donated blood is segregated, such that even a biopolitical imperative to make GIs live operates on multiple distinctions among racialized citizens constructed as the inferior other. Finally, the prison magazine documents the contradictions generated by the fact that inmates marked with civil death are materially energizing GIs, the figures of national patriotism, who are dying to "save" Korea from communism.

Furthermore, I argue that the prisoners' efforts to represent themselves as rightful members of the American family in order to join the Korean War hauntingly mirrors the coercive conditions of citizenship for nonwhite people, especially Chicano/as, Latino/as, Asians, and others who were perceived as foreigners during World War II. The open letter written by William Jones and signed by the prisoners of USP Leavenworth aggressively makes the argument that inmates should be allowed to participate in the Korean War, especially in place of "Asiatics" in the United States. Ironically, for many people of Asian descent, as well as for Black, Chicano/a, Indigenous, and other nonwhite people in the United States, participating in the U.S. military afforded otherwise inaccessible opportunities for both real and symbolic citizenship. This was particularly true during World War II, when many Black and Latinx youth participated in efforts both for and against the war. In *Black Is a Country*, Nikhil Singh quotes a statement from a young student attending a Black college in the South, a statement that succinctly captures the white supremacist tensions of the Second World War: "'The army Jim-Crows us. The Navy lets us serve only as messmen. The Red Cross refuses our blood. Employers and labor unions shut us out. Lynchings continue. We are disenfranchised, Jim-Crowed, spat upon. What more could Hitler do than that?'"[49]

While *The New Era* must conform to nationalist parameters in its articulations of voluntary participation in the Korean War, cultural texts such as James Baldwin's long essay *The Devil Finds Work* (1976) offer alternative knowledges operating in the logic of choice and consent. On the racial politics of the Korean War, Baldwin reflects:

> I began to feel a terrified pity for the white children of these white people: who had been sent, by their parents, to Korea, though their parents did not know why. Neither did their parents know why these miserable, incontestably inferior, rice-eating gooks refused to come to heel, and would not be saved. But *I* knew why. . . . Even in the case of Korea, we, the blacks at least, knew why our children were there: they had been sent there to be used, in exactly the same way, and for the same reasons, as the blacks had been so widely dispersed out of Africa—an incalculable investment of raw material in what was not yet known as the common market.[50]

Baldwin theorizes what *The New Era* articles could not: the incessant algorithm of a capitalist engine appraising the extractive logics of dispossession. Such examples show that, unlike the prisoners of USP Leavenworth who appear to regard joining the military as a means of proving their fidelity to the nation, for Black and Latinx people, the choices for war participation were conditioned by the contradictions of citizenship and the necessity of proving loyalty to the nation. Yet to suggest that the prisoners were only complicit in an empire-building, war-mongering system is too simple. From their particular locations within the penitentiary, the courses they charted to navigate this system triangulated avenues of kinship as well as avenues of combat, both building possible paths into legibility as normative citizens, normative members of the idealized national family.

Carceral Kinships

The stories of post–World War II and post–Korean War adoptions, whether physical or by proxy, offer critiques of dominant definitions of family, which have centered privileged discourses throughout U.S. history. In significant ways, the prisoners' 1954 adoption falls squarely within the normative kinship imperatives of the era—as Elaine Tyler May has noted, "Fatherhood became a new badge of masculinity and meaning for the postwar man. . . . Men began attending classes on marriage and family in unprecedented numbers. In 1954, *Life* announced 'the domestication of the American male.'"[51] Rendered by the state as civilly dead, unable to participate in normative familial relationships, the prisoners of USP Leavenworth navigate alternative relationships to both kinship and the Korean War. With their adoption of Bok Nam Om, the prisoners' access to and remaking of kinship operates within and creates uneven articulations of power, further destabilizing normative registers of family. Inhabiting formations of tenuous carceral subjecthood, the prisoners triangulate and document their encounters with militarized state power, negotiations with civil death, and transnational adoption during the Korean War. Within the framework of an anticommunist, white supremacist war, the prisoners, occupying the contradictions of civil death, discursively claimed Bok Nam Om in an attempt to produce an alternative kinship, one that suggests different kinds of affective relationships that brush against dominant definitions of family.

Literary and ethnic studies scholars locate the emergence of modern transnational and transracial adoption at the end of the Second World War. As they have noted, transnational adoption shares the concerns of a post–World War II phenomenon in which infants represent actual and human capital; in which the accommodation of Asian infants was reflected in the modification of legal restrictions barring Asian immigration during the Korean War with the passing of the Immigration and Nationality Act of 1952; and which shares a prehistory in the white settler colonialist practices of forcible "adoption" of Native children.[52] Before the adjustment of racially restrictive immigration policies in 1952, however, Americans were able to adopt by proxy through various Christian and global relief organizations, such as the Christian Children's Fund, the War Orphan Sponsorship program, and the Save the Children Federation, through letter and photograph exchanges and through financial and material support. Klein states that these post-

Figure 1.3 NASM 4A 32616 "Air Force Activities: Evacuees—Korean" (July 1953).
(Courtesy of the National Archives at College Park)

war "moral" adoptions made possible U.S. cultural imaginings of a global, multiracial family that symbolically enabled visions of democratic, capitalist triumph, especially before racially exclusive immigration laws were lifted.

Korean diaspora and transnational adoption studies scholars have meanwhile analyzed discourses surrounding the post-1945 production of orphans from Korea as consumable, imperiled bodies that require adoption into normative nuclear families. This dominant notion of family is at once inclusive and exclusive, marking the boundaries between trustworthy intimates and unfamiliar others, between those who belong and those who are on the outside. Adoption studies scholars have established that within Korea, numerous factors contributed to the phenomenon of sending babies and children abroad for adoption. The occupying force of the U.S. military since Korea's ostensible liberation from Japan in 1945 not only left intact the structure of Japanese military prostitution but, as Grace Cho and others have revealed, in fact expanded it to accommodate growing U.S. military bases.[53] Sexual encounters between members of the U.S. military and Korean women produced a mixed-race population classified as undesirable by the Korean state and society. The years of war physically devastated the country, which Hosu Kim notes dismantled possibilities for social support within the patriarchal structures of the South Korean state. The conditions of possibility for transnational, transracial, and proxy adoptions were therefore partly formed by the Korean state's responses to U.S. imperial actions, setting the stage for intervention and extraction by such organizations as the Christian Children's Fund.

Proxy and moral adoptions both reinforce dominant understandings of family in the United States and nuance alternative possibilities underwriting kinship. The categories of family and kinship have occupied privileged positions throughout U.S. history. As Judith Butler has observed, "It is not possible to separate questions of kinship from property relations (and conceiving persons as property), and from the fictions of 'bloodline' as well as the national and racial interests by which these lines are sustained."[54] While proxy adoptions enabled Americans who felt excluded from the familial norms of the 1950s to participate in building idealized families, they also enabled prisoners, who occupy hypermarginalized social and political positions, to make claims to the imagined national family, citizenship, and carceral subjecthood. Examining the definitions of kinship in the space of the penitentiary reveals that kinship in this instance is closely affiliated with civil death and militarized state violence. Rather than serving the apparently reifying function of building idealized families, the example of proxy adoption by prisoners instead reveals the inherent instabilities of kinship, instabilities that are critical to unsettling the legitimating foundations of the idealized national family. The proxy adoption and sponsorship of Korean orphans exposes nationalist formulations of the idealized American family, citizenship, and exclusion. In other words, how does the Korean War in particular reveal racialized problems and conundrums constricting dominant conceptions of the American family? As Jodi Kim observes in *Ends of Empire* and as David Eng argues throughout *The Feeling of Kinship*, the gendered and racialized bodies of Asian adoptees labor to shore up both heteronormative white conceptions and queer liberal notions of family. Eng challenges scholars to attend to the racialization of intimacy, the ways race is both exploited and erased in the service of the idealized private family, to uncover the long histories of racialization that organize queer liberalism.[55] This hierarchy and the triangulated relationship among the state, the inmates, and Bok Nam Om bring into relief the fraught and mediated construction of normative kinship. Bok Nam Om's own diasporic status is mobilized through the Leavenworth prisoners' participation in print culture and instantiates a reckoning of U.S. immigration history.

The New Era: Triangulating the Military-, Prison-, and Adoption-Industrial Complexes

The New Era also documents a history that throws into relief the haunting Cold War moment that marks an overlap between the prison-industrial complex and the emerging discourse of the "adoption-industrial complex."[56] The concentration of capital around central constellations of the military apparatus during the period of the Second World War defines what Dwight D. Eisenhower named the military-industrial complex. Drawing critical connections to the logic behind the military-industrial complex, in particular "because of the extent to which prison building and operations began to attract vast amounts of capital," Angela Davis states "the term 'prison industrial complex' was introduced by activists and scholars to contest prevailing beliefs that increased levels of crime were the root cause of mounting prison populations."[57] Tracing this logic back to the significant amounts of capital and profit generated through the system of transnational adoption, I build on the discourse of what Kimberly McKee has called the "transnational adoption-industrial complex" as an analytic that directs us toward a critique of transnational adoption. While all three terms contain different problems in usage, thinking through the emergence of these industries calls attention to the material and discursive formation of the military, the prison, and transnational adoption as interrelated phenomena.

Triangulating the three industries—military, prison, and adoption—works to denaturalize the idea of family, shifting it away from its assumed outcome of representing the nation, in addition to allowing space for a critique of the nation's paternalistic role in global military affairs. Although the *military-industrial complex* and the *prison-industrial complex* are now established terms in both nonacademic and academic discourse, the *adoption-industrial complex* is an emergent term that is useful to examine the Korean War, the USP Leavenworth prisoners, and the proxy adoption of Bok Nam Om. Indeed, such a triangulation couples notions of the heteronormative family to the violence of imperial war and instrumental criminalization, revealing the interconnectedness of national and transnational violence in the service of defending the idealized national family. In this instance, the more familiar prison- and military-industrial complexes serve as known locations to chart the course that a triangulation with the adoption-industrial complex might yield.

Such a triangulation maps the ways family is reinscribed to further entrench nationalism and anticipates the formation of neoliberal economic practices rooted in disassembling the state's management of welfare and increasing state dependence on contracts with private corporations in the post–World

War II era. In other words, examining the triangulation of the military, prison, and adoption industries reveals the interconnections that increasingly rely on privatization and exposes the economic crises that exacerbate such state dependence. The military-industrial complex enabled an economic boom in Southern California during the Second World War, which heralded what Ruth Wilson Gilmore describes as "the 'golden age' of U.S. capitalism (1944–74), [and] the rapidly growing economy both generated and was partly dependent on the now legendary military/industrial complex that Dwight D. Eisenhower spoke of with alarm during his final presidential address."[58] The neoliberal dismantling of social support in California, flexed by "new and reorganizing power blocs that have led the assault on income guarantees and other provisions against individualized calamity," enables state power to define, create, and target criminalized populations, inaugurating the burgeoning prison-industrial complex, or "the state's attempt to produce a geographical solution (incarceration) to political economic crisis."[59] *The New Era* captures the early moments of the military-industrial complex and anticipates the formations of two other "industries"—prison and adoption.[60]

While the United States witnessed the vestiges of the golden age of U.S. capitalism, in South Korea in the 1970s, the capital generated by sex work and by sending babies and children abroad through adoption contributed significantly to the economic development of South Korea.[61] Since that time, "the Korean tourism industry has experienced a boom, hand in hand with the sex industry. At an extreme, government officials have enthusiastically supported prostitution as a way to increase foreign exchange earnings for the Korean government."[62] In the context of Korean transnational adoption from the 1970s, the discourse of biopolitics, of managing the conditions of reproduction and making "abandoned" children live, intersects with a multiplicity of discourses that sustain U.S. liberal democracy—the narrative of masculine salvation, strategically juxtaposed against "a more putatively pernicious Asian patriarchy"; the narrative of liberal feminism, which through "nontraditional (re)productive possibilities" and "middle-class material privileges" delivers the promise initiated by the USP Leavenworth prisoners in the form of proxy adoption; and the illusion of integrating the gendered and racialized recipient of rescue into a benevolent, welcoming capitalist democracy.[63] South Korea occupies an "exceptional" biopolitical position for transnational adoption, not only because it is a developed sending country but also "from the fact that it has the longest history of overseas adoption, and its advanced medical services and streamlined process ensure healthy infants within a short period of time, thereby earning it the reputation as the Cadillac of adoption programs."[64]

Significantly, the production of civil death marks the convergence of subjectivities defined by bare life and constructed by the state. Although situated in radical differentiation from the prisoners of USP Leavenworth, scholars suggest Korean adoptees are also marked by civil death. Eleana Kim writes that for Korean adoptees in the contemporary moment,

> an "orphan hojuk," or orphan registry, served to render the child as a legible, free-standing subject of the state in preparation for adoption and erasure as a Korean citizen. The child was thus registered as a family head of its own, single-person household and solitary lineage. This disembedding of the child from a normative kinship structure and its legal reinscription as a peculiar and exceptional state subject singularize the child as an orphan, without any extant kinship ties. In the context of Korean law, she becomes a person with the barest of social identities, and in the context of Korean cultural norms, she lacks the basic requirements of social personhood—namely, family lineage and genealogical history.[65]

Just as the prisoner is divested from the privileges of normative citizenship, the Korean orphan undergoes "erasure as a Korean citizen." The Korean orphan is made into a "peculiar and exceptional state subject" and expelled from normative kinship ties, similar to the "exceptional" status of the prisoner outside of the idealized national family. In short, both figures are made bare by the state, for the inscription of particular national genealogies to underwrite their conditions of existence.

Furthermore, Jodi Kim extends Eleana Kim's argument to suggest that "the legal production of the orphan renders a social death to the orphan," in light of the fact that adoptees are stripped of social status and because of the natal alienation of birth mothers and adoptees.[66] Yet each of these subjectivities are differentially marked by the legacies of gendered racial capitalism, despite Lisa Cacho's assertion that "to be ineligible for personhood is a form of social death; it not only defines who does not matter, it also makes mattering meaningful."[67] Within such a framework, the figures of the orphan, the birth mother, and the prisoner negotiate differential access to making "mattering meaningful"—in the case of the white prisoner of USP Leavenworth, he can still make claims to kinship in ways that a Black prisoner would not be able to access. While the uses of social death to name the condition of Korean orphans can be generative, I retain the use of civil death in the specific case of USP Leavenworth prisoners and their adoption of Bok Nam Om to highlight the differential degrees utilized for making "mattering meaningful."

In one sense, the civil death of adoptees enables a symbolic reclamation of normative family life and a discursive resurrection from civil death for the prisoners of USP Leavenworth. However, what the prisoners are offering in exchange for such symbolic reclamation and discursive resurrection is in fact their lives, to be read logically within the confines of legitimacy and patriotism. Situated within the emergence of the military-industrial complex, the repeated requests to be released from USP Leavenworth on to the Korean peninsula during the war serve as a harbinger of what will unfold in the next decades as the intimate relationship between the military- and prison-industrial complexes. Furthermore, the prisoners' requests to serve in the Korean War are prescribed against the spectral and proxy body of the Korean orphan, a figure that rapidly assumes corporeal shape in the decades following the war. Reconfiguring the prisoners' relationships to idealized notions of kinship— for instance, the requests for national inclusion via military participation and proxy adoption—refines and reifies liberal state power over incarcerated subjects. Within the framework of the Korean War, the inmates, subject to civil death, virtually claim Bok Nam Om, also marked by civil death, in an attempt to produce an alternative kinship. However, the juxtaposition of the prisoners and Bok Nam Om, bearing various degrees of civil death, which I read as an effort to produce an iteration of normativity, also functions to critique the unquestionable nature of normative and idealized notions of family.

Within USP Leavenworth during the Korean War, the arguments made in *The New Era* suggest the necessity to not only implicitly defend white vulnerability against "the fangs of communism" but also, as I show above, to paternalistically and selectively extend freedom and protection to distant others through adoption. For the USP Leavenworth prisoners, given the civil death imprinted onto the crucible of the penitentiary, the proxy adoption of Bok Nam Om functions as one way to reclaim citizenship, humanity, and a place in the national family, despite the fact that the very same structures created the conditions for their exclusion and incarceration. In other words, for the white prisoners who were recognized as citizens prior to incarceration, proxy adoption served as a critical means of reclaiming it; even as they were stripped of citizenship and humanity through the process of incarceration, proxy adoption opened up new patriotic possibilities tied to the imagined national family. These patriotic possibilities, much like the ability to imagine belonging to the nation that expelled the prisoners in the first place, operate as discursive property for white prisoners. For the Black, Indigenous, Chinese, and Japanese prisoners, not only is the displacement of such possibility the functional logic of the white supremacist nation-state; their own exclusions from the idealized white national family delimit access for participating in this new proxy family. *The*

New Era documents the orchestration of state power via the management of blood, kinship, incarceration, and print culture. I suggest that while some of the prisoners strategically negotiate their whiteness to obtain a certain false liberation, the ostensible ownership of their subjectivities ultimately just transfers them under the governance of the state. The desire to be a GI, and to exercise whiteness as property to attain that status, is mirrored by the fact that GIs, like prisoners, remain legally demarcated as property of the state— as government issue.

"IT'S A BROWN PLACE KOREA IS"

The Asian-Latino Korean War

As far as U.S. military assignments go, serving as radio disc jockey at a base in a noncombat zone is a good one. In June 1950, in occupied Japan, the most pressing concern might be a rogue wave of heat and humidity that could warp the vinyl. But hear that record scratch upon learning this soft gig is rudely interrupted by reassignment to the first U.S. Army combat duty in what's rumored to be a brand-new war. For Rolando Hinojosa, veteran, author, and scholar, this reassignment from disc jockey to infantry found him engaged in ground combat in Osan, Korea, on July 5, 1950. The unit, Task Force Smith, was by any measure a scrappy one: composed of very young and poorly trained GIs, fighting the obsolescence of their own equipment and on the whole infrastructurally unprepared for combat. This is how one of the most important authors in Chicano literature, and American literature more broadly, met the Korean War. Hinojosa's Korean War encounter, a reflection for which is perhaps as yet emergent, "at the very edge of semantic availability," nonetheless exists as "reencounters" in his poetry volume *Korean Love Songs* (1978).[1]

Korean Love Songs is one book in Hinojosa's Klail City Death Trip Series, a multigenre fifteen-volume series narrated through the evolving voices of Rafe Buenrostro, who chronicles stories of the fictional Klail City, located in the Lower Rio Grande Valley in South Texas. Given the series' profound investment in the local color of the Lower Rio Grande Valley, *Korean Love Songs* is unique for its Korean War content and East Asian setting. *Korean Love Songs* presents loosely affiliated meditations ranging from mortality to roving racisms to bespoke kinships. In distinction from his previous works,

which were written first in Spanish, Hinojosa states, "When I began writing
Korean Love Songs in narrative prose and in English, it was easier. But it wasn't
what I wanted, either. Eventually, after reading many of the British World War
I poets, I got the idea that maybe I should use poetry to render something as
brutal as war."[2] While inspired by the British World War I poetry tradition,
perhaps unacknowledged is his radio DJ gig experience: Hinojosa remixes the
subgenre of war poetry by interspersing verse with images, offering a distinct
contrast to the form and extended narrative voice in British war poetry. Hinojosa's attention to the small, the everyday, frames the volume's observations
about something as big and seemingly unknowable as the U.S. Cold War engine
that relies on the labor and lives of the vulnerable and produces new racialized
subjectivities.

Through formal innovations and queer epistemological gestures, *Korean
Love Songs* refuses straightforward narration, is necessarily fragmented, and
destabilizes racially authoritative *knowings* of the Korean War. The Korean
War's nationalist discourses in the United States uphold it as the first deseg-
regated war, in celebratory narratives of Black and white unity in the face of
patriotic anticommunism. Such an imperative to sequester the Korean War as
a proxy for U.S. racial equality fits squarely within, and perhaps anticipates,
state-sanctioned discourses of multiculturalism in the following decades. Disal-
lowing the neat institutionalization of racial progress, cultural texts like *Korean
Love Songs* convene dissonant, unfinished histories of the Korean War. Far from
standing as an isolated outlier, Hinojosa is joined by other Chicano/a cultural
producers in this refusal, fragmentation, and destabilization of Korean War
memories. Inspired by the queer epistemological gestures of José Esteban
Muñoz and Sandra K. Soto, the spinning of retrofitted memory from Maylei
Blackwell, the dissonances theorized by Deborah Vargas, and the meditations
on messiness by Martin Manalansan, I develop a method for perceiving what
might be considered a minor Korean War corpus within Chicano/a cultural
production: Rolando Hinojosa's *Korean Love Songs* (1978) and *The Useless Servants* (1993), Luis Valdez's *Zoot Suit* (1978) and *I Don't Have to Show You No
Stinking Badges!* (1986), Tomás Rivera's *. . . y no se lo tragó la tierra / . . . And
the Earth Did Not Devour Him* (1971), and Rosaura Sánchez's "One Morning:
1952," translated by Beatrice Pita (2000). I attend specifically to the texts'
distanced preoccupation with the Korean War and how such ruminations
emerge through both the direct impact of the war on Chicana/o families and
the provisional, queer longings for alternative and proxy kinships.

In chapter 1, I argue that white Leavenworth penitentiary prisoners asserted their stake in racially configuring the national family through their
engagement with proxy adoption. While the white prisoners mobilized kin-

ship discourses to consolidate their affiliation with white patriarchal nationalism, Chicano veterans of the Korean War negotiated complex challenges of returning to a racially segregated United States and began to write literature that constructed Asia as an alternative, proxy space for building kinships. And even as white prisoners in Leavenworth used the Korean War as an occasion to petition for their release from the penitentiary, Chicano cultural production reveals the extent to which Mexican American subjects were disproportionately recruited for the war. Chicano cultural production about the Korean War further particularizes such contradictions undergirding Cold War racial operations. Theories of Asian-Latino proxies and the continued discussion of the proxy, elaborated through forms, wars, and kinships, guide this chapter. While the Leavenworth prisoners reframe racial discourse occasioned by the proxy adoption and military enlistment during the Korean War, this chapter considers the proxy of the Korean War in Chicano literary discourse as both a site of alternative kinship and a queer temporal and spatial disruption for theorizing war and race in Chicano literature.

Turning Japanese: Proxy Methods of the Korean War

Sonny Ruiz, a significant character in *Korean Love Songs*, performs an astonishing act of proxy personhood, scratching out his own military service in the Korean War. Because "To Americans he looks Japanese," Sonny "filled out and signed his own Missing-In-Action cards. . . . He personally turned them over to battery HQ, / Then simply walked away to the docks."[3] Afterward, Sonny adopts Japan as his home and lives as Mr. Kazuo Fusaro, "now a hundred and ten per cent Japanese."[4] Rafe, the speaker of *Korean Love Songs*, narrates Sonny's marriage to a Japanese schoolteacher and assimilation into Japan, marking his refusal to return to the perpetually racist South Texas of Sonny's speculations. In Japan for medical R&R, Rafe is apprehended by the racist surveillance of the military police, but

> *Just then, Sonny Ruiz passes by and tips his hat, showing,*
> *As he carries, the biggest, the loudest, the most glorious bouquet*
> *In the whole of Honshu.*
>
> *One of them grunts and says:*
> *   "Pipe the gook and them flowers, there.*
> *   Damndest place I've ever seen."*[5]

Sonny performs a double proxy of himself, as someone who fills out and hands in his own missing-in-action (MIA) card, and then continues on as proxy

Japanese. Within such logics of calculation and substitution, the formerly Chicano Sonny exceeds even maximum personhood, as "now a hundred and ten per cent Japanese."[6] Sonny passes by, strolling along in his racial proxy, unknowable to the military police even with "the biggest, the loudest, the most glorious bouquet." Predictably, the U.S. military's comment narrows their scope: "'Pipe the gook and them flowers, there.'" In a beautifully playful gesture, Hinojosa redirects the U.S. military's ocular focus, by tethering the imperialist directive to catalog that which is scrutable—that which is *knowable*—to Sonny's play with inscrutability. That is, the unrecognizably Chicano Sonny performs the inscrutable Asian to the U.S. military that he absented himself from, by turning Japanese. While the hypermasculine, white supremacist U.S. military understandings of the bouquet work to equate "the gook and them flowers" as feminine, rather than perform the presumed emasculation intended by the military police, this moment anticipates, in full bloom, the queer temporalities of the Korean War in Chicano cultural production.

What methods move through the problem of knowledge and, in particular, the spatial logics of speculating unknown coordinates? How might we navigate the *unknown* and, in the language that surrounds and mystifies the Korean War, the *forgotten* presence of the Korean War in Chicana/o cultural production? A serious consideration of Chicano cultural production disrupts historically entrenched understandings of Cold War racialization and offers a speculative meditation on the queer temporalities of the Korean War. Chicano cultural production refuses to authorize nationalist impulses that seek to affix the Korean War within dominant Cold War logics. Rather, inspired by José Esteban Muñoz's theorization, I consider Chicano cultural production to articulate with a queer utopian hermeneutic that desires to be "*epistemologically and ontologically humble* in that it would not claim the epistemological certitude of a queerness that we simply 'know' but, instead, strain to activate the no-longer-conscious and to extend a glance toward that which is forward-dawning, anticipatory illuminations of the not-yet-conscious."[7] Likewise, Sandra K. Soto's framework of "de-mastery," in particular a queer Chican@ reading practice "that wards off ontological impoverishment . . . and epistemological disciplining," invites explicit, expansive engagements with "Chican*o* feminist stories."[8] The possibilities summoned by the queer utopian hermeneutic and the demastery of "reading Chican@ like a queer" functions in distinct contrast to Cold War imperatives to claim comprehensive knowledge about the Korean War. In the formally diverse Chicano/a cultural works examined here, the Korean War recurs as a series of *unknowns*—family members missing in action, the possibility of left-behind children fathered by GIs, the deeply unsettling uncertainty about why the war is happening.

Twinned with the unknowns are the speculations of what may yet emerge, the possibilities unfolding in multiple, recursive, and nonlinear temporalities.

The Korean War is paradoxically narrated as a forgotten war. At this moment, the field of Chicano studies is negotiating the question of what it might mean to be on the verge of being forgotten, whether through the systemic erasure of Chicano/a educational programs or through important, ongoing conversations about the limitations and possibilities of a broader Latinx studies, as theorized by Richard T. Rodríguez in "X Marks the Spot."[9] In *Bridges, Borders, and Breaks* (2016), William Orchard and Yolanda Padilla argue that "Chicana/o literary study remains a vital intellectual field on its own, separate from the broader field of Chicana/o studies and from an increasingly established Latina/o studies that, for some, foreshadows the obsolescence of the Chicana/o project."[10] While the possibilities of converging around Latinx invites important questions about gender, sexuality, language, and more, the academic institutionalization of the Latinx rarely articulates its relationship to anti-imperialist and antimilitary legacies, which remains underdefined. Put differently, if Chicano/a studies, with its specific critiques of the long genealogy of U.S. empire and militarism, is indeed situated precariously in this particular moment, where might we locate the field's significant theorizations about militarized empire in Asia? Furthermore, how might we reckon with the Korean War and its elusive emergence in Chicano/a cultural production, in its unique relationship to Chicano/a studies? These queries signal beyond recovering the *Chicano* experience of the Korean War as a fixed political event. Rather, joining Blackwell, I consider how "structures of remembrance construct an archive of knowledge as well as a Chicana/o structure of feeling," to invite what she calls retrofitted remembrance beyond empirical authorization and epistemological certitude.[11]

And so the question of studying a forgotten war within Chicano cultural production requires a bespoke method, an inquiry into the tangential and subterranean, grounded in an analysis of the *forms* of the Korean War in the literature. The glimpses of the Korean War that surface across disparate forms in Chicano cultural production—poetry, plays, short stories, novels, and *corridos*—emerge speculatively, disclosing both the vulnerabilities and possibilities of the unknown, expressed through kinship formations. The Korean War thus gains form through *the unfixed* in Chicano literary production, through engagements with queer temporalities that refuse to anticipate closure, mirroring the unended status of the war. I observe a remarkable concern with queer temporalities and spatial logics in Chicano cultural production and trace the proliferation of proxy logics in Chicano scholarly discourses about the Korean War.

Indeed, within Chicano/a cultural discourse, considerations of the Korean War have been articulated as a problem of working through the field of Chicano/a studies. The Korean War therefore bears another proxy status, in this instance as a spatial metaphor enabling transnational critique but also, in one instance, by situating Asia as a proxy for South Texas. In *Chicano Narrative: The Dialectics of Difference* (1990), Ramón Saldívar has suggested that Rolando Hinojosa's *Korean Love Songs*, "as paradoxical as this claim may seem, given that the entire action of *Korean Love Songs* is set in Japan and Korea, it can be shown that Hinojosa's poem . . . is about South Texas and Mexican American life in a moment of crucial self-formation."[12] While Japan and Korea are situated as spatial proxy for South Texas in his argument, I am especially interested in the capacity for the Korean War to galvanize Cold War critique in the more recent juncture as a "moment of crucial self-formation" for Chicano/a studies as a field. Such an animation challenges the Cold War "geographical provincialism" of the "Western Hemisphere's temporality," reconfiguring the conceptual space, place-based proximities, and temporal hiatus to mobilize different sets of inquiry.[13] The Korean War in Chicana/o cultural production thus gains further significance for both transpacific critique and for Chicana/o studies, to observe that which has historically been neglected or occluded by limits of academic discipline and to analyze epistemological configurations as systems of power.

Some Chicana/o literary and cultural studies scholars, however, urge against a rash focus on "Asia" in Chicana/o cultural texts. José Limón critiques Ramón Saldívar's work on the folklorist Américo Paredes for reading evidence of Asia where Asia is not present, charging "I certainly see no 'marks' in content, style, or perspective that connect these texts to Asia."[14] Limón's positivist critique, however, misses the apparently tangential yet remarkably indelible presence of the Korean War in the larger body of Chicana/o cultural production, much of which emerged after the ethnonationalist movements of the 1960s but which returns to an earlier Cold War moment. The Cold War's racial liberalism engineered the participation of Chicano GIs in the Korean War through discourses that constructed enlisting and conscription as legitimizing opportunities for those deliberately marginalized from national belonging. And in exposing such logics, Chicana/o cultural production critiques the disproportionate numbers of Black and Latinx peoples impressed into battle against Asian peoples in the Second World War, Korean War, and Vietnam War. This analysis of the minor Korean War corpus in Chicano/a cultural production, while attentive to the lacuna of scholarship on the Korean War's Chicana/o presence, is motivated beyond a directive for inclusion and recovery of the legacies of Chicanos in the war. In part, this distinction from racial recovery projects stems from their particular vulnerability to processes of national-ist neoliberal canonization.[15] How might transpacific analyses evade such incorporative logics? Saldívar offers the importance of transnational analyses of Asia in the works of such authors as Paredes, inviting us to "consider the nuances of [Paredes's] subject position: a Mexican-American soldier in the U.S. Army of occupation; a native of racist, segregation-era south Texas fam-iliar with the history of conquest and occupation in the American border-lands; a journalist and humanitarian aid worker finding himself in a nation which in its own wars of empire and conquest on mainland Asia had been a merciless occupier."[16]

Hinojosa's Korean War experiences approximate the trajectories of occu-pation negotiated by Paredes, advancing significant epistemological, historical, and spatial affinities. A. J. Yumi Lee and Daniel Kim have read Hinojosa's works as establishing a continuum of borderlands in U.S. empire. Lee observes that Hinojosa's Klail City Death Trip Series "insists that we see the Korean War as a part of the history of Chicano life, and the history of Texas and Mex-ico as a part of the Cold War division and consolidation of the two Koreas," locating the U.S.-Mexico War as one "whose crisscrossing lines of descent connect the Korean War" within a broader genealogy of U.S. imperial wars.[17] Likewise, Kim suggests that "the power of Hinojosa's Korean War writings de-rives from how they invite us to see 1848 and 1945 as part of a continuous history, to see the Rio Grande and the thirty-eighth parallel, now the de-militarized zone, as associated segments in the borderlands of U.S. empire."[18] While attending to these important inquiries, I ask in this chapter, how else might analyses of Korean War writings in Chicano/a cultural production advance possibilities for capacious theorizing within both Asian American-ist critique and Chicana/o studies, making them articulate with each other? For the texts I examine, I consider the forms of the works themselves and the cultural productions' play with intertextual proxies: in the space of the theater, the cinematic, the lyrical, and the visual. In addition to their diverse formal innovations, reading the cultural productions as a corpus invites theorizing across textual, generic, and methodological boundaries. Building on these proximities, a queer speculative framework grasps the protean narratives and unanticipated experiences emerging from the Korean War.

Cinematic Encounters in the Transpacific Theater

Caught a double feature at the air base; both are at least two years old: Treasure of Sierra Madre and a western called Red River. . . . As usual, Mexicans got gunned down in both movies, and this is

when Joey said, "Between Bogart and John Wayne, they'll get rid
of all the Mexicans in Hollywood."

—ROLANDO HINOJOSA, *THE USELESS SERVANTS*

The projectionist lifts the 35mm reel out of its canister, examining the film
for any signs of corruption. It's a hot day at Itazuke Air Force Base, and he's wary
of the combustible qualities lurking in 35mm. Goddamn tragic way to go,
he thinks, and ironic too, since the rookies, officers, and old-timers—those
who've been in Korea for a year, since 1950—finally traded in service points
for some R&R in occupied Japan. Imagine going down in flames at a U.S.
military base movie theater, your mind finally off the cold things, the brutal
things you were first witness to and then participant in. He's seen them come
and go; he recognizes a few of the old rookies, their faces now congealed in
disbelief and weathered in shattering maturity. They're old-timers now, he
thinks, and wonders about the others—probably gone, either in a medic's
tent somewhere or a POW camp or blasted to bits someplace in Korea, only
pieces of them left for anyone to mourn.

The movies aren't fresh releases, but it's enough to get some folks' minds
off of Korea. The projectionist thinks about the reel he's screening: *The Treasure of the Sierra Madre*. Not bad. It's the weekend, so officers are showing
up to show off their dates, Japanese girls, sometimes Korean ones, all mixing
together in the heat of the outdoor theater. They'll stay for *Treasure* and for
Red River too. Unfortunate, he thinks, how much the GIs—especially the
rookies—fall for the Asian girls. He's seen enough empty promises, sugary
and blank, of taking them back to the USA, but the army knows better than
that. The cue mark at the end of the reel blinks on, the projectionist nearly
missing it in his ruminations. He changes the reel to *Red River*, slipping back
into reverie, only to be jarred by someone shouting, "Between Bogart and John
Wayne, they'll get rid of all the Mexicans in Hollywood!" accompanied by
raucous laughter near the back. The projectionist's thoughts had been grim,
but now he grins. That was a good one.[19]

Both Hinojosa's service in the war and the poetry and fiction he wrote in
the following decades suggest the embedded histories of the Korean War in
Chicano cultural legacies, as well as the incisive critiques of the war from the
situated perspective of a Chicano subject emerging from that first U.S. action. *The Useless Servants*, through its narrator, Rafe Buenrostro, captures the
terse contradiction of the combat experience as he considers his Purple Heart:
"(For the small pieces of High Explosive wire I caught during Task Force
Smith days last July.) What a trade: I get a Purple Heart for that piece of shit,
and a family at home gets the medal for someone who's not coming back."[20]

Through the small pieces of wire, embedded into flesh, Rafe's meditations on the family who must settle for the proxy of a medal as substitution for their kin in the flesh, and the perverse trade of a Purple Heart for the wounded living, Hinojosa discloses not only the force of critique but also the disruptive intimacies the Korean War imposed onto reconfigurations of family. His observations on militarized disposability are also specifically racialized. In the epigraph above, Rafe records his friend Joey's wry quip about "Bogart and John Wayne . . . get[ting] rid of all the Mexicans in Hollywood," entwining the militarized space they occupy during the Korean War, with the "gunning down" of Chicano GIs in the war eerily mirroring the representations of "Mexicans [getting] gunned down" in the 1948 John Huston film, *The Treasure of the Sierra Madre*.[21]

But here's where the story turns, notices a family resemblance, finds itself kin.

Because Luis Valdez, considered the father of Chicano theater and known for his 1978 play *Zoot Suit*, continues the thematic exploration of how militarism disrupts Chicano lives in his 1986 play, *I Don't Have to Show You No Stinking Badges!* This lesser-known play is replete with subterranean currents of Buddy Villa's experiences in the Korean War. Buddy, father of the Villa household and Korean War veteran, has in fact acted as a Mexican bandit in *The Treasure of the Sierra Madre*, working in bit parts as proletarian soldiers in two imperial theaters—the movie theater, in which he "brought up the rear" in a film that exploits Mexico as a backdrop to the dramas of three working-class white men, and the theater of war, in a forgotten war that secured U.S. military entrenchment in the Asia Pacific region. Imagine the fictional Rafe, watching the fictional Buddy act as a Mexican bandit, in this movie theater on a military base in the Pacific theater of the Korean War even as, in that very moment, Buddy is stationed in Korea for the war.

The title of Valdez's play is borrowed from actor Alfonso Bedoya's legendary line from the film: "Badges? We ain't got no badges. We don't need no badges! I don't have to show you any stinking badges!" Bedoya's line talks back to imperial mandates of legitimacy, repurposed in the Korean War as authoritatively dictating freedom and democracy for both Koreans and for Chicano GIs in the Korean War. Hinojosa's *The Useless Servants* references the ironies of watching the gunning down of movie Mexicans in the Pacific theater, revealing the complex multilayered terrains built into white supremacist structures of war. Within the U.S. imperialist and white supremacist frameworks emerging from the Korean War era, indeed increasingly adaptive Cold War frameworks that exercise flexible methods of incorporating differentially racialized bodies, the cultural texts spin alternative forms of racial knowledge.

Bedoya's line, "I don't have to show you any stinking badges!" therefore embodies the unsettled histories that rearticulate alternative memories of the Korean War. The line also performs a resistance and refusal to assimilate into the totalizing logic of subjugation. Bedoya delivers this line in his role as Gold Hat, the leader of a group of bandits posing as Federales, in response to Humphrey Bogart's character's demand that the bandits show badges proving they are indeed Federales. The initial meanings of the line emerge from an encounter between Bedoya's and Bogart's characters, in which stereotyped representations of Mexican bandits attempt to rob hard-working, *noir*-inflected white American men of their gold dust in 1920s Tampico, Mexico. Although the stereotyped representation of Gold Hat may be meant to function "as a quick and convenient instrument of filmic humor," Juan Alonzo argues "that it is the spectator's ability to critically read the stereotype that makes the circuit of subversion complete."[22] Valdez's own subversive use of *The Treasure of the Sierra Madre* in *I Don't Have to Show You No Stinking Badges!* presents itself in a stage note describing Bedoya's character as a "wily Mexican bandit . . . confronting a scruffy Humphrey Bogart with toothy disdain, somewhere in the wilds of Mexico."[23] Indeed, Valdez's characterization of the Mexican bandit's "toothy disdain" offers an intertextual resonance with Hinojosa's observation in the epigraph: "As usual, Mexicans got gunned down in both movies, and this is when Joey said, 'Between Bogart and John Wayne, they'll get rid of all the Mexicans in Hollywood.'" It directs our attention to the militarized incongruities governing the transpacific theater, as well as the matter-of-fact disposability of "Mexican" lives, celluloid and real, representational and material. Joining the critiques of the Second World War and the Vietnam War as crucibles of racist destruction, Hinojosa and Valdez dismantle fraught avenues promising national incorporation and expose the contradictions of the militarized liberal state.

This interplay between Hinojosa's *The Useless Servants* and Valdez's *I Don't Have to Show You No Stinking Badges!* frames the Korean War within messy racial genealogies and geographies. Their works demand a reading practice reconfiguring multiple histories of the war, which have always been intimate with each other but have been studied as separate and epistemologically structured to remain isolated. Hinojosa and Valdez rescript *imperial returns* through their observations of what Lisa Lowe has called "the survivors of empire, its witnesses, the inhabitants of its borders."[24] The cultural works negotiate an ongoing circuit of racialization produced by the U.S. military during the Korean War, a production built on white supremacist constructions of "gooks" and "chinks," as easily disposable as the "Mexicans [getting] gunned down."

I Don't Have to Show You No Stinking Badges! is attuned to the domestic drama of the upwardly mobile Villa household and shadowed by Korean War memories, which attach stubbornly to Buddy, Connie, and Sonny Villa. Navigating domestic and transnational contexts, *Badges* indulges in exuberant play with racial and sexual stereotypes. Sonny's budding intimacy with the sansei Anita Sakai unnerves his mother, Connie, as it reminds her of Buddy's Korean War relationship (and speculations of a possible child left behind in Korea, fathered by Buddy). Sonny and Anita's romance assumes undercurrents of Buddy's relationship with "an Asian girl" during the war. Sonny, a sixteen-year-old who has dropped out of Harvard to pursue Hollywood acting, attempts to both follow and outdo his parents, who act in minor, stereotyped Latina/o roles. Valdez's play is remarkable for how it "theatricalizes a certain mode of feeling brown in a world painted white and organized by cultural mandates to feel white" and how it ordains so specifically what Muñoz describes as the impoverishment of white affect.[25]

Anita and Sonny meet via a *Village Voice* ad, to rideshare from the East Coast to Los Angeles. During their drive, Sonny attempts to provoke Anita by joking they should make a film called "The Geisha and the Greaser," chronicling their cross-country stopover: "Remember Little America, that truck stop in Wyoming? The one with all the redneck cowboys? It was like a scene out of a movie, wouldn't you say?"[26] Anita dismisses the idea of "The Geisha and the Greaser" as "too weird," leading Sonny to respond, "Precisely. Rednecks won't pay to see us making love. Unless it's a porno."[27] Their banter reminds us of Muñoz's argument on minoritarian identity and how it "has much to do with certain subjects' inability to act properly within majoritarian scripts and scenarios. Latinos and Latinas are stigmatized as performers of excess: the hot and spicy, over-the-top subjects who simply do not know when to quit. . . . Rather than simply rejecting this toxic language of shame, I wish to inhabit it and suggest that as such, it permits us to arrive at an important mapping of the social."[28] Sonny's satiric title, "The Geisha and the Greaser," refits gendered and racialized epithets in order to subvert white supremacist attempts to name, contain, and affix complex subjectivities into static categories of dehumanization.

In the Korean War prehistory of *Badges*, "geisha" and "greaser" also invoke Buddy's romance with "an Asian girl" in Korea, while inscribing Sonny and Anita in the white supremacist imaginary of Wyoming's "redneck cowboys." Yet, like Sonny Ruiz in *Korean Love Songs*, "The Geisha and the Greaser" queers the earnest taxonomy of white supremacy, playfully recoding racial and sexual algorithms to create a story that diverts the "redneck" gaze. Sonny's insistence that the movie will not succeed "unless it's a porno," gesturing to the hypersexualization and exploitation embedded in the very idea of "The Geisha and the Greaser," rescripts "the sparse affective landscape of Anglo North America," toward "a reading of the affect of whiteness as underdeveloped and impoverished." Indeed, their conversation emerges out of an attempt to decenter white settlers as unquestioned occupants of "Little America," denaturalizing the temporally jarring presence of the "redneck cowboys" using cinematic language: "It was like a scene out of a movie, wouldn't you say?" In effect, Sonny redirects the gaze to white people as unnatural inhabitants of a settler frontier.

Alongside Sonny's speculations about his father falling "in love with an Asian girl, when he was in Korea," and the possibility of Sonny's "Korean Chicano" brother, other kinships in Hinojosa's and Valdez's texts enact further racial and sexual transgressions. Hinojosa's *Korean Love Songs* imagines encounters

> *In some well-appointed, hygienic, bug-free,*
> *U.S. ARMY APPROVED and designated brothel.*[29]

Unlike such brothels, not all interactions are stamped with the textually aggressive, magnified, and authoritative badge of "U.S. ARMY APPROVED." Instead, the texts talk back with Bedoya's legendary line: "I don't have to show you any stinking badges!" In other words, sexual representations between Chicano GIs and Korean and Japanese women, sometimes ambiguously described as "an Asian girl, when [Buddy] was in Korea," at other times more explicitly located in a "U.S. ARMY APPROVED and designated brothel," unfix static articulations of racialization and sexuality. Against singularizing narratives of dispossessed, subaltern sex workers and GIs, Hinojosa and Valdez shift attention to possibilities for radical affiliation.

"We're a likely pair, we are; and I'm certainly no Pinkerton / To her Butterfly": *Korean Love Songs*

Américo Paredes, the renowned folklorist, musician, and scholar who self-described as "proto-Chicano," situates the emergence of the corrido in the ballad forms circulating before the mid-nineteenth century, in the material and historical circumstances of greater Mexico and, in particular, the spatial battles of the Lower Rio Grande border. Within the remarkable, sustained impact of Paredes's work, Deb Vargas reminds us, "the corrido's musical and scholarly function, as a form of cultural resistance, has served to authenticate Chicano identity within very limited gender, sexuality, and class parameters."[30] Alongside Vargas, Sandra Soto observes the "cognitive dissonance" of a feminist scholar extending the conversation on "yet another of the male protagonists created by 'Don' Américo Paredes—that imposing father who seems nothing if not the commanding, patriarchal, masculinist, heteronormative *master* of Chicano Studies."[31] Yet, as Soto states, it is his work that is "so queerly enabling in its invitation to a constellation of de-mastering projects" and that these "invitations are too often missed, unseen, unaccepted, or just plain ignored."[32] Within the context of Chicano/a cultural productions on the Korean War, I see such an invitation in perceiving Rolando Hinojosa's *Korean Love Songs* as a Cold War corrido.

As Vargas reminds us, "When we consider the sonic imaginary of the borderlands as constructed by Paredes's corrido or 'border ballad,' it is one constructed along heteronormative spatial and temporal configurations of masculinity, namely, through conflict (privileging race and class conflict between Anglo and *mexicano* men) and territory (as a defended 'homeland')."[33] I suggest that Hinojosa remixes this, too, in *Korean Love Songs*: the corrido form's play with *love songs*, the spatial contexts of territorial defense in Korea and South Texas, and the temporal alignments of the Korean War as a conflict. In *Korean Love Songs*, Rafe's spatial proxy, affiliating Korea and South Texas, tethers both terrains in an uneasy cartography of empire:

> It's a brown place Korea is; hilly, too.
> And cold, but the summers can be
> South Texas hot.[34]

"It's a brown place Korea is"[35] charts an unlikely affinity of profound significance—the underknown *brownness* of the Korean War, twinned to a melancholy familiarity for "South Texas hot." Hinojosa conceptualizes proxies in that Korea *is* a brown place, Korea *can be* South Texas hot. Hinojosa's poetic approximations, suggesting what is and can be, recall Muñoz's queer horizon, and I consider Muñoz's own proxy engagements and epistemological disquiet: "Brownness is not white, and it is not black either, yet it does not simply sit midway between them."[36] Muñoz observes brownness through what it is *not* (white, black, midway between them), but offers *feeling* brown as "a mode of racial performativity, a doing within the social that surpasses limitations of epistemological renderings of race."[37] In a clause, Hinojosa reiteratively declares the unambiguous brownness of Korea; in his affective refusal to approximate, Muñoz theorizes the very performativity of that brownness, in excess of how race can be *known*.

The conceptualization of spatial proxy recurs in Hinojosa's work, assuming visual form in *Estampas del valle y otras obras*, remapping the Asia Pacific

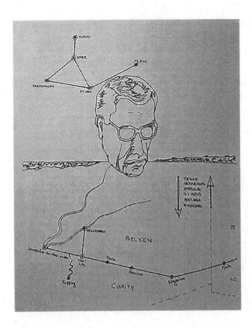

Figure 2.1 Map in Rolando Hinojosa's *Estampas del valle y otras obras*. (Courtesy of Quinto Sol / Bilingual Press Review)

and South Texas in a remixed geography.[38] Héctor Calderón writes of Hinojosa's "schematic map of his invented world which appears in *Estampas del valle*. At the top portion of the map toward the left, hanging in space, Hinojosa situates Kobe, Tokyo, Panmunjon [*sic*], Fort Sill, and Fort Ord with lines of relation to each other. These are the cities that through the Korean War will affect the Mexican families of Belken County."[39] This visual representation of Hinojosa's world remaps the intimate geographies of the Asia Pacific and South Texas, creating a counterrepresentation to a Cold War map that attempts to fix hard lines demarcating first, second, and third worlds. The dominant Cold War map presumes rigid and stable power relationships among capitalist, communist, and nonaligned nation-states while erasing past and ongoing colonial legacies and anticolonial movements. In contrast, the illustration invites a different sort of understanding, asking viewers to reflect on a map that exclusively renders both the imperial borders drawn in the Asia Pacific and South Texas. The exclusions in this illustration are critical omissions—while the borderlands of Kobe, Tokyo, Panmunjom, and Belken County exist in mutually connected spatial relationships, other places remain off the map or are represented in a list. Furthermore, the lines connecting different sites in Asia hover behind the figure of the head, serving as an ongoing haunting presence that colors his perspective of South Texas.

The fictitiousness of both Panmunjom and Belken County denaturalizes national borders. Belken is a fictional county located in the Lower Rio

Grande Valley; by creating a name rather than using one of the formal county names in the region, Hinojosa shifts attention to the constructed nature of borders and boundaries, especially significant in the South Texas region, which harbors the histories of the Civil War and the U.S.-Mexico War. While Panmunjom is the recognized name for the political space marking the border that divides the Korean peninsula, and the site in which the armistice agreement was signed, it too marks an imperial border signaling political instabilities. Panmunjom exists in tension with its incomplete past, as South Korea never signed the Korean Armistice Agreement that halted the armed conflicts but not the war. That the two sites are exclusively rendered within the same map casts into relief the imperial positioning of the Asia Pacific and South Texas.

Within this spatial proxy, *Korean Love Songs* makes a significant intervention into the corrido tradition, offering a unique occasion to theorize the lyrical occupations of the Korean War. When read as a corrido, *Korean Love Songs* builds queer kinships imagining radical elsewheres to the white supremacist and settler imperatives of the U.S. military as represented in military songbooks, which I examine in relation to Hinojosa's poetry. Chicana/o scholars, in particular Ramón Saldívar, have read *Korean Love Songs* as a corrido, especially in its structure and themes of border justice: "Hinojosa's *Korean Love Songs* tells the corrido story of border conflict and social justice in the symbolically displaced form of the long narrative poem and the ideologically different context of the Korean War."[40] Recalibrating Saldívar's claim, I consider too Deb Vargas's conceptualization of the "*vato* vernacular," defined as "the sustained attention to Chicano voices, the coveted masculine homosocial spaces of conversation, and dominant historiography methods."[41] Vargas's intellectual interruption of the "*vato* vernacular," especially among José Limón, Ramón Saldívar, and José David Saldívar about "Asia," makes space for transnational feminist readings of Hinojosa's Cold War corrido.

Hinojosa binds border ballads in Korea to border ballads in Texas and, in doing so, exposes a specifically positioned challenge to the white supremacist, heteropatriarchal masculinity of the U.S. military in the Asia Pacific. If the border ballad functions to mediate, document, and critique the violent doings of empire, military ballads function to illicitly celebrate the same violent doings. Indeed, the two forms constitute two sides of an imperial coin in the context of the Korean War, embedding and replicating military masculinity but also providing fissures for subjectivities working against white supremacist empire building. Hinojosa's construction and imagination of *love songs* is significant, especially in contrast to unofficial U.S. Air Force songbooks, such as *Songs My Mother Never Taught Me* and *The Fighter Pilot's Hymn Book*, which express the heteropatriarchal anxieties sutured to U.S. nation building in a series of misogynist collections of lyrics sedimented with imperial violence.[42] My intention here is not to privilege or delegitimate the corrido as a form. Rather, I ask what emerges in considering misogynist military songs that also operate as another kind of transnational border ballad. Given the accumulation of masculinities embedded into the military songs of the Korean War era, I consider what it may mean to imagine Korea, in both the military songs and in *Korean Love Songs*, as a corrido setting.

The U.S. military songs document the fluctuations of borders and the vexed genealogies of misogyny and settler nationalism through multiple imperial and settler wars. *Songs My Mother Never Taught Me*, for instance, issues a "word of warning" for readers with "tender sensibilities" and explains that "many of these lyrics were adopted to the Korean 'situation' after becoming popular among the same warriors during WWII, and at least one or two were sung around the compfires [*sic*] of the eve of Gettysburg. It follows, therefore, that they are not the product of a particular generation."[43] The temporal disavowal of the word of warning recalls ongoing heteropatriarchal legacies that inform the long genealogy of U.S. settler colonialism, beginning at least on the eve of Gettysburg. Other song lyrics, such as "Taegu Girls," reprinted below from *The Fighter Pilot's Hymn Book*, archive the blatant racist misogyny of elite U.S. military officers during the Korean War:

> *We are from Taegu, Taegu are we*
> *We don't believe in virginity*
> *We don't use candles we use broom handles*
> *We are the Taegu girls*
>
> *And every night at twelve on the clock*
> *We watch the white man piss on the ROK*
> *We like the way he handles his cock*
> *We are the Taegu girls*[44]

The lyrics of the U.S. Air Force song "Taegu Girls" entangle the violent erotics embedded within formations of nationalism, gender, and sexuality in U.S. military expansion during the Korean War. In particular, the fantasy that "Taegu Girls" "watch the white man piss on the ROK" and "like the way he handles his cock" animates the illusion of both a masculine and racially homogenous United States degrading an implicitly feminine, burgeoning Republic of Korea, bolstered by the willing sexual desire of Korean "girls." In the context of the emergent nation-states on the peninsula, the song suggests that the nation-building enterprise itself is mired in misogynist ideology. Indeed, the lyrics of "Taegu Girls" appear to presage white supremacist claims to what would become a significant military acquisition for the United States, as the U.S. military occupation of South Korea represents a U.S. military station from which to police Asia.

Furthermore, the military circulation of the lyrics demonstrates that U.S. nationalist white supremacy does not operate independently of processes of gendering and sexualization, both discursively in the feminization of "the ROK" and in the sexual availability of Korean girls and women ("We don't believe in virginity"). Contrary to the dominant legibility of the Korean War as a masculine discourse, the maintenance of the U.S. military empire depends on such constructions of sexually available Asian women to ensure enlistment.[45] Furthermore, the military *circulation* of the lyrics also points to class differentiations within militarized masculinities, as the rehearsal and circulation of the songbooks enable elite members of the U.S. military to also perform their privileged class status, as one former naval officer describes:

> I was in an elite status . . . mine and bomb disposal, which with a few exceptions, attracted top-ranking university grads from all over the USA as officers. This officer group exchanged ROTC and fraternity songs and limericks. Copying meant mimeographing in those days, and few of us typed well. . . . We were dependent on Yeoman, the Navy's secretaries and clerks, all male. . . . They did not enjoy literary erotica, and were even disgusted by some limericks. . . . At the same time, they themselves typed and circulated page after page of descriptions of lurid, boring, repetitive heterosexual fantasies. Nonetheless, by position of rank and other favors, we were sometimes able to get our collections typed and copies for exchange.[46]

Not only do the songbooks document the misogynist and nationalist erotics underpinning the elite corps of the U.S. military; the material process of creating the artifacts also requires the complicity of "Yeoman," including military personnel who themselves had been conscripted.

Returning to *Korean Love Songs*, Hinojosa's lines from "Old Friends" offer a rebuttal to white supremacist misogyny, through Rafe's tenuous position as a member of the occupying U.S. military force. Unlike the officers and pilots of the air force, Rafe is a working-class Chicano situated at multiple border-lands—the U.S.-Mexico border in Texas, the shifting borders constituting the evolving Korean states, the complex borders of racialization in which he is *feeling brown* (not white, not Black, not midway between them), and fighting alongside both racialized groups against Asian adversaries. In "Old Friends,"

Rafe references the 1904 Italian opera *Madama Butterfly* in his disidentification with Pinkerton, who represents the deplorable white U.S. Navy lieutenant stationed in Japan. Butterfly is the young Japanese girl whom Pinkerton abandons upon his departure for the United States. Rafe disarticulates his "old friend," Mosako Fukuda, a sex worker at Shirley's Temple of Pleasure Emporium in Kobe, from the tragic figure of Butterfly from the opera:

> *We're a likely pair, we are; and I'm certainly no Pinkerton*
> *To her Butterfly*[47]

Rafe constructs an alternative theorization of mutual racial belonging bypassing the fantasy of whiteness when he declares, with iteration, "We're a likely pair, we are." In this line, we hear a remix of the echo, "we are the Taegu girls," but with mutual affinity rather than misogyny. Rafe's disidentification with Pinkerton suggests a disidentification from whiteness, and the use of enjambment (Pinkerton / To) also indexes a remove from the tragic exploitation of a young "Butterfly." In addition to asserting the intimate possibility of the Chicano and Japanese pair, the lines also suggest an implicit impossibility riding on the currents of formal laws and informal violent reprisals against miscegenation throughout U.S. racial history, in this case reaching across the Pacific. Rafe's disidentification with Pinkerton suggests not only his disidentification from whiteness but also a remove from the salacious exploitation of a young "Butterfly." Indeed, Mosako Fukuda labors with

> *no pretense here:*
> *Her parents know where she works,*
> *And I, learning the ways of the world,*
> *Do not add insult to their injury*
> *By visiting their home.*[48]

Despite Rafe's sensitivity, having "learn[ed] the ways of the world," he still functions within the operating structures of overlapping patriarchies and empires, deeply saturated with and replicating imbalances in power. For Mosako Fukuda's parents, her labor reads as "injury," and Rafe himself, as a Chicano GI, represents a racialized "insult" to that injury. Furthermore, Rafe allegorizes through Mosako Fukuda the U.S. occupation of Japan as an injury and simultaneously denaturalizes his own position in the role of liberator. Learning "the ways of the world" for Rafe includes a consciousness that race, gender, and class are not separate but are rather mutually constitutive. In this Cold War corrido, Rafe simultaneously affirms heteropatriarchal masculinity through his relationship with Mosako Fukuda and challenges another imperial war in the Pacific, demonstrating the necessity of an antiracist, anti-imperial feminist framework that dismantles existing structures of power toward other ways of being.

The formation of the militarized subjectivities above focuses on a multiplicity of desires, though I am not suggesting an easy equivalence between the subjectivities constructed through the performance of "Taegu Girls" and the theorizations of "Old Friends." That GIs sing and reiterate the lyrics, which are from the perspective of "girls" in Taegu, points to a perverse discursive occupation of the subaltern, one that amplifies the tensions of white supremacist and misogynist roots of empire building emerging from the Korean War. And while existing scholarship formulates important arguments about Hinojosa's imperial critiques, there are fewer transnational feminist readings of his works. Yet the pairing of the two generates provocative inquiries on the unruly methods and unended histories of the Korean War and, indeed, "how the Chicana feminist critique of ethnonationalism, explicit engagement with racialized sexuality, and proactive collaboration and dialogue with other women of color all have something important to tell us about the usefulness of Latin@ Studies and comparative ethnic studies."[49] U.S. military songbooks and Chicano cultural productions about the Korean War theorize both the patriotic desire and the desire for sexualized and racialized bodies, constituting two sides of the same imperial coin. These desires are articulated with each other, mutually constituted, and perform the contradictory functions of embedding and replicating military masculinity, as well as directing a critique of the U.S. military expansion in Korea.

"I Hope You're Not Talking about Korea?": Zoot Suit and I Don't Have to Show You No Stinking Badges!

Recall Hinojosa's representation of the R&R at Itazuke Air Force Base in Tokyo, in which Rafe and his friend Joey watch *The Treasure of the Sierra Madre*: "As usual, Mexicans got gunned down in both movies, and this is when Joey said, 'Between Bogart and John Wayne, they'll get rid of all the Mexicans in Hollywood.'"[50] Rafe and Joey's observation of easy death during the Korean War carry precedence, with the "gunning down" of Chicano GIs eerily mirroring the cinematic "Mexicans [getting] gunned down" in *The Treasure of the Sierra Madre*. This moment of spectatorship, of a film Rafe notes is "at least two years old," reflects and recasts the unglimpsed memories of the Korean War in Chicana/o cultural production.

Luis Valdez's *I Don't Have to Show You No Stinking Badges!* highlights the struggle behind finding complex roles for Chicana/o actors. The play zooms in on the Villa household in Monterey Park, narrating Buddy and Connie Villa's struggles to find acting roles that are not flat stereotypes of Latina/os. Buddy performed a role as a bandit in *The Treasure of the Sierra Madre* and is also a Korean War veteran, working in bit parts as proletarian soldiers in two imperial theaters—the movie theater and the theater of war, in a so-called forgotten war that solidified U.S. military entrenchment in the Asia Pacific region.[51] In Sonny's conversations—permeated with Buddy's experiences in the Korean War—with the Japanese American Anita, Sonny discloses his dad's affair with "an Asian woman" during the war and wonders if he has a "Korean Chicano" half brother somewhere in Korea.[52] *Badges* traces several genealogies stemming from the Korean War—the wartime experiences of racialized and gendered subjectivities, the anxieties about the possibilities and limitations of kinship, and the fraught relationships between the "illegal border crosser" and sexualized "model minority," or as the language of the play articulates, "The Geisha and the Greaser."

Badges theorizes part of its resistance to narratives of legitimacy through form. The play already makes use of the theatricality of the stage and upends single-genre storytelling, by framing *The Treasure of the Sierra Madre* as a metanarrative in the stage directions: "Behind BUDDY VILLA, the VCR on, a rack comes on, playing a scene from 'The Treasure of Sierra Madre.' On the studio monitors: A wily Mexican bandit is confronting a scruffy Humphrey Bogart with toothy disdain, somewhere in the wilds of Mexico."[53] *Badges* plays with form and the performative by using the film as an overarching point of reference. Yet the space given to the film in the play is minimal, just as Buddy's role "somewhere in the wilds of Mexico" in the film is extra and just as Buddy's role as a veteran "somewhere in the wilds" of Korea is marginal. Indeed, formally, Valdez treats the Korean War as it is treated in dominant U.S. history—almost forgotten, lurking in the edges, "somewhere in the wilds" of other, realer, more contained history.

Valdez subverts this marginal representation, however, by rendering the Korean War both haunting and spectral. As Avery Gordon observes, "To be in the seemingly old story now scared and not wishing to be there but not having anywhere else you can go that feels like a place you can belong is to be haunted."[54] In the context of *Badges*, "the seemingly old story" is the Korean War, a past experience only Buddy is privy to, the others in the play "not wishing to be there" but nevertheless "not having anywhere else" that escapes that story. Even if the characters were to discount or willfully ignore Buddy's Korean War experiences, the U.S. nation-state's Cold War logics continue to erupt as hauntings in their lives as actors: a rare speaking role for Buddy arrives in the form of "a Costa Rican General," presumably in a film (casting Jack Nicholson in the lead role) about the 1948 civil war, presaging Costa Rica's Cold War entanglements.[55] In an attempt to placate Sonny, Connie tells him about a role, as "sort of a soldier . . . a *guerrilla*. The story takes place in Central America, see? And there's this American Marine who's down there advising the *contras*. Well, you're one of the boys he's training."[56] Ironically, in the play, the only viable possibility for Sonny in Hollywood is that of playing a bit part as a proletarian soldier, this time in an anticommunist U.S.-backed force: "Who's financing this thing, the Sandinistas or the CIA?"[57] Sonny dismisses Connie's own appearance in the film as the owner of a "whorehouse," indignantly exclaiming his disdain for such roles in films that glorify the United States in its anticommunist repressions in Central America.

Badges is also a play about movie actors and underscores Buddy's bit part as a bandit in *The Treasure of Sierra Madre*. As I discuss in previous sections, Hinojosa's characters Rafe and Joey view the film during the Korean War. They would have recognized Buddy in the film as a marginal character, as part of the background, yet Buddy would not have been invisible to them, as he is intended to be for mainstream white audiences. Indeed, Buddy's work as an extra might have served as an occasion for Rafe and Joey to recognize their own positions as marginal participants in the Korean War. Buddy is a Mexican getting "gunned down" in Hollywood, just as they consider their own possibilities of getting "gunned down" in Korea. That Buddy's labor is officially recognized by the U.S. film industry as "extra" also resonates with Rafe and Joey's labor for the U.S. military, which Rafe narrates in the poem "A Matter of Supplies":

> *It comes down to this: we're pieces of equipment*
> *To be counted and signed for.*
> *On occasion some of us break down,*
> *And those parts which can't be salvaged*
> *Are replaced with other GI parts, that's all.*[58]

Badges also renders the Korean War as spectral, in the phantom nonpresence of Sonny's Korean Chicano brother and his mother, the "Asian girl": "My dad fell in love with an Asian girl, when he was in Korea. Wanted to marry her, but the Army discouraged him. . . . So he came back to the states, promising to send for her. He never did. The family pressure was so against it, he ended up marrying my Mom instead. Rumor has it he might even have left a son behind. . . . I guess he'd be older than me now—poor bastard. A Korean Chicano . . ."[59] The identity of the "Asian girl" remains unclear, as do the circumstances under which she and Buddy met. Reading between the actors' lines and silences, the fact that "the Army discouraged him" and that "family pressure was so against" their marriage suggests the illicit nature of their relationship.[60] While the U.S. military regarded prostitution and the dehumanizing exploitation of Korean women as a mundane reality, the military routinely discouraged GIs from marrying Korean women, which would endow the women with the possibility of U.S. citizenship during a war that chaotically redrew the terms of national sovereignty. For the spectral "Asian girl," "immigration to the United States through marriage represents an opportunity for the Korean woman who is associated with military sex work to shed the stigmas of the past by legitimizing her sexual labor, to the extent that it is no longer legible as sexual labor."[61]

Badges thus raises, through the hidden contours of the Korean War, important questions about kinship. As a normalizing U.S. state project regulating and legitimizing kinship, the management of marriage extends to Korea, demarcating the transnational reach of the state institution. During the Korean War, U.S. military authorities relied on normalized understandings of "proper," heteronormative intimacy as a measure of social control, especially as marriage grants belonging to a nation forged through the ideology of white supremacy. Sonny Villa's wistful invocation of his "Korean Chicano" brother, on the other hand, suggests an affective desire for kinship exceeding heteronormative boundaries. Sonny Villa's pitying speculation that his brother would be a "poor bastard" indicates not just the presumed material poverty of his hypothetical brother nor just the sensitivity to racism his brother might confront but also his illegitimacy within any intimate, societal, and national parameter.

In contrast, Hinojosa's Sonny Ruiz, in the poem "Nagoya Station," considers kinship as a communal experiment forged of mutual desire, in his marriage with a Japanese schoolteacher. Yet Sonny Ruiz too must construct kinship within a national framework, invisible to the U.S. military. After "he filled out and signed his own Missing-In-Action cards," Sonny Ruiz "simply walked away to the docks."[62]

> *Not long after, cards started to arrive from Nagoya and*
> *   signed*
> *By Mr. Kazuo Fusaro who, in another life,*
> *Had lived as David Ruiz in Klail City,*
> *And who, in this new life,*
> *Was now a hundred and ten per cent Japanese.*[63]

Sonny Ruiz's marriage operates on the precondition of his assimilation into Japan, adopting an identity that is Japanese even in excess of his past life. Valdez's and Hinojosa's works thus theorize the multiplicity of kinships. Such improvisational kinships reorient the presumed stabilities of kinship. Despite the insistent regulation of marriage by the U.S. military, both works imagine other possibilities for articulating intimacies that exceed legitimate channels of familial belonging.

I present a brief reading of another Valdez play, which also glimpses the Korean War. *Zoot Suit*, like *Badges*, plays with theatrical conventions and chronicles the 1942 Sleepy Lagoon murder case, which tried and convicted seventeen young men for the murder of José Diaz, and which is regarded as the precursor of the 1943 Zoot Suit Riots. Valdez's theatrical reworking of the murder trial follows the story of Henry Reyna, who along with his friends is wrongfully condemned for the murder, and the efforts of his family, friends, and other communities to clear their names. In the play, Henry is released from incarceration but faces another encounter with the police, which culminates in a series of possible endings. In one, Henry Reyna's younger brother, Rudy, states: "Henry Reyna went to Korea in 1950. He was shipped across in a destroyer and defended the 38th Parallel until he was killed in Inchon in 1952, being posthumously awarded the Congressional Medal of Honor."[64] As an alternate ending, the play refuses an epistemologically secure closing. And in the process, *Zoot Suit* presents a perhaps unanticipated meditation on form and the unended status of the Korean War. Although the play directs most of its critique toward the military apparatus of the Second World War, this line establishes the Korean War within critical genealogies speaking back to state power. The fact that it is Rudy, Henry's younger brother, speaking this line intensifies the impact of multiple imperial wars within this particular Chicano family. As with Hinojosa's works, the play theorizes the dizzying, queer temporalities of the Korean War. Henry is outlived by the Korean War, which to this day continues to outlive him, as an unended war, as a decolonial hiatus.

All from Memory: Rosaura Sánchez's and Tomás Rivera's Audio/Visual Retrofits of the Korean War

Lo-fi by necessity, but in keeping with time, Rosaura Sánchez and Tomás Rivera spin a different set of what Maylei Blackwell might call retrofitted war memories. Like Hinojosa and Valdez, Sánchez and Rivera consider the Korean War's aural and visual forms, revealed in absences of those lost in action (Rivera's "The Portrait") and in the low volumes of an early morning radio broadcast (Sánchez's "One Morning: 1952"). Sánchez's short stories, previously published during the years 1976–1992, have been translated from Spanish into English by Beatrice Pita and collected in the 2000 book *He Walked In and*

Sat Down, and Other Stories. Rivera's 1971 . . . *y no se lo tragó la tierra /* . . . *And the Earth Did Not Devour Him* also takes a series of short stories and vignettes, collected into a Premio Quinto Sol award-winning novel. While I focus on one short story from each collection, the two books represent two of the most foundational Chicana/o literary works. And both "The Portrait" and "One Morning: 1952" consider loss, memory, and the unknown in the Korean War.

Similar to Valdez's portrayals of the Korean War, Rivera's and Sánchez's texts both set the war as a backdrop within domestic, familial story lines. "One Morning: 1952" opens with the unnamed masculine narrator's interior monologue on building a bathroom for the family home, as he prepares for the day's work. He listens to news on the radio as his coffee percolates, "but he kept the volume low."[65] The next line invokes the Korean War, on which the narrator ruminates: "His brother-in-law was out there, somehow caught up in that mess of Chinese, Koreans and *gringos*."[66] There's kin here, to be sure, but the "somehow" as antecedent to "that mess of Chinese, Koreans and *gringos*" conjures all the uncertainty and unknowns situating his brother-in-law in "that mess." Martin Manalansan has argued for taking "mess" as a queer analytic that operates against colonial epistemological logics of empirically measured, quantitatively assured knowledge production. Sánchez's use of "mess" here suggests the word's "alternative, often underused, meaning as plentitude," that lost within the sheer numbers of "Chinese, Koreans and *gringos*"—implied to be the expected racialized actors for the Korean War—is his brother-in-law.[67]

But back to that radio news broadcast. Because after the narrator turns the radio on, "he kept the volume low. The war in Korea continued; it seemed it was going on forever."[68] Like *Zoot Suit*, "One Morning: 1952" ruminates on the unanticipated temporality of the Korean War, which not only "continued" but, with the internal suspension engendered by that not quite relational punctuation, the queer semicolon, "seemed it was going on forever." And like Valdez suggests through his use of form the Korean War's obscured role in U.S. domestic history, the narrator's haunting meditation in the story, to leave the "domestic" undisturbed, "kept the volume low."

Fading out of "One Morning: 1952" into Rivera's "The Portrait" discloses meditative qualities of uncertainty and forgetting in both texts. "The Portrait" describes a traveling portrait salesman's swindle of Don Mateo's family, who purchase an enhancement of their one photograph of their son Chuy as an adult, who was "lost in action" in Korea.[69] As with the other vignettes in Rivera's novel, "The Portrait" is narrated by an unnamed protagonist, who recalls the portrait salesman's arrival from San Antonio into their South Texas community. With Chuy's photograph, the salesman promises, "We will not only enlarge it for you but we'll also set it in a wooden frame like this one and with inlays, like this—three dimensional, as they say."[70] Doña Mateo considers this enhancement for Chuy's photograph: "It's the only picture we have of him. We took it right before he left for Korea. Poor m'ijo, we never saw him again. See . . . this is his picture. Do you think you can make it like that, make it look like he's alive?"[71]

What the portrait salesman offers is nothing less than a resurrection, "three dimensional": Chuy not only brought back to life but overlaid with military enhancements, once the salesman realizes that "he left for Korea." Don Mateo insists, "You take good care of that picture for us because it's the only one we have of our son grown up. He was going to send us one all dressed up in uniform with the American and Mexican flags crossed over his head, but he no sooner got there when a letter arrived telling us that he was lost in action."[72] The salesman promises to put Chuy in uniform for the portrait, even as Don Mateo points out, "But he's not wearing a uniform in that picture."[73] Chuy, "lost in action" in Korea, has no say in the enhancement of his photograph, no voice in his own proposed resurrection, to be rendered "three dimensional" in ersatz military uniform.

After the salesman takes their money and the only photograph they have of Chuy as a young man, he disappears, while the family waits for Chuy's enhanced picture. A group of children finds the photographs, "all worm-eaten and soaking wet" after a series of heavy rains, not certain they are photos at all except they have "faces that could just barely be made out." When Don Mateo encounters the salesman at the market one day, he insists that the salesman restores Chuy's photo, remarking that the salesman "had to do it all from memory," given the faded image. The salesman delivers Chuy's finished portrait, and prompted by Don Mateo on his thoughts, the narrator says, "Well, to be honest, I don't remember too well how Chuy looked. But he was beginning to look more and more like you, isn't that so?" With the loss of the photograph, Chuy is lost in action all over again, his "worm-eaten" image standing in as the family's nearest confirmation that Chuy may in fact already be dead in Korea. His visual resurrection, "all from memory," belies the suspended uncertainty on whether he lives, staring out from a photo that may not be Chuy at all, in a U.S. military uniform that he may never have worn. The portrait displays its own spectral agency, larger than life and three-dimensional, made to "look like he's alive" but as yet refusing to disclose its genealogy.

3

SLEUTH CITIES

East LA, Seoul, and Military Mysteries

Even as the genealogy of Chicano/a literature about the Korean War indicates subversive departures from U.S. Cold War preoccupations with racial knowing as a usable state project, contemporary fiction by the Chicano author Martín Limón indexes the U.S. military's continued contradictions in the war's afterlife. Limón's popular Sergeants Sueño & Bascom mystery series features George Sueño as the Chicano military detective from East LA. The early novels in the series take place during the 1970s in Itaewon, known for the long-established U.S. Army base originating in the Korean War. The series offers considerations of spatial proxies in cities, which are themselves affiliated in the language of kinship. Inhabiting the detective's role as empiricist compiler of evidence, Sueño registers the liberal incorporation of racialized and gendered subjectivities, as well as the contradictions emerging through such incorporation. In other words, this Chicano military police procedural series produces knowledge about the Korean War's liberal contradictions in a series of nested hierarchies entangling Korean sex workers, Korean houseboys, nonwhite U.S. military personnel, and representations of liberal white womanhood.

Beyond the proxy spatial function represented in Limón's series, the urban spaces of East LA and the U.S. military districts of Itaewon and Tongduchon were critically, *infrastructurally* shaped by the Korean War. Limón's military police procedural genre functions as an aperture into white supremacy, gendered exploitation, militarization, and the expansion of U.S. frontiers from California to Korea. More explicitly, sexual violence at the intersections of race and empire haunt Sueño in *The Wandering Ghost* (2007), during his investigation of sex work and rape in East LA and Tongduchon, and in *Slicky Boys* (1997). That Limón's series begins with *Jade Lady Burning* in 1992, the year of the LA uprisings, and continues through torrents of global U.S. police actions and wars marks the series as one that registers the concomitant eruptions of racially and sexually oppressive institutions through the extension of U.S. military power. Limón's series functions in part as a litany of violence fundamental to the U.S. military and as an open index of U.S. white supremacy's temporal and spatial scope. Limón's portrayals of white supremacy, xenophobia, and sexual exploitation in East LA and throughout Korea trace the transnational circuits of racial formation and at the same time locate Sueño as an unwitting guard of heteronormative masculinity. Building on the spatial proximities to racialized empire generated by Limón's series, this chapter considers the Korean War's remnant subjectivities: sex workers, houseboys, nonwhite U.S. military personnel, and the white woman U.S. Army lieutenant.

Transpacific Space in Hard-Boiled and Detective Fiction

Limón's *Slicky Boys* and *The Wandering Ghost* take place in the militarized spaces of 1970s Itaewon, Tongduchon, and East LA, an important transpacific frame that attends to both the legacies of the Korean War and the shifting dynamics of industrial capitalism. In addition to shaping the military and infrastructure development of Los Angeles, the Korean War forms the prehistory for Sueño's deployment to Korea as corporate disinvestment and deindustrialization empty the city of jobs. The deindustrialization of Los Angeles was devastating for nonwhite labor forces that relied on manufacturing and processing work, even as "deindustrialization in the advanced industrial countries occurred in tandem with industrialization in the newly industrialized economies," such as South Korea.[1] The accelerating avenues of transpacific neoliberal exploitation foreground Sueño's migration to Korea, as part of the occupying U.S. military presence.

Because of Southern California's development as a production center of the military-industrial complex, many newly enlisted recruits received training in San Diego before crossing the Pacific to Korea. The same military defense production plants that sustained the economy of such Southern Californian cities as San Diego and Los Angeles demanded segregated labor forces, mirroring the de facto segregated military units during the Korean War and during 1970s Itaewon and Tongduchon. While cultural and literary studies have focused on Los Angeles as a transnational noir city, Limón's mystery

series disrupts such readings by rejecting representations of "hordes" of perilous Asians and other racialized groups infiltrating Los Angeles that appear
in dominant versions of the noir tradition. Instead, Limón's work depicts
a sympathetic Chicano narrator's memories and experiences in negotiating
racial and class oppression in East LA, which prove to be critical for solving
military crimes in Itaewon and Tongduchon.[2] Itaewon and Tongduchon during
the 1970s also figure as "seedy" districts for military prostitution and transactional sex in the transnational cultural imagination, a representation that Limón
embeds into Agent Sueño's narratives. It is at this intersection that I read
Limón's mystery series as one that binds East LA, Itaewon, and Tongduchon
as interconnected sites of war, poverty, and gendered racial exploitation that
inspire a critique of state power.

Framing Los Angeles and Seoul as layered spaces in Limón's military
mystery series reveals entwined legacies of militarization and their production of overlapping spatial temporalities. The military development timelines
of both cities provide a critical geographical framework for understanding
Limón's novels. Los Angeles burst into economic development during the
Second World War, with an intensity of activity in the defense industry and
military preparation for war personnel. Roderick Ferguson suggests the insidious correlation between the expanded economic opportunities for nonwhite workers in the defense industry and U.S. empire in East Asia: "The
state used that labor as the motor for establishing hegemonic authority in
Asia through war and economic imperialism."[3] In light of the multipronged
impact of wartime development in Los Angeles, the urban historian Norman
Klein shows that Los Angeles did not serendipitously become a privileged site
of development but that the city was aggressively promoted by city and county
officials. According to Klein, "Competition to attract government defense
money was fierce during the war. L.A. became the center for military industries serving the Pacific, and many of these remained afterward, as part of
the huge postwar defense industry here."[4] As much as the city was a center for
military industries, Los Angeles was a microcosm for wartime contradictions,
from segregated defense plants to explicit white supremacist hostility and
violence. For the city's Chicano/as, participation in the booming war industries, which represented a militarized state's main avenue of access, changed
little of prevailing white supremacist social attitudes. Indeed, following the
war, the county of Los Angeles engineered explicit disruptions of Chicano/a
communities.

The military language during this period performed a supple function,
used to describe war strategies as well as city development plans. The development and use of militarized language to justify the unsettling of Chicano/a

communities for urban renewal closely mirrored the larger U.S. public's support for devastating military actions in Korea. While the growth of Los Angeles in this era was fueled by military development, Seoul (and the rest of the Korean peninsula) suffered widescale attacks by the U.S. military during the Korean War: "Between 1950 and 1953, U.S. bombers dumped as much as 600,000 tons of napalm over the Korean peninsula; in Churchill's words, it was 'splashed' over the landscape. This was more napalm than had been used against Japan in World War II and more than would later be dropped over Vietnam."[5] The U.S. military "promiscuously" strafed living and working spaces on the Korean peninsula, making it impossible for civilians to remain stationary, thereby adding to the ever-increasing refugee population on the move from indiscriminate aerial attacks. The movements of refugees tautologically necessitated further aerial bombing, as the U.S. military made no effort to distinguish civilians from North Korean, Chinese, and South Korean troops. The discourse of anticommunism and white supremacy absolved U.S. military attacks on civilians, justifying the military's actions as necessary to protect South Koreans against communist North Koreans.

Significantly, Raúl Homero Villa and Norman Klein document the military language used in urban planning discourses in Los Angeles, in particular freeway development in the 1950s: "Urban-planning campaigns 'took on the spirit of wartime propaganda, particularly aerial bombings,' suggesting the urgent need for scorched-earth policies to raze the 'infected' central-city neighborhoods."[6] The people "infecting" these Los Angeles neighborhoods were Black, Mexican, and Chicano/a residents, and urban planners used the language of blight, rot, and decay to justify urban renewal programs in nonwhite neighborhoods underdeveloped or impoverished by prior instances of racist city planning. It is no surprise, then, that the military language used by planners directly correlates to the concurrent Korean War. The rationale for using military language in city planning discourses is brought into forceful relief when we consider the popular support for napalm and popular opinion against communism in the wider U.S. public: "The scorched-earth policy and the widespread use of napalm were unquestioned, even celebrated. The American war propaganda of the time unabashedly and affectionately termed its new weapon 'flaming death' when captioning aerial photographs of napalm bombings. 'Burn 'em out, cook 'em, fry 'em.'"[7] While the horrific use of napalm in Pacific wars is not tantamount to the aggressive discourse and practices of razing neighborhoods for freeways, these events share deep ideological roots. The common dehumanizing language of infection and decay, of burning and frying "gooks," is conceptually bound to liberal progress and modernity—for bringing modern development to Los Angeles, accompanied by accruing profits for the powerful, and for delivering freedom from communism to Korea.

In postwar South Korea, the development and gentrification of the spaces around military bases emerge through gendered discourse. Jin-kyung Lee observes that "one of the ways in which modernization was made concrete was through the ongoing and fast-paced urbanization. The constantly changing landscape of the old city, Seoul, included the continual construction of buildings, the ever-expanding network of the mass transit system, and the growing ubiquity of squatters and their slums."[8] In the 1970s, U.S. military bases were expanded as powerful emblems of modernity, while the impoverished peripheries were inhabited by those who worked feminized, devalued jobs. As Min-Jung Kim observes, "Women in [camptown] prostitution are in an especially vulnerable and defenseless position because of the dynamics of U.S. imperialist relations to South Korea that further set the context for the vast power differences of race, gender, sexuality, nationality, and language."[9] Building on critical foundational research by such scholars as Katharine Moon, Seungsook Moon, and Ji-Yeon Yuh, Kim reminds us that misogynist disposability was explicitly engineered by a U.S.-supported military dictatorship: "During the Park Chung Hee regime, the South Korean government promoted camptown prostitution as a way both to keep the American forces in South Korea happy and to bring in foreign currency. In 1961, Park Chung Hee had declared prostitution illegal with the Prostitution Prevention Law, but he revised his stance a year later, designating 104 special districts as exempt from the law, 60 percent in camptowns."[10] The U.S. military and Koreans with access to capital were joined in misogynist structures of exploitation: "The men in charge of these camptowns—the local bar owners, the wealthy landowners, and even national legislators—extend geopolitical domination into the back alleys of places like Itaewon and commodify women as products for rent."[11]

The significance of such critical feminist scholarship cannot be underplayed, particularly when considered along the work of such scholars as G. Cameron Hurst III, who approaches the development of Itaewon from a reactionary area studies perspective. While on the faculty at the University of Kansas, he published the field report "It'aewon: The Gentrification of a Boomtown" in 1984. The introduction states: "While not yet a bastion of establishment respectability, It'aewon has become a shopper's paradise and perhaps the most comfortable international environment in metropolitan Seoul."[12] For Hurst, Itaewon's gentrification proceeds along familiar routes of consumer-driven capitalist development, out of what he characterizes as the unwanted effects of the Korean War. Hurst's selective recognition of Itaewon belies the violent toll of modernization and exposes the troubling ideological parameters of Cold War area studies logics. Along with the report on Itaewon's gentrification, Hurst acknowledges as an afterthought the sedimented histories of militarization that construct the social and political space of Itaewon: "The Japanese military establishment was located at Yongsan (the U.S. military simply took over the same facilities after the Japanese left)."[13] Nor does Hurst contextualize the U.S. military's role in why Itaewon is not "respectable": "While no longer a boomtown, It'aewon has not completely cast off that stigma as yet. . . . Most telling, It'aewon still has the whores and the GIs."[14] His account of the "stigma" permeating Itaewon situates sex workers as an a priori development of Itaewon and erases the militarized order of operations: U.S. military occupation's and South Korean military dictatorships' prerequisite in the presence and exploitation of sex workers, some of whom had been forced into sexual slavery for the Japanese Imperial Army during the Second World War.

Furthermore, Hurst displaces the rationale underlying sex work in Itaewon solely to Korean patriarchal cultures: "That war, poverty, and colonial rule contributed to social breakdown and encouraged some Korean females to turn to prostitution as a means of survival is neither debatable nor unique to Korea. . . . The real source of the industry's proliferation is Korean male chauvinism, not Japanese and American depravity."[15] Misogyny in Korean society absolutely requires critical challenge, but Hurst's motive for introducing "Korean male chauvinism" is to obscure the official military infrastructures constructed by both Japan and the United States to produce racialized and sexualized violence. Indeed, Hurst directs his efforts toward absolving the U.S. military of any influence in Itaewon's "stigma": "Given the long-established cultural patterns underlying the industry, it is hard to determine what impact boomtowns have had in this area. Once these were the main avenues through which foreign influences filtered, and no doubt American attitudes toward male-female relations penetrated the country through boomtowns. . . . [But] there are magazine [*sic*], movies, and other influences; an increasing number of Koreans are going abroad, even as tourists. So how much comes through boomtowns is difficult to gauge."[16] Not only is the "stigma" of Itaewon justified by "long-established cultural patterns underlying the industry"; Hurst suggests that Korean tourists in the early 1980s were somehow related to the militarily sanctioned, racialized institutions of mass rape of women by the Japanese Imperial Army dating back to the Second World War. Hurst's account attempts to excise the U.S. military's "penetration" of foreign influences and absolves the Japanese Imperial Army of their perpetuation of militarized sexual violence.

Hurst's understanding of Itaewon, initially deployed to assert a neutral perspective on the district's gentrification, settles into a strange and defensive denial of culpability for sex work. Furthermore, the gendered orientalism of his language rehearses deep-seated global asymmetries: "Once weak and helpless, Korea welcomed U.S. military support and the tremendous economic advantages the large U.S. military presence provided. But as Korea becomes economically more secure, as her international status increases . . . South Korea feels a greater degree of self-confidence. This makes it difficult to maintain the same harmonious relationship with the United States, which still enjoys a sort of 'semi-colonial' rule over the country."[17] Hurst's portrayal of Korea as a victim of patriarchal violence, "once weak and helpless" but when "economically more secure," feeling "a greater degree of self-confidence," is especially appalling when he writes about the U.S. difficulty to thus "enjoy a sort of 'semi-colonial'" power over South Korea. Hurst evacuates from this discourse how Korea came to be "weak and helpless" in the first place and the role of the United States in creating the peninsula's extreme vulnerabilities. Feminist scholars have critiqued the U.S. military's binary rationales, arguing "that the very maintenance of the military establishment depends on promoting gendered notions of femininity and masculinity, weakness and strength, conquered and conqueror."[18] Hurst's bald acknowledgment of the U.S. "semi-colonial" enjoyment of Korea depends entirely on the exploitation of poor and uneducated people, especially women, from rural districts. This is the context for Limón's hard-boiled novels, with Itaewon and Tongduchon entangled in spaces of devastating desperation, human disposability, and notions of criminality.

The concept of the criminal is central to the detective fiction genre in the Western literary tradition, which dates to the early nineteenth century and follows established conventions of questioning, interrogating, and observing in attempts to gain empirical knowledge and truth, with outcomes oriented toward neat resolutions and restorations of the social order: "The detective story is the realm of the happy ending. The criminal is always caught. Justice is always done. Crime never pays. Bourgeois legality, bourgeois values, bourgeois society, always triumph in the end. It is soothing, socially integrating literature, despite its concern with crime, violence and murder."[19] Mainstream detective fiction manufactures anxieties in attempts to reconcile readers with the current social order, often functioning to restore faith in justice systems; the figure of the criminal justifies the upright social system. For scholars of cultural studies and racial history in the United States, detective fiction can function to individualize violence and criminality, to the effect of foreclosing any critiques of the system. Yet the genre also builds in a certain degree of self-conscious discovery, at least for the narrator, as scholars of detective fiction argue that "in a diverse array of mystery novels . . . time and again the detective also unravels a mystery about him- or herself. The novel is as much his or her story as it is the story of the crime."[20] Even so, readers' perspectives are often confined to the narrators' ideologically normative positions, including latent racism and more blatant heteropatriarchy, and readers may find themselves reaching beyond those limits to formulate social and political critiques.

Hard-boiled crime fiction, recognized as the U.S. response to more conventional bourgeois detective fiction emerging from Britain, can be traced to the years following World War I.[21] Moving away from exclusively individualized and private motives for crimes, the hard-boiled genre often focuses specifically on the corruption of the powerful, featuring detectives or investigators that work for a living rather than solve mysteries as a hobby. Although grittier, more explicitly violent and sexual, less respectful of authority, and more attentive to working-class perspectives, the hard-boiled genre still carries over conventions from traditional detective fiction, often modifying them and creating different possibilities for critique. The genre's built-in features challenging various forms of modern authority—economic, racial, and social, among others—allow for critical modifications to its ideologically white masculine emergence.

Raymond Chandler's work perhaps exemplifies a template for the conventions of the U.S. hard-boiled detective story, which in turn influenced U.S. film noir in the 1940s and 1950s, significant here because of film noir's role in representing the blight of Los Angeles and because of Chandler's own racist characterizations. Kelly Oliver and Benigno Trigo argue that "in an important sense, film noir is born out of the hard-boiled racism of Chandler's style."[22] On noir fiction, Klein remarks in *The History of Forgetting*, his study of erasure and memory on Los Angeles: "As much as I love *noir*, and find it exotically compelling, it is nevertheless often utterly false in its visions of the poor, of the non-white in particular. It is essentially a mythos about white male panic. . . . The hard-boiled story cannot help but operate, very fundamentally, as white males building a social imaginary."[23] Yet such noir novels as Chester Himes's *If He Hollers Let Him Go* absolutely disrupts the process of "white males building a social imaginary" and instead theorize critical interrogations of white supremacy within the genre. Klein's admission of the exotically compelling nature of noir and the hard-boiled story recall the military recruiting slogan during the Second World War "Join the Army, See the World." The world in the slogan, imagined from a white masculine subjectivity, invites deployment to "exotic," feminized locales, such as Korea and Japan.

Such exoticism, whether in Asia or U.S. urban spaces, serves an appealing function for some readers. But for queer people of color, immigrants, and others against whom the normative U.S. subject is defined, the exotic in mainstream detective fiction are often just racist snapshots, saturated by white supremacist scripts. Over the past few decades, however, detective fiction by people of color, as well as scholarship on multiethnic and queer detective fiction, has flourished. Ralph Rodriguez addresses the critical possibilities of the genre for Chicana/o writers, arguing that given the feeling of alienation many Chicana/os confront in the United States, the voice of the alienated hero or detective functions as an ideal mediator.[24] In Limón's novels, George Sueño—the alienated Chicano hero of the series—delivers for readers both a seedy urban place and a layered discursive space that position his insights about transnational racism, critiques of the military power structure, and memories of East LA.

"Koreans Might Be Inscrutable to Most of the World, but They Aren't Inscrutable to Me": The Chicano Detective in *Slicky Boys*

The militarized developments in Itaewon and East LA and their operative ideologies become even more entwined in Limón's 1997 novel *Slicky Boys*. *Slicky Boys*, like all of Limón's military mysteries, chronicles the adventures of Sergeant George Sueño and his partner Ernie Bascom as they solve various military cases in their capacity as detectives for the Eighth Army, based in Itaewon during the 1970s. Their encounters often entail brushes with South Korean civilians, state entities, gangsters, and business girls, a euphemism for sex workers. Rarely do they solve their crimes and mysteries the official way, instead opting to work with shamans, business girls, and black market racketeers, especially since the perpetrators of the crimes are often military officials or personnel, complicit in or directly committing violent crimes against civilians and lower-ranking military personnel. Sueño and Bascom also operate at odds with various U.S. military agencies since the criminals are often representatives of the U.S. military. The detectives' investigations usually showcase Sueño's desire to understand, protect, and accurately represent South Korean society against the bald apathy of the U.S. military. While Sueño attempts to function as a voice and champion for South Korean civilians, he is nonetheless situated as a representative of the Cold War U.S. military, his position rendered more complex for his status as a Chicano soldier.

This section analyzes *Slicky Boys*, first focusing on the transnational circuits of racism that layer the home spaces of East LA and Itaewon and then exploring critiques of gender, labor, domesticity, and "coolie labor" through the character of Mr. Yim, who works as a houseboy for GIs. The novel follows Sueño and Bascom as they investigate a series of gruesome murders, starting with the murder of a UN guard. Their initial suspects are "slicky boys" in a highly organized network of black market gangs. The slicky boys have roots in the intense poverty and suffering created by the Korean War, when some lives depended on pilfering food and other necessities from the U.S. military. The agents discover with the help of the gang leader, named Herbalist So, that the murderer is Lieutenant Commander Bo Shipton, a white Navy Seal who disappeared after he was rebuffed by a Korean woman, the daughter of a Korean official, who planned to marry him. The twists include the Korean official's cover-ups of the murders and the Texan Shipton's hatred of Mexicans. While Shipton's racism is especially explicit, interrogations of white supremacist logics underpin the novel's development.

Limón's military mystery series embeds Sueño's childhood and adolescent memories of East LA into Itaewon in the 1970s. In doing so, the novels urge a comparative examination of the militarized development of both spaces and frame a transpacific racialized lens across South Korea and the United States. In *Slicky Boys*, Sueño notes that "Mexican or Anglo, we were all just Americans in the eyes of a Korean policeman. When I was growing up in Southern California that attitude would've come in handy if more people had shared it. Saved me a few lumps."[25] By using both East LA and Itaewon as frameworks for Sueño's observations on race and racisms, the novel considers the optics informing citizenship, national identification, and the transnational circuit of racialization. Sueño considers the benefits, however problematic, of a "colorblind" Southern California that overlooks race in favor of a U.S. national identification. Describing himself, Sueño states, "I'm dark, tall, big, Mexican, and used to being stared at."[26] Sueño's consideration privileges a U.S. nationalism closely linked with citizenship, and his self-description captures the complex history of racism against Chicana/os in the United States; that Chicana/o "symbolic status within the United States nevertheless remains in question as long as the nation continues to conflate citizenship with having an Anglo appearance."[27] Sueño's self-description belies his consideration of a colorblind Southern California, instead pointing to how his U.S. citizenship is already called into question when he is "being stared at." As in the World War II slogan "Join the Army, See the World," when Sueño joins the army, he becomes the world that both Americans and Koreans stare at. Sueño's reflections on U.S. racism in relation to South Korean state power suggest the Cold War complexities indexing race, nationality, and citizenship.

Sueño's recall of his East LA childhood is paired with a ventriloquizing lesson on the American Dream. His father leaves for Mexico after Sueño is born, and from that point, Sueño is transferred from foster home to foster home: "I was brought up by the County of Los Angeles—in foster homes. It was a rough existence but I learned a lot about people, how to read them, how to hide when it was time to hide, and how to wait them out."[28] He reverses the dominant optic directing the American Dream, reading and hiding his way into corners of that dream. Sueño's name, translated from Spanish into English as "dream," reflects his untranslatable and contradictory relationships with the ideologies undergirding the American Dream.[29] Recounting his difficult childhood, Sueño asks, "What was I grateful for? For having a real life, for having money coming in—not much, but enough—and for having a job to do. I was an investigator and I wore suits and did important work. A status I never thought I'd reach when I was a kid in East L.A."[30] Given the structural lack of opportunity permeating Sueño's life in East LA, his "real life" unfolds in the camptowns of South Korea. Sueño serves as an ill-formed template of the rugged individual, wearing empire's suits (a haunting reminder of the military uniform added to Chuy's portrait in Tomás Rivera's vignette) and doing important work he never thought possible as "a kid in East L.A." Sueño's location in a militarized U.S. neocolony to achieve this dream speaks volumes about the structured lack of economic possibility and the U.S. state's Cold War representational investment in optics of racial equality, which send him to Korea to serve at U.S. empire's Pacific edge.[31]

Yet Sueño's childhood in East LA allows him access to less stereotypically saturated ways of understanding Koreans and to feeling at "home" in Itaewon: "Koreans might be inscrutable to most of the world, but they aren't inscrutable to me. I grew up in East L.A. speaking two languages, living in two worlds, the Anglo and the Mexican. . . . So learning a third language, Korean, hadn't intimidated me. . . . And living in the Korean world hadn't bothered me either. Their culture was just another puzzle to unravel, like so many that I'd faced when the County of Los Angeles moved me from home to home."[32] Sueño's learning the Korean language records the linguistic topography of the Cold War: the shifting parameters of Korea's provisional third world statuses are reflected in Sueño's learning of a third language. His understanding of Korea and Koreans is contingent on spatialized Cold War knowledges that approximates the U.S. state's liberal logics of racial and linguistic incorporation. Sueño's usage of "home" further registers in reverberating decibels of overlapping empires. Within the County of Los Angeles, he has no home, though his spatial identifications are firmly with East LA.

His sense of ambivalent belonging implicitly critiques the U.S. annexation of Southern California from Mexico and the ever-stringent surveillance of the U.S.-Mexico border in the "two worlds" of East LA: "This feeling of being on the outside, being the alienated other, thematizes the hero of the detective novel and resonates especially well with Chicana/os, who though subjects of the nation are often represented as alien to it."[33] Sueño's presence in Korea shifts this argument, considering his position as a racialized U.S. subject who travels abroad on the circuits of Cold War militarization. When Sueño does leave East LA, "living in the Korean world" becomes his job, his new homeland, in the neocolonial military outpost of Itaewon. His claim that "living in the Korean world hadn't bothered [him]," that Korean culture was "just another puzzle to unravel," suggests an epistemological orientation he braids together from his lived entanglements with power: his foster home experiences, his racialized brushes with alienation and belonging in East LA, and his participation in the U.S. military.

In the context of Korea, world, culture, and home carry multiple valences in the continuing deferred decolonial condition of the unended Korean War, as the thirty-eighth parallel engineers the peninsula into separate worlds and cultures, fragmenting the Korean homeland. In addition to the partition, the aerial and terrestrial destruction of the peninsula created millions of homeless refugees. Sueño's statement urges consideration of the militarized borders between the United States and Mexico and between North and South Korea. Sueño's discussion of the simultaneity of two worlds reveals the sedimentation of imperial histories near the U.S.-Mexico border, remapped in Korea during the 1970s when the peninsula is negotiating with the aftermath of Japanese colonialism, the presence of U.S. military occupation, and the U.S. conscription of South Korea's engagements with the Vietnam War.[34] Sueño's reflections on home denaturalize these national borders, revealing the artificiality of national spaces. Sueño's very presence in the U.S. military in Korea evokes the twinned threat of communism and nuclear war that North Korea represents in the U.S. imagination, noxiously articulated as part of an "axis of evil" by George W. Bush. Sueño's use of home thus evokes Homeland Security, in the imagined threat embodied by Mexico and the looming presence of North Korea.

While Homeland Security ostensibly directs attention to a stable and vulnerable U.S. domestic space, another border that Sueño's use of home disrupts marks the gendered confines of domesticity. In consideration of the GI exploitation of domestic labor performed by houseboys in *Slicky Boys*, Sueño's articulations of South Korea as home offers a rethinking of the term *domestic*. As Rosemary Marangoly George states in *Burning Down the House*,

"The close association between women and the domestic arena is of such long standing that it is sometimes perceived as a natural affinity that draws the two together."[35] The naturalized association between domestic and feminized labor opens up considerations about houseboys to further critique ideological configurations of domesticity, gender, and race in relation to military discourses. Dating back at least to the Second World War, "native" boys and men sustained livelihoods by doing domestic work for occupying military personnel around the globe. Similar to the Filipino, Japanese, and Korean workers serving these functions in the United States, the male workers, regardless of age, were called houseboys. The very name links engrained understandings of domesticity in "house" to a presumably undeveloped masculinity in "boy," a designation stripped of an ostensibly threatening masculinity and made instrumental by the military in Korea and middle- and upper-class families in the United States.

In *Slicky Boys*, Sueño interviews a houseboy named Mr. Yim for their investigation, mediated through the patronizing, orientalist filter of Sueño as a U.S. military subject. Sueño describes Mr. Yim's life as "an endless chain of shining shoes, washing laundry, ironing fatigues, and putting up with GI bullshit," despite the fact that Mr. Yim's "English was well pronounced. Hardly an accent. I knew he'd never gone to high school—probably not even middle school—or he wouldn't be working here. He'd picked it up from the GIs over the years. Intelligence radiated from his calm face. When I first arrived in Korea, I wondered why men such as this would settle for low positions. I learned later that after the Korean War, having work of any kind was a great accomplishment."[36] Sueño's description of Mr. Yim suggests tightly bound, normative understandings of domestic labor as private, unpaid labor performed dutifully by women. Limón's discussion of houseboys in *Slicky Boys* occasions a rethinking of the term *domestic* in relation to transnational gendered and racialized divisions of labor. As Rosemary George reminds us, "What is truly remarkable are the ways in which dominant domestic ideologies and practices have become globally hegemonic as a result of colonial and capitalist expansion and modernization, even as they have entered into contestation with other local forms of domesticity."[37]

Sueño's narrative of Mr. Yim shows the globally hegemonic manifestation of domestic ideologies in several ways. First, Sueño's questioning of "why men such as this would settle for low positions" belies his assumptions about domestic labor as both gendered and classed. That is, women might perform the labor but not men. Moreover, Sueño perceives something innately "low" and demeaning about the work itself, rather than the uneven logics of power that enable the devaluation of both the labor and the laborers. Second, colonial and capitalist expansion and modernization carve routes that allow U.S. GIs to maintain masculinist approaches to strictly policed military regulations, such as "shining shoes, washing laundry, ironing fatigues," by exploiting the work of houseboys. That Korean men in the U.S.-occupied militarized space of Itaewon perform this labor functions to uphold the masculinity of GIs against the feminized bodies of Asian men, which has a long-standing tradition in the United States, and is used as justification for exercising repressive mechanisms.

The devaluation of gendered labor operates multiply in the racialized labor of Korean men in Itaewon, as globally hegemonic U.S. domestic ideologies entered "into contestation with other local forms of domesticity," given that South Korean patriarchy regards domestic work as demeaning for men. Sueño attempts to dignify workers like Mr. Yim, as Mr. Yim is described as "lucid, calm, smart, sober," and laboring to value his work, though "houseboys were so low on the social scale that nobody took their testimony seriously." Domesticity then reveals normative associations of feminized labor, a distinct private/home sphere, and unpaid or low-paying work, but Limón's depiction of Mr. Yim potentially reframes masculinist power structures, questions the layering of private/public spheres, and critiques devalued notions of domestic work. Similarly, the word *houseboy* appears to affirm U.S. masculinity and generosity and denigrates the status of "native" men, but Mr. Yim registers a particular affect that shows him to be "lucid, calm, smart, [and] sober," in comparison to "GI bullshit." Thus, houseboy, a "positionality that has been rendered unthinkable by the dominant culture," accrues possibility in Mr. Yim's performance to dislodge normative discourses, to gain traction to critique, and to create accessibility to different ways of understanding the unthinkable.[38]

During the Korean War and its aftermath, U.S. military personnel exploited devalued forms of labor, allured by the availability of the ostensible "coolie labor" they perceived through orientalist lenses. In his 1950 essay "The Simple Art of Murder," Raymond Chandler declares that "the fellow who can write you a vivid and colorful prose simply won't be bothered with the coolie labor of breaking down unbreakable alibis."[39] Chandler's reference to "coolie labor" must be situated within the global histories of racialized labor. In California during the 1870s and 1880s, Chinese workers were wedged to bolster white labor claims against immigration, manifesting in the Chinese Exclusion Act (1882). Indeed, the figure of the *unfree* "coolie" in the United States was instrumental for consolidating the idea of the autonomous white liberal individual, despite the legal status of Chinese workers as free labor.[40] In the early nineteenth-century transatlantic context of British colonialism, the figure of the Chinese "coolie" gains political traction as one mediating the global transition between slavery and freedom, while in the late nineteenth-century transpacific context of Mexican colonization, versions of the Chinese "coolie" trade continued under pretexts of open immigration and economic development policies.[41] Chandler's formulation of "coolie labor" in relation to detective fiction hinges on the figure's ambivalent register and the shifting variables demarcating freedom and unfreedom. But his "coolie labor" registers as well in that other gendered racial figure, the Asian houseboy.

With Chandler's insistence on describing certain elements of writing detective stories as "coolie labor," I assert the historical and material significance of "coolie labor" in the figure of Mr. Yim as a houseboy and also in Chandler's formulation of masculine writers of detective fiction. In addition to Chandler's formulation of detective fiction as the gendered discursive territory of "fellows," he also imagines a rigid binary of "vivid and colorful prose" and "the coolie labor of breaking down unbreakable alibis," in which the flamboyance of vivid writing is incommensurate with the mechanical, unimaginative work of narrative consistency. Sueño's interview with Mr. Yim belies Sueño's own participation in Chandler's notion of "coolie labor" as a racialized, diasporic subject of U.S. empire. Chandler's usage in reference to detective fiction is significant in light of his definitions of the hard-boiled genre and the ways in which, as I note earlier, his visions of orientalism saturated the blighted cinemascapes of Los Angeles in film noir. Of further significance is the historical appropriation of the "coolie" for anti-Asian trade unionism in California: As "mere tool, the Asiatic lacks independent agency. The figure's docile qualities are the effect of the physiological rigors imposed by cheapening wages as well as the training of industrial discipline."[42] In this light, Chandler's racialization of detective fiction writers (and, by extension, such detective protagonists as Sueño) through their "coolie labor" draws on the legacy of the racialized and gendered body of the Asiatic "coolie," who functions as a docile tool with no independent agency and who, with mechanical discipline, performs the work of dismantling watertight alibis in detective fiction. Thus, Sueño's own racialized status as diasporic U.S. subject is twinned with the "coolie labor" of the military detective work he conducts. As such, Sueño hovers in the liminal space manufactured by fantasies of the American Dream, as a racialized U.S. subject in the Pacific circuit of empire performing the jaggedly doubled "coolie labor" putatively limited to characters like Mr. Yim.

While *Slicky Boys* explicitly narrates representations of houseboys, I juxtapose an archival document that more implicitly theorizes Cold War labor and empire. Figure 3.1 portrays a letter from the Center for the Study of the Korean War, written by Y. H. Kim and addressed to Sgt. Cleveran, found among Cleveran's archival effects. Y. H. Kim's letter shares a similar critical

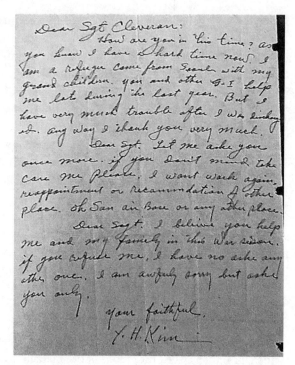

Figure 3.1 Letter from Y. H. Kim addressed to Sgt. Cleveran. (Courtesy of the Center for the Study of the Korean War)

spirit as the novel's representations noted above, recoding the "unthinkable" and refusing to disqualify its positionality. The text reads:

> Dear Sgt. Cleveran: How are you in (t)his time? As you know I have a hard time now. I am a refugee came from Seoul with my grand children. You and other G.I help me lots during the last year. But I have very much trouble after I was discharged. Any way I thank you very much.
>
> Dear Sgt. Let me ask you once more. if you don't mind take care me please. I want work again, reappointment or recommendation of other place. Oh San air Base or any other place.
>
> Dear Sgt. I believe you help me and my family in this war time. if you refuse me, I have no aske any other one. I am awfully sorry but aske you only.
>
> Your faithful, Y.H. Kim.

The letter is written in perfectly cogent, grammatically imperfect English. Though the letter is signed, the initials make the writer's gender ambiguous. Given that most girls and women did not have automatic access to formal education in Korea until after the Korean War and given that Y. H. Kim states having "grand children," Y. H. Kim likely attended school during the Japanese colonial era. Although it would be safe to assume that the letter is written by a grandfather, I suggest that its ambiguity is generative for rethinking domesticity and labor. Queer readings of Y. H. Kim's letter direct different outcomes, and the letter provides potential for critical gender analyses if we imagine and situate the writer's multiple positionalities.

Y. H. Kim's letter is significant for its discursive engagements with theoretical benevolent liberation and actually enacted military violence. While the purpose of the letter is to ask for "work again, reappointment or recommendation of other place," it also encapsulates Lisa Yoneyama's argument on the U.S. imperialist myth of *liberation and rehabilitation*, which "presents both violence and liberation as 'gifts for the liberated.'"[43] Not only does this imperialist myth bolster U.S. nationalism, but the notion of indebtedness that accompanies the "gift of freedom," according to Yoneyama, "has serious implications for the redressability of U.S. military violence. The injured and violated bodies of the liberated . . . do not seem to require redress according to this discourse of indebtedness, for their liberation has already served as the payment/reparation that supposedly precedes the violence inflicted upon them."[44] Reading Y. H. Kim's letter alongside this argument discloses that, in addition to the "gift of freedom" allowing the United States to portray itself as the generous liberator ("You and other G.I help me lots during the last year"), the imperial myth legitimates in advance any sort of military action ("But I have very much trouble after I was discharged") that would again be reinforced by U.S. narratives of generous and benevolent liberation ("Any way I thank you very much").

Yet the sentence "As you know I have a hard time now" is revealing not just of Y. H. Kim's dire situation but also the sharp implication behind "As you know." Sgt. Cleveran might know better than anyone, except for the Koreans suffering the impacts of war, how and why Y. H. Kim would "have a hard time now." While the letter vacillates between gratitude and pleading, Y. H. Kim offers damning critiques of the war and the U.S. military. "I am a refugee came from Seoul with my grand children" could be read as an indictment, directing attention to how Y. H. Kim became one of the millions of refugees during the Korean War, how Seoul was destroyed and multiply occupied, and how Y. H. Kim's movements with "grand children" implies the absence of their parents as a haunting reminder of the human loss of war. When Y. H. Kim states "I believe you help me and my family in this war time," "war time" (전쟁시절) could also translate into English as "war season."[45] Read in this way, the cyclical language of "seasons" accounts for prior wars of U.S. empire, foretells U.S. wars and police actions to come, and strings them temporally through a strand of domestic labor. As much as Y. H. Kim "aske[s]" for work, the letter also holds "Dear Sgt." accountable for the Korean War's violence and destruction, ultimately disrupting the imperialist myth of liberation and rehabilitation.

Readers could easily imagine Mr. Yim from the novel writing this letter, despite the fact that "he'd never gone to high school—probably not even middle school." And while Mr. Yim's life might be "an endless chain of shining shoes, washing laundry, ironing fatigues, and putting up with GI bullshit," if we situate Y. H. Kim's gender as female, then her sexual labor might be exploited along with domestic reproductive labor. Read in this light, Y. H. Kim's request to find work at "Oh San air Base" (Osan Air Base), located approximately thirty-eight miles south of Seoul, resonates with the ongoing contemporary sexual exploitation of workers at Osan Air Base. Osan Air Base, like many other military bases in South Korea, serves as a nexus for gender and sexual exploitation, particularly for poor, uneducated rural women and women trafficked from nations in Southeast Asia, South Asia, and Africa, as well as Russia. The explicit reference to "Oh San air Base" in a letter from the Korean War era requesting work exposes the bleak continuity of the U.S. military "war season" and its imperial legacies in creating and maintaining gendered and sexualized exploitations.

With this critique of sexual exploitation, while I argue that the figure of the houseboy indexes critical histories of militarism, empire, domesticity, and gender, I do not wish to elide the everyday laboring experiences of girls and women who do the same reproductive labor under more rigid and exploitative constraints. Centering the "unthinkable" figure of the houseboy should not exceptionalize the domestic labor of boys and men, and tracing this figure should not selectively valorize their labor. Rather, my aim is to make thinkable a critique of how feminized labor and domestic work itself are demeaned and described as "low" labor, which justifies the ongoing exploitation of the workers. The next section investigates the limitations imposed by the racial hierarchies constructed by a white liberal feminist framework in the gendered exploitation of labor and in militarized sexual violence against women. I investigate Sueño's maintenance of heteronormative masculinity licensed by the differentially racialized bodies of women in *The Wandering Ghost*.

Transnational Circuits of Race, Sexual Violence, and Militarism in *The Wandering Ghost*

Like *Slicky Boys*, Limón's novel *The Wandering Ghost* (2007) depicts gender and sexuality at the intersections of race and militarized power. *The Wan-*

dering Ghost follows Sueño and his partner Bascom to Camp Casey, a U.S. military camp approximately forty miles north of Seoul and located near the demilitarized zone (DMZ), established at the Korean War ceasefire in 1953. While Itaewon was installed in a former Japanese military base after the Japanese defeat in 1945, Camp Casey was not constructed until 1952. Camp Casey is located near several other U.S. military camps close to the small city of Tongduchon. The main mystery in *The Wandering Ghost* is the disappearance of Jill Matthewson, "the first woman MP ever assigned to the 2nd Division Military Police," with rumors and suspicions of sexual harassment and assault guiding Sueño and Bascom's search for Matthewson.[46] As with Limón's other novels in the series, Sueño and Bascom rely on the assistance of sex workers, shamans, and reluctant lower-ranking U.S. military personnel to solve the multiple crimes surrounding Matthewson's disappearance: the U.S. military's attempts to cover up the GI killing of a schoolgirl named Chon Un-suk, several mysterious deaths, and black marketeering by high-ranking U.S. officials. As in the other novels from the series, and following hard-boiled fiction conventions, Sueño states, "I worked for the little guy. We worked for the private or the sergeant or the Korean civilian who'd been stepped on by criminals or by the system."[47] Yet Sueño's own masculinist identity comes to depend upon the unevenly feminized bodies of racialized women.

While *Slicky Boys* upholds Mr. Yim as a dignified houseboy, *The Wandering Ghost* represents other exploitative factors that undergird gendered labor, such as different forms of sex work and the complex racial hierarchies within reproductive labor performed by women. The same patriarchal ideology that constructs domestic work as demeaning to men, thereby devaluing the labor of houseboys, allows for the gendered exploitation by the U.S. military of girls and women who work to support their family members. In *The Wandering Ghost*, Pak Tong-i, an entertainment booking agent, explains why one of his workers, Kim Yong-ai, might have owed money: "'Stripper always owe money,' he said. 'That's why they get into business. Maybe their mom owe money, maybe their daddy owe money, maybe they have younger brother who want to go to school. Very expensive, how you say, hakbi?'"[48]

Hakbi translates into English as "school fees" or "tuition," and the phenomenon of young women participating in the sex work industry to support their male siblings' tuitions is well documented. Jin-kyung Lee discusses this phenomenon taking place in the 1960s and 1970s:

> Under the new economic policies of the Park Chung Hee regime . . .
> young girls and women who had previously contributed to family
> farming and domestic work were now compelled to leave for the

urban centers. There, they would be able to make more contributions to family finances, by supporting themselves and sending the rest of their income home to help with their male siblings' education. The traditional undervaluing of daughters placed the burden of helping to educate the male heirs of the family on the shoulders of these young women.[49]

Young women engaging in sex work to support their brothers' tuitions emerges as one of the hallmarks of Korean and Korean diaspora camptown writing. In one South Korean camptown short story, Kang Sok-kyong's "Days and Dreams," a sex worker named Ae-ja states, "And I've heard that some of the girls are squeezed for money by their own families. If their families can't pity them, how can they take money the girls make by having their crotches ripped open and then use it for someone's tuition?"[50] Elaine Kim states, "During the long decades of military rule in South Korea, beginning with the 1961 military coup d'etat and extending to the end of the 1970s . . . I heard many stories of women tricked or lured into working as prostitutes and 'service girls' to support families in the countryside or to send younger brothers through school."[51] Korean economic policies implemented by the U.S.-supported military dictatorship form one condition of possibility for gendered labor exploitation, a condition that Sueño layers with his memories of gendered exploitation in East LA.

In *The Wandering Ghost*, Pak Tong-i's statement that female sex workers labor to pay for their male siblings' tuitions foreshadows the multiple and uneven instances of gendered labor and violence in the novel. In one case, Sueño's memories of a Chicana friend who becomes a sex worker in East LA coincide with his investigations in South Korea, spinning a complex web of transnational racialized gendered exploitation. These memories haunt Sueño, and they partially explain his motivations to save the "little guys." He recalls, "One of my classmates, Vivian Matatoros, started hanging out with gang members. Everything about her changed. . . . She slid down from the classes that held the top students to the lowest rung of academic hell."[52] Sueño remembers cornering Vivian, "forc[ing] her to talk," and she tells him that she started hanging out with gang members because nobody was paying attention to her. When Sueño offers to help her, she "looked at [him] with contempt. 'Where were you when I needed you?'"[53] Eventually, he hears about Vivian "working a corner off Whittier Boulevard."[54] Sueño states that his friends "wanted me to go look—and laugh and shout names at her—but I couldn't do it. I remembered the Vivian who used to help me with my algebra. The girl who'd shared a sandwich with me when I had no lunch. That

Vivian was the only Vivian I wanted to remember. The only Vivian I could bear to remember."[55] Sueño constructs Vivian Matatoros exclusively as an object of rescue, whom he then chooses to remember only as a top student. In "forc[ing] her to talk," not only does he take credit for attempting to save Vivian, but also by selectively remembering her, his response indicates that he individualizes the entire responsibility for her circumstance. For Sueño, Vivian does not own her actions in either case, and as Neferti Tadiar reminds us, "Women are themselves produced as the objects to be exchanged by men. *How they are produced* hence becomes a crucial question, on which the elaboration of a static system of exchange forecloses. Instead, women are viewed as finished products whose subordinate status in society is a result of their place in an already operative system of relationships."[56] Sueño's characterization of Vivian forecloses ways of understanding her own mode of navigation through various structures differentially charged with power. Instead, Sueño can only regard his relationship with Vivian in terms of benevolent regret that ultimately bolsters his own sense of primacy within her transformation.

In contrast to the representations of Kim Yong-ai and Vivian Matatoros, both of whom Limón generally portrays as victims, he represents Jill Matthewson exercising more agency, though the portrayal is narrated through Sueño's objectifying gaze. As a white woman U.S. military police officer, Jill Matthewson's relationship to the nonwhite women in the novel is fraught with racial tension. Many of the Korean women in the novel either remain victims, even though the military cases depend on their cooperation and participation, or need to be saved, like Vivian Matatoros. Limón represents Matthewson as a white liberal feminist, and such representation comes at the expense of portraying Korean sex workers as voiceless and abject. In one instance, Limón creates a troubling portrayal of Korean sex workers idolizing Matthewson as a savior figure. In the excerpt below, as Matthewson walks through the streets of Camp Casey, the business girls spot her leading Sueño and Ernie to their destination:

> They'd seen uniformed MPs before, plenty of them, but they'd never seen one shaped like this. . . . Even beneath her bulky fatigues one could see that her waist was small and her ample bosom had to be firmly held in place. . . . They elbowed one another, pointed, and stared in awe as Jill Matthewson waded through them. . . . It was clear to me that these young, put-upon, Korean business girls, had just seen something akin to a miracle. A woman in a position of power. A woman leading men. A woman wearing a pistol and a uniform, set on her own self-determined goal, not letting anything stand in her way.[57]

Limón shapes a tangled narrative of gender, race, and power in the passage above. Sueño's attention to Jill Matthewson's body is commensurate with an objectifying gaze at women throughout the series. What is exceptional here, however, is that he displaces his gaze to the business girls so that they see Matthewson's normatively feminized body, "even beneath her bulky fatigues." Given that Sueño uses similar language to describe women—especially sex workers—throughout the series, what "awes" the business girls is not Matthewson's body, and not just the MP uniform, but what from Sueño's perspective is the unlikely combination of the two. Furthermore, Limón uses the imagery of a tall, blonde woman "wading" through a group of Korean women who regard her as a "miracle," painting Matthewson as the feminist savior that Sueño failed to become, at least for Vivian Matatoros. More troubling, by portraying Matthewson and the business girls in this way, Limón bypasses both official and unrecorded legacies of feminists throughout Korean history, many who militated against Japanese colonialism and many who continue to agitate against U.S. neocolonialism. Finally, even if Matthewson functions as a sort of role model for the business girls who see her, it is in her role as an imperial soldier, as part of the occupying force in South Korea. The only kind of feminist power that is legible to Sueño is a phallic one, "a woman wearing a pistol and a uniform."

Limón's attempts to construct a visibly feminist figure in Jill Matthewson are directly related to her hypersexualized construction in the novel. He addresses early in the novel not just the issue of sexual harassment in the U.S. military but also the speculation "that someone had sexually assaulted her, murdered her, and then disposed of her body."[58] A higher-ranking officer, Lieutenant Colonel Alcott, attempts to throw suspicion to "a Korean" based on the normative hyperlegibility of Jill Matthewson's sexuality: "'A woman on the street,' Alcott persisted. 'An American woman. Tall. Blonde. A much more tempting target than a Korean would have seen before.' 'So you think her creamy white flesh drove some Korean mad with lust,' Ernie said. Colonel Alcott nodded vigorously. 'And why not?'"[59] Alcott invokes the U.S. white supremacist myth of the Black male rapist, lethally prevalent during—but certainly not limited to—the nineteenth century, to criminalize Black men and to paradoxically subordinate *and* embolden white women with racial power.[60] Alcott's glib remark, "And why not," indicates the saturation of the U.S. military structure in misogyny and casts suspicion back to his character. Rhetorically, both Alcott and Bascom attempt to empty Korean women of personhood when they use "a Korean" and "some Korean" interchangeably to mean "Korean man," remarkable in a sentence in which the actual perpetrator—Alcott—is trying to displace blame for his crime of raping Matthewson.

The novel ends with Matthewson "pulverizing" and starting to "gouge out . . . eyeballs" of another military officer who had previously assaulted her and is attempting to rape her again. Readers discover that a primary catalyst for Jill Matthewson's feminist consciousness is her desire for revenge against the three military officers who raped her. However, despite the discourse surrounding the sexual harassment and assault of female military personnel throughout the novel, Sueño initially misreads the evidence documenting Matthewson's rape in a photograph that clearly shows three men, "all naked. All working on some poor young woman who'd been bound and gagged. The lighting was dim. I studied the woman. I expected her to be the stripper, Jill's friend, Kim Yong-ai. But then I realized that she wasn't Kim. She wasn't even Korean. She was American. And then I realized who she was. The impetus for Jill Matthewson's rage became clear to me."[61]

Sueño's misreading of the photograph is significant for several reasons. His matter-of-fact expectation that the victim would be a Korean woman speaks volumes about the embedded reality of sexual assault against South Korean women near U.S. military bases during the 1970s. The revelation that "she wasn't even Korean" appears to be a surprise, implicitly revealing that sexualized violence against Korean women by U.S. military personnel is a mundane occurrence. The expression of Matthewson's rage suggests that although sexualized violence against Korean women is condoned, it would be punished if the violence were directed at a white American woman. Furthermore, Matthewson appears to be the only woman with agency to pursue the men who raped her, despite the fact that Sueño frequently encounters many Korean women attempting to resist harassment and assault by military personnel. Given such representations, the novels frame the U.S. military as a misogynist institution, a rendering delivered through the objectifying complicity of the narrator. Past and present charges of sexual assault in the U.S. military are not exceptional deviances from an otherwise upright norm but rather a sexualized instantiation of the gendered and racialized violence that structures the institution itself.

As in *Slicky Boys*, Sueño again conflates "American" with "white," despite the fact that he represents a tensely multiracial U.S. military throughout the series. That he chooses to employ the word "American" rather than "white" reiterates the presence of the occupying force in Korea, a presence that fights back rather than remains abject, as Sueño suggests a "Korean" might. Jill Matthewson was "bound and gagged" but ultimately breaks free to seek revenge, aided by both her whiteness and her American citizenship, posing a very sharp contrast to most of the South Korean business girls Limón portrays, who figuratively remain "bound and gagged." Indeed, throughout the novel,

Matthewson speaks for Kim Yong-ai, whom Matthewson rescued from her financial debt to the booking agent Pak Tong-i and was unable to rescue from rape by higher-ranking military officials: "Sullenly, Kim Yong-ai followed [Matthewson] but rather than speaking . . . she kept her eyes averted, ducked through the small entrance to the cement-floored kitchen, and shut the door behind her."[62] Rather than leaving Kim Yong-ai to refuse to speak with Sueño and Bascom, which would enable Kim Yong-ai to choose her silence, Limón instead shows Matthewson speaking on her behalf: "She's not comfortable with men."[63] Although Limón represents Matthewson as a white liberal feminist, perhaps a bold move for an author who began the series with Sueño wholeheartedly enjoying the services of business girls, such a representation can only portray Korean sex workers as voiceless and abject.

4

CONFEDERACY IN KOREA

*Archiving the United Daughters in
Susan Choi's* The Foreign Student

I n *The Foreign Student* (1998), the titular Korean protagonist—Chang Ahn,
seeking refuge at a university in Sewanee, Tennessee, following the Korean
War—receives tutelage on the logics of white supremacy during his first
Thanksgiving dinner in the United States, in 1955. Chang's college roommate,
Crane, invites Chang to his home in Atlanta, assures Chang that "they don't
hang Orientals," and then ruminates on whether or not Chang would be mistaken for Black and lynched.[1] Crane's father, Grand Dragon of the Ku Klux
Klan, stages for Chang a putative choice between white and dark meat during
dinner, thereby allegorizing one U.S. racial binary through a Thanksgiving
turkey: "When you look back, Mr. Ahn, on your first years in America, on
your first lessons in things American, you will think of the Cranes. I am giving you white meat and dark. You will develop a preference in time. You may
develop a preference right away. If you do, exercise it."[2]

As a high-ranking representative of white supremacy, the Grand Dragon
establishes his family as all "things American," the universal, rational, and civilized template that attempts to define Chang's "first years in America." Through
the occasion of Thanksgiving, a holiday firmly entrenched within ever renewing
settler colonial processes, the Grand Dragon dictates to the foreign student
the "first lessons in things American": white supremacy reigns through the
execution of conquest, terror, and imperial aggression. Rather than succumb-
ing to the absurd scenario "of some noble aim like the creation of peace and
understanding between a Grand Dragon of the Klan and a young Oriental,"
the narrative instead propels Chang from a civil war hijacked by Cold War

geopolitics on the Korean peninsula and embeds him in the violent racial terrain of the U.S. South in 1955.[3] While Chang is relieved that Crane is not inviting him to dinner for "some noble aim," the very notion that "the creation of peace and understanding between a Grand Dragon of the Klan and a young Oriental" is conceivable speaks to Chang's position within the obdurate spectrum of anti-Blackness in the United States.

What is unimaginable becomes imaginable due to Chang's liminal status modulating the apparently contradictory inclusiveness of white supremacy and the lethal rigidity of anti-Blackness, and the degree to which this foreign student is produced by ongoing settler logics and U.S. imperial wars in Asia. Indeed, Chang's exceptional presence in the Grand Dragon's Atlanta home for Thanksgiving dinner demarcates a site within what Jodi Kim calls "settler modernity," or "the nexus of U.S. militarism, imperialism, and settler colonialism . . . an ensemble of relations significantly structured and continually reproduced through spatial exceptions."[4] Given the novel's further exceptional status among Asian American literary studies and American studies, what does it mean to consider *The Foreign Student* within Lisa Yoneyama's query on "the ways a transpacific framework can relate geohistorically distinct, ongoing critical engagements in ways that can expose the uneven yet intersecting and simultaneous workings of power?"[5] Moreover, how does the novel propel us temporally to consider beyond the historical bindings of discipline, to configure the Korean War's future history within these critical frameworks?

Crane further demonstrates an extension of white supremacist racial operations after declaring, "They don't hang Orientals. . . . There aren't any down there to hang. I don't think they'd know one if they saw him. I wonder if they would hang him. They might mistake him for a nigger and hang him, or have the sense to see he's not a nigger and *not* hang him just because of that."[6] In Crane's racial calculus, Chang's potential lynching can only be possible within the long history of anti-Black violence: a lynch mob would either hang Chang because of their "mistake" in seeing him as Black, or they would "have the sense" to recalibrate this particular white supremacist terror exclusively for Black people. Either way, in Crane's speculations, Chang would not be lynched merely for being "a young Oriental," but only insofar as "there aren't any down there to hang." Especially significant is Crane's observation that "I don't think they'd know one if they saw him": within the racially polarized charge of the 1950s U.S. South, Chang is legible either as a "mistake" or unplaceable as both not-white and not-Black yet residually harboring the markers of "Orientals" established in the nineteenth century.

This chapter traces the genealogy of Korean illegibility in the United States from the Reconstruction era, a moment that constructed the Klan itself, to the aftermath of the Korean War in the U.S. South. Along the way, I examine the parameters of racialization exploited by disparate precursors and inheritors of area studies, who include nineteenth-century orientalists and the United Daughters of the Confederacy. I suggest that such nineteenth-century orientalists as William Elliott Griffis, the emergence of Korean War archives, and the United Daughters of the Confederacy attempt to secure Korean War narratives within white nationalist confines. By contrast, Choi's novel contests such attempts and urges us to remain attentive to the shifting yet closely affiliated geographies of power that constitute Cold War knowledge production about the Korean War. These disparate sites code and recode the Cold War ideologies that in turn animate orientalist and white supremacist specters from the nineteenth century. Yet *The Foreign Student* imagines peripheral voices responding to those ideologies, forming alternate histories that vividly contest the dominant templates of white supremacist, capitalist nation and empire building and illuminating possibilities that thwart the typeset of those orientalist templates. The novel also captures what the misleading density of archives does not, providing narratives that exceed the seductive quality of archives that promise to contain and bridge spatial and temporal affects, moments, memories, histories.

"The Pivot of the Future History of Eastern Asia Is Corea": Back to the Future of Nineteenth-Century Orientalism

The history of U.S. knowledge production about Korea prior to the Korean War faithfully adheres to the degrees of "unknowability" that characterize the ongoing neocolonial, militarized relationship between the United States and the Korean peninsula. In 1882, the minister and author William Elliot Griffis published *Corea, the Hermit Nation*, a general history written with complete authority despite his lack of knowledge about Korea. Yet it is telling that orientalists such as Griffis were quite popular, animating and confirming the exotic fantasies and benevolent impulses of eager, avid readers. Even this history, one of the earlier attempts at glimpsing the "sealed and mysterious" state, dubbed "the hermit kingdom,"[7] is initially framed not only as unknowable but also barely worthy of being known: "Many ask, 'What's in Corea?' and 'Is Corea of any importance in the history of the world?'"[8] Most telling is Griffis's admission that he had not written this authoritative text from any substantial contact with Korea: "In one respect, the presentation of such a subject by a compiler, while shorn of the fascinating element of personal experience, has an advantage even over the narrator who describes a country through which he has travelled. With the various reports of many witnesses, in many times and places, before him, he views the whole subject and reduces the many impressions of detail to unity, correcting one by the other."[9] Griffis illustrates the existing paradigms for *knowing* Korea, a template that chroniclers only just marginally modified during the Korean War and its aftermath. From the vantage point of a U.S. subject borne of liberal modernity, the matter of Korea merely needs a distant and ostensibly objective "compiler" to organize complex histories, "correcting" discordant narratives into an earnest linear history.

Such a temporally sincere construction of Korea is nestled within the late nineteenth-century genealogy of Western attempts to simultaneously disavow and underwrite the humanity of racialized nonsubjects. Griffis speculates on the future of Korea, making claims that in retrospect appear to establish *Corea, the Hermit Nation* as a handbook for U.S. imperial actions in East Asia: "At this stage of affairs, when Corea ceases to be a 'hermit nation,' and stands in the glare of the world's attention, we bring our imperfect story to a close. The pivot of the future history of Eastern Asia is Corea. On her soil will be decided the problem of supremacy, by the jealous rivals China, Japan, and Russia."[10] Griffis himself casts a long, imperfect shadow—the overt threat of the implicit division "stands in the glare of the world's attention," though ominously absent from this glare is the long U.S. history that sets conditions of possibility for the division. Thus, the division of the peninsula renders a simultaneous and contradictory construction of a belated, atavistic north in contrast to an ultramodern south, braced with U.S. military and economic authority. Griffis's phrasing "the pivot of the future history of Eastern Asia" is provocative, because again it suggests a history from which a major player is absent from the list of "jealous rivals[,] China, Japan, and Russia," a major player that is ever redirecting its geopolitical and neocolonial imperatives in its "Pivot to Asia."

Griffis did his work, primarily writing about and lecturing on Japan, within certain hallmark moments of U.S. empire, documenting key histories illustrating various tenets of American exceptionalism. In describing the Reconstruction-era 1871 U.S. military expedition to Korea, Griffis recalls a member of the U.S. military who died in the U.S.-Mexico War; the war, which took place from 1846 to 1848, enabled claims "that contiguous lands were part of the continental 'domestic' space rather than foreign territory . . . promot[ing] an exceptionalist understanding of the United States as a nonimperial nation."[11] Griffis himself participated as a soldier in the U.S. Civil War,[12] with his orientalist template of Korea manifesting in the Civil War legacy of both Choi's *The Foreign Student* and in the archival efforts of the United Daughters of the Confederacy. *Corea, the Hermit Nation* was initially published in

1882, the same year of the Chinese Exclusion Act, which was designed as the first racially specific immigration legislation in the United States and was fueled in part by the same orientalist fantasies animating Griffis's book. The Chinese Exclusion Act (one of the U.S. state's earlier pivots away from Asia) itself echoes the legacies of fugitive slave acts, which attempted to restrict the migration of free and enslaved Black people among states and which failed to contain abolitionist movements, ultimately exposing comparative racializing measures in the legal frameworks of the nineteenth century. Griffis's book was reprinted in nine editions well into the twentieth century, reiterating and justifying claims about the unknowable, heathen, and uncivilized parts of Asia, just as the United States moved toward acquiring Spain's Pacific possessions and places for business interests to profit from, including the Philippines, Guam, Cuba, and Puerto Rico, as well as annexing Hawaii in 1898.

These moments in the history of U.S. expansion, while certainly not comprehensive, nonetheless operate to consolidate and materialize the ideologies driving American exceptionalism, the premise that the United States was, as Shelley Streeby puts it, "an empire that was not one."[13] The roots of such ideologies go deep, provoking the United States throughout the nineteenth century to acquire more lands and entrenching justification for further imperial development, continually eliding the histories and the presence of Indigenous peoples and enslaved peoples in the United States. Indeed, "assertions of American exceptionalism cannot always be taken at face value, but rather should often be seen as nervous attempts to manage the contradictions of ideologies of U.S. empire-building."[14] The notion that the United States occupies a unique position as *free* and more democratic, in particular compared to Europe, is coupled with the idea that the United States therefore has a duty to spread freedom, progress, and democracy around the globe. The idea of American exceptionalism persists as stubbornly as the phrase "hermit kingdom," now selectively applied to a North Korea labeled as recalcitrant, and indeed both concepts reify each other in tenacious ways: a bold, modern, yet civilized United States (and its subempire, South Korea) operates most explicitly in contrast to a reclusive, backward, and barbaric nation allegedly bereft of rational capability. As the Cold War's conceptual condition of possibility, the state remixed the ideology of American exceptionalism to include strident anticommunism in its movements toward global supremacy and domestic containment. The ideology of American exceptionalism, harboring a genealogy that drove U.S. capitalist expansion throughout the nineteenth century, manifested in the U.S. military occupation in Korea during the post–World War II period, ostensibly protecting the southern part of the newly liberated peninsula from the Soviet Union. This moment of American exceptionalism also unevenly incorporates those heretofore known as "gooks," instrumentally assimilating the remainders of U.S. imperial war in a post–World War II era of racial formation, as an active strategy of Cold War liberalism. The calibrations of American exceptionalism do more than just persist—they couple with the U.S. state and military to combat ideologies hostile to capitalism and constitute the conditions of possibility for the ongoing becoming of the nation.

This partial genealogy of American exceptionalism traces a cruel history of orientalism and racial violence and reveals how such exceptionalism affixes itself to white supremacy by claiming the metaphor of kinship. In other words, the discursive and affective qualities of genealogy and kinship are instrumentally employed in the service of perpetuating white supremacy. Within the genealogy of the Korean War in the United States, then, the war becomes conscripted to a terrible *family* history—one written by white supremacist narrators, such as Griffis, who heralds later formations of area studies. Strands of exceptionalist epistemology constitute understandings of U.S. history in specifically gendered and racialized configurations: sites of knowledge production about the Korean War within archives and area studies formed within Cold War frameworks. I trace one such strand to a privately funded archive, the Center for the Study of the Korean War, founded in 1989 and located in Independence, Missouri. Although the center operated as a politically neutral nonprofit organization until its incorporation into the Truman Library, it received support from the Daughters of the American Revolution and the United Daughters of the Confederacy. The women's groups signify the members' fidelity to and perpetuation of gendered kinship, explicitly in relationship to U.S. nationalist projects. The United Daughters of the Confederacy, with its explicitly white supremacist discourses, functions both as domesticized ventriloquists of the Klan and as persistent Confederate survivors, due precisely to their gendered status as daughters, inheritors, preservers, and cultural transmitters. Tracing the history of the Daughters and their support for the center yields disquieting questions about the relationship to the center's knowledge production on the Korean War. Furthermore, the archive's own underpinnings legitimate ongoing narratives of the war as a benevolent intervention liberating Korea from a communist enemy.

Choi's novel subverts the imposition of a linear temporality composed of stubborn nineteenth-century orientalist discourses, replete with ideas of belatedness. Racialized imperatives toward possessing complete and fundamental knowledge, emerging from the long genealogy of area studies, constitute the Korean War as a possession of U.S. history. The epistemological formation of "Orientals" from Griffis's *Corea, the Hermit Nation* to the center's mission to *study* the Korean War thus highlights the disciplining mechanisms of U.S. state-sponsored area studies and the efforts of the Daughters. Given such knowledge production about the Korean War, what kind of memories does such literature as *The Foreign Student* recall? How do such memories, otherwise subject to disciplinary erasure, trouble the prevailing knowledge production of the war? Beyond enlisting cultural productions to elicit counternarratives of the Korean War, this project compels readings of historical artifacts, such as authoritative histories, archives, and records, as cultural texts. Grace Cho has argued that assimilation into the American Dream pays the cost of historical unintelligibility and that haunting, as a method, produces tensions that were not present before—something else that did not previously exist in linear, homogenous accounts of the war. This chapter thus insists that literature and other cultural productions create productive tensions and fractures within dominant knowledge production.

Furthermore, what practices offer a more complex and illustrative alternative that is not animated by white supremacy, and what methods enable the learning of historical specificities, as abstract as they might appear? While this chapter takes seriously the generative possibilities of haunting tensions, it also remains attentive to the fraught incapacities and limits of singularly discursive countermemories. I do not mean to suggest that the tensions and fractures generated by cultural productions inexorably capture material specificities and social conditions. Nor do I mean to suggest that the frayed edges of authoritative histories that betray ideological inconsistencies alter the tangible qualities of collective subjection. Rather, countermemories craft practices of theorizing through loss—specifically in *The Foreign Student*, Chang's inability and unwillingness to seamlessly recover an absolute account of the Korean War. Theorizing through loss places pressure on locations of power—in this case, the orientalist impulse of area studies, the uneasy formations of archives, and the work of the Daughters—to expose the obstinate pursuit of pure recovery and the untroubled accumulation of empirical data. Through such theorizations, we might imagine visions that exceed the ostensibly authoritative, prevailing, and objective history of Korea.

The Foreign Student unravels dominant knowledge production about the Korean War through its narration of Chang. The novel captures early moments in the informal formation of postwar area studies and documents Chang's perverse complicity as a part-time educator on the subject of the war. The next section pairs critiques of early moments in Korean area studies with close readings of *The Foreign Student* to tease out the tension between the imperatives of Cold War knowledge production and the memories that exceed such a regime of knowledge. Analyzed alongside the Center for the Study of the Korean War and the United Daughters of the Confederacy, *The Foreign Student* disrupts the sanitizing discourses of white supremacist kinship that tether the Korean War to U.S. nationalist histories. As I suggest in the opening of this chapter, the novel inserts the presence of the Ku Klux Klan into memories of the Korean War, thereby writing into these memories the masculinist counterpart to the United Daughters of the Confederacy and the organization's efforts of white supremacist nation building. Supplementing each of these critiques with a reading of the literature ruptures uncontested, naturalizing, and linear narratives of the Korean War. The imperatives of postwar area studies and uneasy archives sustained by white supremacist women's groups perform and constitute Cold War and post–Cold War knowledge production. Analyzing such disparate, unlikely sites of knowledge production troubles the ongoing militarization in Asia and the Pacific region. And to conduct readings of archives in addition to *and as* cultural productions works to destabilize the homogenous historical assimilation of the memories and histories encircling the Korean War, identifying nuanced spaces for recasting knowledge construction calibrated to critiques of power.[15]

Double Salvation, Area Studies, and the War that "Defied Explanation"

Nationalist Cold War texts consistently and authoritatively frame Korea as backward, atavistic, innocent of modernity, and requiring direction and guidance toward modernity, progress, and civilization. Such throwback ways of knowing Korea produce the ideological justification for military police action, narrated as liberating the peninsula, first from Japanese colonization and again from the specters of communism. The Korean peninsula is therefore discursively fettered to terrains replete with an emergent U.S. military power and violence for the United States to demonstrate an updated exceptionalism and to ensure the triumph of the core concepts of liberalism.[16] This double salvation and dubious welcome to modernity disallowed Korea's independence and instead caused Korea's confinement in deferred decolonization. And while Korea's passage into modernity may arguably be entwined with Japanese colonization, the ongoing U.S. military occupation of South Korea lends another layer to the peninsula's militarized conscription. Within the military purview of the United States, the now near-requisite passage through such a terrain fosters the claims for the necessity of U.S. participation in the Korean War.[17]

Critical feminist scholars have made some of the most incisive critiques of this self-fulfilling logic, of double salvation from colonization and communism, of the processes leading up to the formation of a new political border and the rationalizing force for occupation following the Korean War. Grace Cho states that "military efforts to deal with 'the refugee problem' resulted in a self-perpetuating cycle of destruction and displacement. The massive dislocation of Korean civilians meant that battle lines often became obstructed with hordes of moving refugees whose origins could not be identified."[18] The military thereafter executed further destruction, which in turn created more refugees, which then rationalized even more "use of lethal force against civilians as a means of clearing traffic jams."[19] A declassified military memo from July 27, 1950, provides just one example of retroactively justified violence against civilian populations: "All civilians moving around in combat zone will be considered as unfriendly and shot."[20] The U.S. imperialist myth of liberation and rehabilitation does more than buttress U.S. nationalism—the notion of indebtedness that accompanies the *gift of freedom* also preauthorizes future violence. While the gift of freedom allows the Cold War representation of the United States as the generous liberator, this imperial myth legitimates in advance any sort of military gesture that would again be reinforced by and reinforce dominant U.S. narratives of progress and democratization. In addition to the self-justifying logic that permeates the U.S. liberation narrative of the Korean War, even the gift of freedom necessarily operates on the condition of homogenous nonpersons belated to enlightenment that characterizes Cold War knowledge of Koreans. *The Foreign Student* exposes the underbelly of nationalist knowledge formation and deconstructs Cold War knowledge production that presents itself as a neutral arbiter and mediator of the recipients of benevolent freedom.

Attentive to the contradictions embedded in the formation of area studies, and that knowledge production is situated in political particularities, I briefly trace the financial sources of area studies, address the necessity of charting a genealogy of Korean War knowledge production, and present a reading of *The Foreign Student*'s subversions against the emergence of Cold War knowledge production. While Bruce Cumings is heralded as a U.S. academic authority on the Korean War, *Parallex Visions* extends beyond Korean history and the Korean War, by interrogating the formation of area studies. *Parallex Visions* (1999), on U.S.–East Asian relations, presents an inquiry into the specific sources of funding, including the Ford Foundation, that enabled the formation of area studies. Cumings writes that the scholar Philip Mosely, the ruler of the Russian Institute at Columbia and influential shaper of U.S. foreign policy during the Korean War era, "was a central figure at the Ford Foundation throughout the formative years of American area studies centers, which Ford supported to the tune of $270 million."[21] Although Mosely was a Soviet specialist and worked closely with the Ford Foundation to develop

Soviet area studies, his reach into foreign policy and state department affairs gave him clearance into confidential information that extended to various hot regions during the Cold War. Mosely's declassified files reveal, among other institutional histories, that "the Ford Foundation's decision in the late 1950s to pump at least $30 million into the field of China studies (to resuscitate it after the McCarthyite onslaught, but also to create new China watchers) drew on the same rationale as the Russian programs examined above."[22] The idea of creating new "China watchers," though an attempt to "resuscitate" China studies in the United States amid stringent anticommunism, marks the emergence of methods following the geopolitical imperative to acquire untroubled knowledge about and conduct surveillance on an unquestioned communist enemy.[23]

Examinations of Philip Mosely's and the Ford Foundation's files show how U.S. knowledge production about the Cold War during the Korean War era constitutes a tense balance of state-sanctioned knowledge acquisition and the degrees of alternative accounts that constantly threaten to depose that knowledge production. The implications for knowledge production about the Korean War include maintaining tensions in the histories of the war, emerging from institutional studies but troubled by memories that exceed those studies. The emergence of these particular institutional studies, presented by "incomplete but important evidence from the Mosely papers suggests that the Ford Foundation, in close consultation with the CIA, helped to shape postwar area studies and important collaborative research in modernization studies and comparative politics that were later mediated through well-known Ford-funded SSRC projects."[24] U.S. studies of the Korean War must reckon with this fraught genealogy and recognize the discursive violence embedded in its emergence, in order to urge accountability for the contours of its militarized knowledge production. Furthermore, declassified files suggest that "this interweaving of foundations, universities, and state agencies (mainly the intelligence and military agencies) extended to the social sciences as a whole. . . . Official sources in 1952 reported that 'fully 96 percent of all reported [government] funding for social sciences at that time was drawn from the U.S. military.'"[25] Attending to these disciplinary origins makes possible the analyses of Korean War narratives that exceed logics of untroubled inscrutability and rehearsals of Cold War ideologies.

One such declassified document, a "Development Program" from the public policy think tank, the Council on Foreign Relations, dated June 1, 1951—nearly a year into the Korean War—specifically argues for the objective necessity of area studies programs that are concomitant to the U.S. role on the global stage. The document presents arguments reflecting a growing anxiety about creating and maintaining a line of scholars who conform to nationalist masculine norms, in particular to direct and appease a homogenously and paternalistically portrayed U.S. public:

> The American people are faced with a situation of great tension in international affairs which may continue for some years. Our national existence may depend on their ability to stand the strain without surrendering to either the appeasers or the warmongers. The propaganda of pressure groups and the dogmatic assertions of columnists and radio commentators tend to increase the strain by bringing about an artificial polarization of opinions. To the man in the street, and even to many intelligent laymen, their plausible solutions and ready-made answers are a welcome substitute for the painful processes of independent judgment.

According to the document, the program's concern about "our national existence" depends not on the U.S. government's flexing of the recently fortified military-industrial complex but rather on "the strain" introduced to the U.S. public by "pressure groups and the dogmatic assertions of columnists and radio commentators," who serve to circulate "an artificial polarization of opinions." The program operates in the assumption that the scholars they recruit will produce true, non-"artificial" knowledge about the vaguely identified "situation of great tension in international affairs," correcting the problem of the apparently un-American acts of expressing ideas. The document addresses concerns for a U.S. public imaginable only as masculine, "the man in the street," even "many intelligent laymen," who appear to struggle with "the painful processes of independent judgment."

The document continues its paternalistic representation of Americans and their ability to comprehend the true matter of foreign affairs, stating: "Most Americans now acknowledge that their country is firmly committed to international collaboration. They go even further; they understand that, because of America's great power and wealth, it must assume the role of leader in world affairs. . . . Americans, especially the leaders of opinion, must be helped to understand world affairs and to make up their minds what policies are to be followed." In addition to naturalizing the role of U.S. state power on the global stage, which it necessarily "must assume," the program explicitly seeks to influence policymakers, "helping" them "to make up their minds" on the policies generated by the think tank, which are then unquestionably "to be followed." The program's recommendation for implementing an expansion of research and publication is "to add to its staff three young men of the rank of assistant or associate professor in the age group, 30–40, who are particularly competent in political science and modern history." The document explicitly identifies the producers of competent knowledge as young men in authoritative social science disciplines, which coalesce into Cold War area studies. These criteria for selection reveal the ideologies undergirding Cold War liberalism that shape the state's knowledge producer.

The formation of Cold War knowledge production has been sustained through such attempts to shape knowledge in the educational, political, and cultural spheres. The declassified Council on Foreign Relations document's insistence on university appointments for "young men . . . who are particularly competent in political science and modern history" signals an intensification of the construction of exceptionalist knowledge in the Korean War era. While it might appear axiomatic that such "young men" responsible for culling and creating knowledge on international regions of interest to the state are implicitly marked as white, it is equally significant to call into question how knowledge producers are positioned and naturalized. While the focus on funding in reports included in Cumings's *Parallex Visions* is necessary, an inquiry into how Cold War policy and university knowledge producers are situated is also essential. Such contexts underpinning knowledge production naturalize the universal subject of knowledge production rather than inquiring into both the structures and people participating in the formation of "disciplinary divisions that suppresses the history of racialization and racialized exclusion from citizenship."[26]

The Korean War era isolates the genealogies of American exceptionalism and dominant knowledge production in the post–Cold War era. Considerations of both the well-worn and more obscured paths that attend to how the Korean War continually unfolds is critical. The Korean War *continues to become* in the present as a war that was never a war for the United States but a police action and as a war that has not ended but is current. And so critical studies of the Korean War unsettle the presumed fixity of "the present" and engage a "genealogy . . . focused more on the conditions of possibility that enabled various claims to be made at different times, how claims, once made, came to be regarded as tenable, and what the political result of that outcome was."[27] The Korean peninsula, like all the regions geographically demarcated as constituting East Asia, has accrued meaning in the United States within nineteenth-century orientalist and exceptionalist Cold War contexts. Both contexts experiment with the ornamental habitation of complex subjectivity in attempt to define the liberal contours of the Western subject. Yet both dominant and marginal accounts of the Korean War expose fissures of such ideologies, fissures that include the very attempts made by the state to truncate access to official files.

Challenging the Korean War narratives shaped by area studies, a field sustained by nineteenth-century roots in such texts as Griffis's *Corea, the Hermit Nation*, Susan Choi's *The Foreign Student* upends area studies logics fueled by large private foundations and the U.S. military. In the novel, Chang Ahn flees Korea in 1955 to become a foreign student at the University of the South in Sewanee, Tennessee, where he meets Katherine Monroe, a white woman who constantly challenges and thereby threatens the rigid social order of the small town. The novel cuts among Chang's life in the United States, his memories and experiences of the war, Katherine's adolescence, and the relationship they develop with each other. Significant moments in the novel include Chang's memories and nightmares of the events leading up to (and his own excruciating torture during) the war, Katherine's sexual relationship with her father's colleague (which began when she was fourteen and he was forty), and Chang's shifting modes of racialization as he encounters differentially racialized groups in different parts of the United States.

By translating and rereading the narrative of the war, Chang generates critical tensions between what readers may know as historical truth and his own uneasy, ill-fitting didactic lectures in exchange for his education in Sewanee. The scene in which Chang delivers a slideshow of Korea for the members of St. Paul's Episcopal Church, located in Jackson, Tennessee, is a particularly productive one for American cultural studies scholars, because of Chang's attempts to make the Korean War legible and palatable for a white southern audience. This scene disrupts the understandings of the war disseminated through the emergent area studies channels I discuss above. In his presentations, Chang is "called upon to deliver a clear explanation of the war. It defied explanation. Sometimes he simply skipped over causes, and began, 'Korea is a shape just like Florida. Yes? The top half is a Communist state, and the bottom half are fighting for democracy!' He would groundlessly compare the parallel to the Mason-Dixon line, and see every head nod excitedly."[28] The Korean War "defied explanation," which I suggest applies to Chang, whose memories and experiences of the brutal war punctuate the novel, as much as it applies to his audience.[29]

Indeed, Chang's attempts to situate the Korean War within the history of the U.S. Civil War, by "groundlessly compar[ing] the parallel to the Mason-Dixon line," stems from the necessity to position the war in relation to a history his white southern audience can grasp but, more importantly, reframes the scope of the war from one provoked by a northern communist invasion to one that is resituated as a civil war. The passage offers striking asymmetries in the rehearsals of orientalist knowledge claims—Chang's white southern audience may well compose the "many" in Griffis's 1882 statement, "Many ask,

'What's in Corea?' and 'Is Corea of any importance in the history of the world?'"[30] Yet Chang not only retrofits the Korean War into the U.S. Civil War but also juxtaposes two distinct wars motivated by capitalist expansion and ideologically justified by the deliverance of liberation. Chang's subtle reframing of the Korean War as a civil war rather than as a conflict with unquestioned origins in the North's communist invasion of the South registers as a quietly radical move. Indeed, within the racially bifurcated U.S. South, in which Chang's very presence disrupts white supremacist binaries, his comparison of the two wars invites consideration of what Lisa Yoneyama calls "'catachrony,' or temporal discombobulation, and its effects on knowledge."[31]

As a refugee and newly stateless individual, Chang's anxious and coerced relationship with the white supremacist U.S. South compels his gratitude, yet even in such a space, he resists demonizing either communism or North Korea by lecturing that "the Soviets, on their side, enabled the return from exile of a great people's hero, a revolutionary who had fought the Japanese throughout the thirties."[32] By stating Kim Il Sung as "'this man become the leader of Communist North Korea,'" Chang asserts a revolutionary, "a great people's hero," a man who challenges and resists both Japanese and U.S. imperialisms, as the leader of the North. Such representations brush against the grain of dominant U.S. knowledge production during the Korean War era and create possibilities of thinking otherwise about narratives with totalizing anticommunist imperatives. Though Chang and his audience are situated fifty years after the first publication of Griffis's *Corea, the Hermit Nation*, Chang "realizes that Korea, if known at all to his audience, exists primarily through racialized and primitivist tropes."[33] Chang's use of the slideshow, snapshots projected to accompany his lecture, serves as isolations of a static history and a country stuck in time, which he is expected to thaw for this audience. I quote at length from the novel to trace the circuit from Griffis's 1882 accounts of Korea to Chang's refusal to rehearse the dominant narratives of the war:

He punched the slide-changer now, and Korea After 1945 was replaced by The U.S. Infantry Coming out of the Seoul Railway Station, a soap-scrubbed and smiling platoon marching into the clean, level street. . . . People were often surprised by the vaulted dome of the train station, and the European-looking avenue of trees. "That's Seoul?" a woman asked, vaguely disappointed. The file of troops looked confident and happy, because the picture had not been taken during the Korean conflict at all, but in September 1945, after the Japanese defeat. The photo's original caption had read, "Liberation feels fine! U.S. and their Soviet allies arrive to clean house in Korea." No one was dreaming there would be a civil war. He followed the U.S. Infantry slide with Water Buffalo in a Rice Paddy, and then Village Farmers Squatting Down to Smoke, which satisfied the skepticism of the woman who had asked about the Seoul railway station. Everyone murmured with pleasure at the image of the farmers, in their year-round pajamas and inscrutable Eskimos' faces.[34]

Chang deliberately reorders the chronology of the war in his slides, projecting an image of "a soap-scrubbed and smiling platoon" that "looked confident and happy, because the picture had not been taken during the Korean conflict at all, but in September 1945, after the Japanese defeat." By literally resequencing these moments in history, Chang is able to manipulate his narrative of the Korean War in suggestive ways. In place of a picture "taken during the Korean conflict," Chang instead inserts into this narrative chronology the beginning of U.S. occupation, following a Korean liberation that was little more than an afterthought for the United States, merely arriving "to clean house in Korea." The unmistakably domestic and paternalistic overtones of cleaning house situate the United States in a position of establishing order, while simultaneously recalling both the U.S. military's use of Korean houseboys during the occupation and the war, and Chang's own domestic role at the university's dining hall near the end of the novel. One of the dominant narratives of the U.S. military involvement in Korea, leading up to the Korean War, is its deliverance of double salvation, first from Japanese colonization and then again from the North Korean, Chinese, and Soviet communist forces, ironically captured in the caption for one of the images as the United States "and their Soviet allies." However, Chang's slideshow links Japan and the United States as occupiers and thereby displaces the narrative that the United States served as liberators.[35]

Conspicuously absent from Chang's slideshow are images of the peninsula's devastating destruction during and after the ceasefire of the Korean War. Instead, "most of his pictures were from a set of National Archive photographs of Korea, in which it looked dim, impoverished, and unredeemable. . . . He understood that people liked something to look at, and that even the least seasoned audience eventually lost interest in looking at him."[36] Chang's audiences, however, do not have access to the slides' origin and instead rely on Chang as the transparent source of cultural authenticity in relaying information about Korea. This is, of course, just as long as Chang conforms to the audiences' expectations so that "everyone murmured with pleasure at the image of the farmers, in their year-round pajamas and inscrutable Eskimos' faces," an audience who are "vaguely disappointed" with "skepticism" and "often surprised by the vaulted dome of the train station, and the European-looking avenue of trees."[37] That the National Archives photographs serve as a proxy for Chang as the "something to look at" suggests not only his own objectification in the eyes of his audience but also their attempts to situate him within the national gaze. Indeed, Chang's "exotically" racialized presence in the U.S. South underwrites such an attempt, yet "that even the least seasoned audience eventually lost interest in looking at him" ironically frames his inclusion of the proxy image, the photograph of farmers with "inscrutable Eskimos' faces."

Chang uses the National Archives photographs perversely, reworking images collected by the U.S. state to inscribe "dim, impoverished, and unredeemable" portraits of Korea, for the purpose of subverting the dominant narrative of the U.S. role in the Korean War. To project slides that do capture the ruins and wreckage of the war would demand that Chang elaborate stories of a war that "defied explanation" and would demand a more thorough examination of why he is in Tennessee, to supplement his statement "that his presence before them was the direct result of MacArthur's Inchon landing. 'I'm not here, if this doesn't happen.'"[38] In contrast to his presentation, "which sought to be generic and not surprising or unpleasant," the fantastic violence of Chang's torture scenes, spliced through the narration of his experience in the U.S. South, suggests the untranslatability of certain histories in the contradictory spaces generated by the imperialist moves of the United States.[39]

Chang's refusal to display violent images of the conflict, in contrast to the vivid dreamlike spectacles of his own excruciating torture during the war, also functions to blur the temporal boundaries of the Korean War. During the war, Chang is apprehended by the nascent, U.S.-backed Republic of Korea Army and "arrested by the National Police on suspicion of espionage" on Jeju Island, where he had hoped to meet his insurgent friend, Kim.[40] Chang's presence on the island during the war, guided by his communist friend, is significant because of the prior South Korean and U.S. anticommunist repression of the island's inhabitants: as Grace Cho states, "the peasant uprising on Jeju Island on April 3, 1948, and the subsequent counterinsurgency authorized by the Rhee Syngman regime and backed by the U.S. military" constituted one of the most violent post–World War II clashes in Korea.[41] Furthermore, Chang's capture on the island during the Korean War recalls that "the mass killing of Jeju villagers in the name of anticommunism was a precursor to the events of June 25, 1950, one whose visibility casts doubt on the accepted narrative about when and how the Korean War started."[42] Read alongside Chang's temporal resequencing of the National Archives slides for his church audience, his presence and arrest on the island during the Korean War also creates an alternate chronology of the war that rewrites the origin myth of benevolence and liberation into the prehistory of violent anticommunist repression.

While Chang is imprisoned by the National Police and tortured for information about communists on Jeju Island, his humanity becomes legible only through temporal mediation. Chang is, among other inflictions, brutally beaten, his head pulled "backwards by his hair until he thought his neck would break," "made to swallow his vomit," given "putrefying meat to eat."[43] After the National Police chains break his right wrist, "he was shackled by his left hand now. He learned to haul himself up by it, to gash the inside of his right forearm against the sharp end of the bolt. He made a new gash every night. The marks spread across his arm, crisscrossing sometimes, but still readable, like the lines on his palm. He did not know how else to keep track of time, and he was determined to control at least the passage of his body through time. He could not control anything else."[44] Chang's body harbors the echoes of anticommunist counterinsurgencies, echoes of torture that, like the war itself, "defied explanation."[45] Indeed, during Chang's incarceration, no other passage is possible, confined as he is by shackles and pain, so that "the passage of his body through time" appears to be the exclusive source of movement. Yet his very body also becomes a type of passage, an organic palimpsest etched with Chang's deliberate acts of pain, to document the remnants of violence that are "still readable," a passage that he later refuses to read to a white southern audience only interested in "an exciting, simple minded, morally unambiguous story."[46]

As an act of empire in the Pacific, U.S. military aggression in Korea creates an occasion for a circuit of migration, with Chang's own migration interrupting the ongoing racial formation in the U.S. South. Through a pedagogically cloaked palimpsest, Chang's mission for the purpose of his tuition—telling people what they might want to hear about a place called Korea—mirrors both the legacy of racialization and racial violence inscribed into the emergence of the United States through an anticolonial renarration. At the same time, however, his very presence, translatable only as utterly foreign and inassimilable, disrupts his own incorporation into the U.S. cultural matrix and throws into relief the renewed processes of racialization required to explain his presence in the U.S. South. The next section stays in the U.S. South and examines the role of the United Daughters of the Confederacy, a white supremacist organization that exerted significant influence in building monuments dedicated to the Confederacy, as well as the unanticipated relationships created through their support for the Center for the Study of the Korean War.

Wicked Falsehoods and Embracing the Villain Within:
United Daughters of the Confederacy and the
Center for the Study of the Korean War

The Center for the Study of the Korean War was a private archive created by
Paul Edwards, a Korean War veteran and a historian of the war. The center,
founded in Independence, Missouri, was established in 1989, to function as a
repository for the artifacts of Korean War veterans, who were at that time beginning to die of advanced age. In 2015, the center's collections were donated
to the Truman Library, under the administration of the National Archives,
which further solidifies its relationship to the state's knowledge-producing
capacity. In its prior function as a private archive, the center has two central
goals: to expand its collections as an archive and library and to further the study
of the Korean War so that such conflicts might be avoided in the future. Yet
the center operates from an investment in a dominant nationalist history of
the war, intimating the idea that archives are neither static nor perfectly authoritative but are rather dynamic, shifting, and actively working to suppress
histories as much as illuminating them. This section analyzes Paul Edwards's
book *To Acknowledge a War: The Korean War in American Memory* (2000),
reads the archive itself into the history of the United Daughters of the Confederacy (who provide support for the center), and teases out the complex relationship between archives like the center and their relationship to literature,
in particular *The Foreign Student*.

Significantly, as a historian, Edwards himself criticizes the discipline of
history for failing to remember or even acknowledge the "forgotten war," but
his deeply reactionary critique is directed toward what he implicitly frames
as a multicultural and subjective history. Edwards writes that

> In the last half-century or so, events of the past have often been dis-
> missed as more representative of "memory" than of "meaning." Thus,
> we are often found searching for meaning not in what has happened
> but in the coincidences of separate environments, special emphases,
> and cultural explanations. . . . Out of a sense of national guilt—guilt
> for having been successful and reasonably happy—we have elected to
> "embrace the villain within" and moved toward a separate-but-equal
> concept of history. . . . The historical disciplines [have never] been so
> dominated by inquiries in such limited and unrelated fields.[47]

Edwards constructs a binary of memory and meaning, in which meaning
inhabits the teleological certainty of "what has happened," and "memory" is

relegated to the racially coded realms of "*separate* environments, *special* emphases, and *cultural* explanations" (emphasis added). Separate, special, and cultural all register accounts of history that exceed the dominant narrative of the war, traditionally written by white historians beginning in the 1950s.

Indeed, Edwards's decision to describe what he perceives as a diluted history as separate but equal recalls significant legal moments in U.S. racial history—"separate but equal" is the language of *Plessy v. Ferguson* and *Brown v. Board of Education*, two Supreme Court cases that legislated the possibility and mandated the reversal of Jim Crow laws and anti-Black attitudes in the United States. What initially appears to be a curious choice of words for Edwards to use in describing the lacuna of the Korean War in U.S. history becomes clearer when we consider that the shift in history he critiques happened "in the last half-century or so," since the 1954 *Brown v. Board* decision. The unambiguous, politically authoritative, and U.S. exceptionalist understanding of history (fashioned by scholars such as the "young men" recruited by the Council on Foreign Relations during the 1950s, which I discuss in the previous section) is the history Edwards asserts as harboring legitimate meaning. Edwards also claims that approaches to history since the Korean War era have been afflicted with "a sense of national guilt—guilt for having been successful and reasonably happy—[and] we have elected to 'embrace the villain within.'" The unexamined, unified *nation* he invokes in this statement is categorically homogenous and refers to those with access to the American Dream, those who "hav[e] been successful and reasonably happy," a nation implicitly marked as white and propertied. In one formulation, "the villain[s] within" are the carriers of *white* "national guilt," who then attempt to alleviate this anxiety in the discipline of history with concessions to "inquiries in such limited and unrelated fields." In another interpretation, however, "the villain within" may refer to the people on the margins, who persistently expose U.S. white supremacy.

Edwards operates within the narrative of political correctness, suggesting that the teaching of a complete and absolute history has been "rewritten, reinterpreted, or selectively remembered for the sake of political correctness and to appease a national lack of self-confidence."[48] Indeed, Edwards claims that the teaching of the Korean War "would be a nightmare to those needing some politically correct presentation."[49] What emerges through his narrative of "a national lack of self-confidence" is the desire for an authoritative, comprehensive version of history, a *universal* version that does not succumb to "some politically correct presentation." Furthermore, as evidence that "the number of Korean War poetry, short stories, novels, academic works, and even films is small indeed," Edwards cites literary scholar Paul Fussell, who "finds that the Korean War 'generated virtually no literature.'"[50] Such claims gloss over the significance of the Korean War literature in English by non-white writers, much of which was in print in 2000, the date of publication for Edwards's study. In addition to anxieties about "politically correct" and therefore partial histories of the Korean War, the fact that he finds "virtually no literature" about the war, in particular ignoring literature written by Chicana/o writers and members of the Korean diaspora, suggests Edwards's narrow definition of literature and its producers. And so the ideological imperative driving the center is not neutral or objective but rather saturated in nationalist discourses, discourses that remain white and masculine.

The United Daughters of the Confederacy (UDC), which supports the Center for the Study of the Korean War and other U.S. military and U.S. military veterans' organizations, also claims a similar nationalist discourse in its mission. I trace here a brief legacy of the Daughters, from its emergence in the late nineteenth century to their recent activities supporting the Center for the Study of the Korean War. I frame this manifestation of white supremacy as the Confederate preoccupation with epistemology, which I'll briefly contextualize with two points. The first is that the cause of the Confederacy was taken up with renewed zeal during the early Cold War era, a moment in which racial liberalism coincided with the U.S. Civil War centennial. As civil rights challenges to school segregation emerged in different contexts throughout the United States, the Confederate cause pushed the naming of schools after Confederate leaders. The second is the idea, based on turn-of-the-century eugenicist conceptions of race and blood, that a proper southern subject was not defined by geography, since being a southerner was based on blood descent.[51] The white supremacist objectives of the Daughters, founded in Nashville, Tennessee, in 1894, were "to honor the memory of those who served and those who fell in the service of the Confederate States . . . [and] to collect and preserve the material for a truthful history of the War Between The States."[52] Membership to the organization is contingent on showing evidence of lineal blood descent from veterans who participated in supporting the Confederate States of America or from members of the Daughters. The gendered language of kinship that identifies the women of the organization affirms their investments in the status as true daughters and thus the legitimate inheritors of the Confederate nation.

The Daughters also invoke naturalized discourses not just of feminization and infantilization but also as the descendants and reproducers of the Confederacy, ensuring a living genealogy as well as preserving Confederate traditions, which the Daughters articulate as "a glorious heritage from a nation that rose so pure and white."[53] The process of racialized gender formation for members of the Daughters in the post-Reconstruction Jim Crow South must not be understated, especially in relationship to the construction of Black masculinity as a threat to the racial and sexual "purity" of the nation. Thus, the racialized gender formation of the Daughters made it dangerous for Black people to "publicly criticiz[e] white women in the Jim Crow South. They could criticize the message, but not the messengers."[54] The UDC's gendered kinship status as legitimate "daughters" of the nation afforded them decisive impunity for reproducing, transmitting, and retrenching white supremacy. The gendered ideologies driving the Daughters intersect of course with white supremacy and with ideologies intent on preserving elite class status.[55] While members of the Daughters exercised their power in fundraising for memorials, overseeing the construction of veterans' houses and organizations, and creating libraries and archives, they are also kin to the people that wield tremendous power in making and enforcing laws. In their role in ensuring the success of the Confederate legacy as well as supporting the U.S. military after Confederate defeat, members of the Daughters work to protect and preserve the histories of the U.S. military and to record its practice of extending freedom abroad.

Because the Daughters to this day explicitly funds veterans' projects, the organization creates a direct circuit between white supremacist, southernborn organizations and military interventions abroad. Indeed, the discourse informing the emergence of the Daughters is a militarized one, advocating for the Confederacy. The UDC awards a Korean Conflict Cross of Military Service to lineal blood descendants of Confederate veterans of the Korean War. The words "Korean Service" are encased in the starred cross that fashions the Confederate battle flag, and the dates for the U.S. Civil War—1861–1865—are listed on the background Cross of Honor, embedding the white supremacist contribution in the Korean War within the Confederate legacy of the U.S. Civil War. The "blue, white, blue, stripes denoting [the] Korean Nation" also mimic the colors of the United Nations, endowing the UN with this particular Confederate honor, ironically configuring the UN's liberal claims for universal human rights.[56] According to the 1959 *Handbook of the United Daughters of the Confederacy*, "The Southern Cross of Honor was designed by the United Daughters of the Confederacy in 1898," and "the Crosses of Military Service are the outgrowth of the Cross of Honor—all 'symbols linking the present with the past and memorializing the heroic deeds of our Confederate ancestors and their lineal descendants.'"[57] The temporal ambitions of the cross, "linking the present with the past," link also with U.S. imperial interventions abroad, to include the Spanish-American War Cross of Military Service, the Philippine Insurrection Cross of Military Service, and the Global

War on Terror Cross, in addition to the Korean Conflict Cross of Military Service. And on the geographical unboundedness of the Confederacy, the UDC also issues a Pioneer in Space Award, presented to men and women who are lineal blood Confederate descendants and who have traveled to outer space. All of these crosses are fashioned in the image of the Confederate flags, "sacred to the people of the South and people of Southern descent."[58]

Within the contexts of the Confederate preoccupation with epistemology and the geographically unbound reach of white supremacy, the Daughters actively archived and supported Confederate projects during the Korean War, as William D. McCain, the director of the Mississippi Division of Archives and History,[59] evidences in his praise of the Mississippi Daughters' work in 1952: "Your unselfish efforts to preserve and maintain the priceless records of our Southern heritage and to keep that heritage fresh in the minds of our citizens have done much to keep us from being engulfed in the chaos and slavery that the Communists and their sympathizers seek for us in this country."[60] Mc-Cain's use of slavery to evoke antipathy against communists, in his support of the Daughters in Mississippi, strangely realigns those in the Confederate cause as inculpable victims and resistance fighters working to protect southern heritage, the destruction of which was apparently in McCain's mind the primary aim of communists. The real threat in McCain's statement, of course, is the work the UDC is engaged in "to keep that heritage fresh in the minds of our citizens," which manifests in material reminders of white supremacy in the form of monuments and buildings celebrating the Confederacy.[61]

While the UDC's direct support for the Center for the Study of the Korean War took place after the center's establishment in Independence, Missouri, in 1989, the UDC's connection to Missouri is bound up with the organization's origins: "Ironically, the first group of women to call themselves 'Daughters of the Confederacy' was organized in a non-Confederate state, Missouri, in 1890."[62] The UDC's Independence, Missouri, chapter organized support for the Center for the Study of the Korean War, a trenchant reminder of the deep white supremacist roots that underpin dominant knowledge construction. Indeed, the UDC support for the Center for the Study of the Korean War itself extends from a longer history of Confederate archive building: "Soon after its founding in 1894, the UDC became the Confederate organization most actively engaged in combating what one Texas Daughter called 'wicked falsehoods.' Many UDC leaders spoke about the importance of impartial history, but their organization's efforts to preserve history were also concrete and systematic. The Daughters collected artifacts for museums and supported their male counterparts in setting up state departments of archives and history."[63]

Notably, the "'wicked falsehoods'" about and the "impartial history" of the Confederacy could be corrected through collecting "artifacts for museums" and supporting "their male counterparts in setting up state departments of archives and history." History, in this case, must carry certain and objective masculine authority, especially if supported by faithful Daughters. The very idea that the Daughters are able to participate in the creation of state archives, moreover, demonstrates their access establishing legitimacies that are foreclosed to others, especially for Black residents of the U.S. South. The UDC's attempts to establish a singular and universal history of the Confederacy resonates with broader Cold War ideological imperatives to fasten U.S. nationalist narratives to unquestioned discourses of freedom and democracy. To build an image of the Confederacy in response to "wicked falsehoods" vilifying the Confederacy is to repress the vein of white supremacy that runs deep in the establishment of archives. However innocuous the Center for the Study of the Korean War's funding from the Daughters might appear, such actions are embedded within racially saturated ideologies and create new relations of power that channel knowledge production in certain ways.

The UDC connects the preservation of white supremacy domestically to their support of nationalist wars (coded in the language of freedom, benevolence, and democracy) abroad, in particular the Korean War. Cultural texts such as *The Foreign Student* show, then, what happens when people like Chang, who index the impact and violence of empire, move into the imperial center, in a place such as Sewanee, Tennessee, which is saturated in the restrained and overt expressions of white supremacy. For this section's reading of the novel, I return to the scene in which Chang and Katherine travel together to Jackson, Tennessee, for Chang's lecture on Korea for the members of St. Paul's Episcopal Church. Instead of returning to Chang's lecture itself, which I argue above engages in both a perverse complicity in reiterating dominant knowledge claims about Korea and asserts a critique of those same knowledge claims, I first turn to a conversation between Katherine and the priest who greets them on their arrival to the church. I argue that this scene critically captures the racialized and gendered anxieties occasioned by Chang's presence in the South and subtly records the embedded impact of the Daughters.

The white supremacist state's investment in managing the intimate boundaries of white racial purity in the novel, and social and legal antimiscegenation policing, complicates Chang's putative desire for whiteness. The sexual policing intrinsic to maintaining Confederate genealogies emerges in Chang's audience, mostly older white women who interrogate his mere physical proximity to Katherine—who drives and accompanies him to the church—with "a subtle, unremitting scrutiny, disguised as politeness."[64] Rather, richer critical possibilities emerge in examining the racial recalibration required in the U.S. South to explain Chang's condition of possibility at all in Sewanee. Constructions of white womanhood and the hint of potential miscegenation characterize this scene, which takes place just before Chang's lecture about Korea. After their arrival at the church, "they saw the priest coming across the yard, frowning and nodding in welcome. 'I'm Katherine Monroe,' she announced when he'd drawn near, rising to offer her hand. He was looking at [Chang] as he groped for it. 'I didn't realize Mr. Ahn would be accompanied.'"[65] While the priest was expecting the arrival of the foreign student to present his lecture on Korea and the Korean War, Katherine's unexpected presence jars the priest into assessing and policing the possibilities of their relationship. In this scene, Katherine decides not to stay for Chang's lecture, stating that her presence would only make him nervous, and asks the priest, "Did you think of anything I should see, Father?"[66] After some light banter, the priest responds, "'If you were a southerner, I could think you'd take an interest in our monument square, but you might find it interesting anyway.' Katherine laughed again. 'I am a southerner, Father.'"[67]

While a relatively minor moment in the novel, it nonetheless directs readers to the heart of the racialized and gendered anxiety that Chang's presence generates and hearkens to the legacies of the Daughters. The fact that the priest does not perceive Katherine to be a southerner registers her limited viability in representing respectable white womanhood, a proper southern Confederate "Daughter" to his status as "Father." Furthermore, the priest's suggestion to "take an interest in our monument square" alludes to the fact that "the Daughters successfully campaigned to build monuments in almost every city, town, and state of the former Confederacy. . . . Monuments were central to the UDC's campaign to vindicate Confederate men, just as they were part of an overall effort to preserve the values still revered by white southerners. . . . Significantly, southern blacks, who had no stake in celebrating the Confederacy, had to share a cultural landscape that did."[68] Bound up in this moment, in which Chang, Katherine, and the priest negotiate a renewed racial crucible in which to alter the existing Black/white racial framework, is the physical evidence of a white supremacist landscape shaped by the efforts of the gendered subjects of white supremacy.

The novel inserts the presence of the Daughters and the Ku Klux Klan into memories of the Korean War, thereby writing into these memories the contradictions inherent in the formation of the U.S. nation-state and contesting histories that seek to whitewash the long litany of violence that constitutes the essential foundation of the nation. While the monuments to the Confederacy constructed by such groups as the Daughters and the Klan may not be legible to Chang as physical manifestations of white supremacy, he might have encountered Confederate flags in Tennessee with a flash of recognition, as A. M. Rivera Jr. of the *Pittsburgh Courier* reports, "Rebel Flags in Korea: Confederate Banners Fly Anywhere!!!" While passing through Georgia, Chang's gaze might linger on the vague familiarity of a Confederate uniform as well. Chang did not need to be present in Tennessee to witness the cultural artifacts of white supremacy; he, along with Black, Latinx, Indigenous, and Asian GIs in the U.S. military, may have already known them in Korea. The fantasy of integration and equality necessary for justifying the emergent U.S. role as a global power capable of democratizing nations on their way to freedom is absolutely shattered by Choi's novel. Thus, *The Foreign Student* refuses to forget the contesting histories of U.S. empire and enables a reading practice that discloses the disjunctures and continuities of the long shadow of racialization in the United States, concentrated in the novel's memories of the Korean War.

CODA

To perceive the Korean War, in particular from a U.S. context, compels a paradoxical recognition of its forgotten condition. It often demands arguing for its occurrence at all, much less grasping why the war is foundational to unfolding global geopolitics. *Warring Genealogies* has considered the significance of that which has been obscured and the purposes such a diversion have served, with a focus on Cold War epistemological frameworks. Contextualized within renewed global attention to centuries of racial violence, this book's argument on Korean War knowledge production and how discourses of race and kinship shape conceptualizations of the war engages contemporary calls for racial justice across long-standing institutions: the disciplinary university, Confederate memorialization, and the abolition of police and prisons, among others. In his critique of the liberal academic establishment as a white academic field, Nelson Maldonado-Torres writes: "The logic is that what benevolent white liberal and even so-called radical scholars do in their traditional disciplines has priority over inter- and transdisciplinary research that addresses race and racism—as if many of the founding figures in disciplines were not themselves inter- and trans-disciplinary scholars; as if disciplinary divisions do not have a history; as if some disciplines did not disappear along the way, new ones emerged, and others could still disappear or transform into something else."[1] As chapter 4 demonstrates, U.S. Cold War historiography is constitutive of what he calls the white academic field, itself a white supremacist formation developed in continuance with orientalist genealogies.

The specific continuity from late nineteenth-century epistemologies on Korea, which structured U.S. Cold War engagements in Asia, impacts disciplinary histories in this moment. In other words, the late nineteenth century represents much more than a historical moment to be studied with narrative objectivity. We each carry specific relationships to these histories, yet tracing such often subversive genealogies appears to confound existing disciplinary methods, logics, and pedagogies. Indeed, Danika Medak-Saltzman theorizes academic erasures of Indigeneities, in part located in disciplinary containments of periodization, which could be disrupted

> by reframing and reconfiguring how we conceptualize traditional fields and historical periods, what they mean, and why this matters. For embedded within standardized understandings of historical periods are assumptions about the past that the specters of colonialism are invested in maintaining. . . . Thanks to the way that academic disciplines have been siloed and how time has been demarcated into specific and bounded historical periods, the specters of colonialism have been able to render the fact and consequences of settler colonialism invisible by making it arduous to work across disciplinary and temporal boundaries in attempts to call attention to subjects other than those privileged by conventional periodization.[2]

This is where *The Foreign Student* requires our faith in deferring teleological impulses and our infidelity to temporally assured intellectual habits. In the novel, Chang Ahn is perpetually suspended in his proximities to race—his association with "Red" comrades in Korea, his immersion in southern whiteness in the United States. His physical proximities to racial minorities—with Black workers in the university dining hall, with those relocated after Japanese internment in Chicago—as minor as they seem, require material interaction. His known engagement with Indigenous peoples, however, remains purely discursive and geohistorically broad. From the reference of Korean farmers' "inscrutable Eskimos' faces" in his slideshows, to his history paper on "the American Indian," to the grotesque lessons about race at a Thanksgiving dinner hosted by a Grand Dragon of the Klan, Chang's relationships with Indigeneities hinges on misrecognition and on not knowing. It hinges on his proximity *to*, on his proxy *for*.

But especially relevant to the white academic field and its colonial attachments to periodization is Chang's academic essay: "For history he had written an impassioned, grammatically reckless paper on the mistreatment of the American Indian which his professor had lavishly praised. Seeing it again he didn't recognize it. If he had been accused of plagiarism at that moment he would have surrendered."[3] While the paper is a class assignment, it is also *for* history—not just the course but for the discipline and for the imagined collective *pastness* that history represents. Although "mistreatment" is a radical diminution to the homogenized imprecision of "the American Indian," the foreign student persists in his "impassioned, grammatically reckless" critique of colonial power. Such grammatical recklessness might enfold the tense—making a mess (as Martin Manalansan might say) of the past, present, and future tenses that resist the relegation of Indigenous sovereignties for history; the tense affect engendered by Chang's impassioned critique and his history professor's lavish praise. The significant tension of Chang's not recognizing his own paper, of his preemptive surrender to the hypothetical plagiarism for a work that only he could have written, allegorizes Cold War racial epistemology.

This book examines as well other sites and narratives that have been obscured because of the forgetting of the Korean War in U.S. historiography. The consolidation of the U.S. security apparatus and refinements of aerial and chemical military strategies through the Korean War must also engage the selective circulation of misogynist ballads of the U.S. Air Force and other units, which themselves trace to the settler occupation and heteropatriarchal foundation of the United States. If the aerial, with its accompanying logics of surveillance and civilian bombing, authorizes sweeps of violence from above, the racialized misogyny of ballads "on the ground" lays bare any claim to just war. And even as such military ballads supplemented ideas of "Asia" in feminized vulnerability, works like Rolando Hinojosa's *Korean Love Songs*'s engagements with verse, corrido, and form theorize kinship, interdependence, and a queering of femininity in ways that more than write back to racist heteropatriarchy. In addition to what Rosaura Sánchez and Beatrice Pita call "subversive subterfuge," *Korean Love Songs* also imagines new kinships and utterly upends fixed logics of race for the Chicano GI.[4] Yet this literature is obscured too, nestled layers deep in a forgotten participation in a forgotten war, even as it could mediate in key ways the specific tensions animating Latinx and Chicanx compositions. Through queer reading practices, how does the *Latinx* encounter the Korean War, the Cold War?

Another obscured narrative, which bears what at first glance appears to be a strange relationship to the Korean War, is the United Daughters of the Confederacy. We witness the symbolic power of Confederate monuments recently toppled by those participating in protests against anti-Black violence and for racial justice. And movements—especially those led by Black women to make visible, to undo, to rename—have long been ongoing mobilizations, building on early legacies of critiquing the practice of Confederate memorialization itself. The current removal of Confederate memorials is also catalyzed by white women's participation in policing race, and Blackness in particular. But the histories of white women, and the United Daughters of the Confederacy specifically, as key figures who got those memorials up in the first place, must be understood as well. Indeed, during the Korean War era, as I discuss in chapter 4, they were especially active in funding and supporting Confederate memorials, libraries, and archives. One archive benefiting from United Daughters of the Confederacy support is the Center for the Study of the Korean War. But beyond this, *The Foreign Student* has offered its meditations enveloping Korean War and Confederate histories through literature. Considering the unknownness of the Korean War, it may seem jarring to think about it in relation to recent mainstream discussions about the Confederacy, as a precursor to some of the rhetoric mobilized leading up to the January 6, 2021, U.S. Capitol insurrections. In *The Foreign Student*, the genteel, conversational lesson of white supremacy from the Klan's Grand Dragon in his Atlanta home, as a benevolent domestic space, is particularly disconcerting when considered along recent discussions of white supremacists at the Capitol as "domestic terrorists." They were *already* at home, they made themselves *at home* in the Capitol building, and white supremacist structures made sure that they couldn't be *seen* as white supremacist terrors. As Toni Morrison depicted in her Korean War novel, *Home*, and stated in her essay by the same name, we already "live in a redesigned racial house."[5] If we are surprised, however, we might examine why. As with Chicano Korean War narratives and U.S. military ballads, the question to confront this surprise may ask, what conditions disallowed such conceptual scopes? And after all, and after all this time, what is surprising about the global reach of white supremacy?

In addition to genealogies as epistemological concerns, what is our relationship to the Korean War and to the affinities discussed in this book? When I teach the war, and when I assign oral history projects, students come to realize that they had not known that their family members (most often grandfathers) had served in Korea. Paul Edwards discusses this in relation to the center as well, with family members learning only upon the deaths of their husbands and their fathers, that they had been in the war at all. What is our relationship to the war? Ongoing disruptions of normative kinship and adoptions represent one of the most important impacts, even as proxy adoptions were leveraged to refine whiteness in the carceral confines of Leavenworth, as I discuss in chapter 1. What is our relationship to the Korean War when the continuation of the Cold War with North Korea, in which the United States as supreme nuclear power, is both absented and naturalized? And what is our relationship to the Korean War, in the U.S. responsibility in the suspended, deferred decolonization of Korea, even as we commit to material decolonization and recognition of Indigenous sovereignties in the United States, even as we commit to struggles for radical redistributions of wealth and recalibrations of property? What is our relationship to the Korean War, in sustaining ongoing, ever rich legacies of cross-racial political affiliations? What is our relationship to the Korean War? Crystal Baik's diasporic memory critique frames the everyday scope of this relationship and the political possibilities and ethical limitations offered by the Korean diaspora. What is our relationship to the Korean War?

I'm born in the southern part of the Korean peninsula. In 1988, I'm part of the Korean diaspora, a military empire's settler diaspora, to the U.S. Midwest. I grow up in Kansas, learning early on to field questions about whether I support North or South Korea, to navigate expectant gratitude from random white U.S. veterans of the Korean War. As a kid, I go with my dad to the Truman Library and Archives in Independence, Missouri, which is a thirty-minute drive from where we live in Kansas. I find it all to be pretty boring; I want to play Tetris on my Gameboy instead. A few years later, there's famine in North Korea, newspapers vibrantly inked with photos of emaciated children, babies. They blame it on water, a series of droughts and floods, on natural disasters, although, of course, there's no such thing as a natural disaster. They don't mention U.S. sanctions, only U.S. aid, or when they do mention sanctions, it's in the bewildered way of "why these miserable, incontestably inferior, rice-eating gooks refused to come to heel, and would not be saved"—the perspective of white parents who've sent their children to fight in the Korean War, as observed by James Baldwin.[6] Continuing the visitation of archives, I go with my dad to the Center for the Study of the Korean War, then housed in Graceland University, now part of the Truman Library.

Here, on ancestral Osage and Kaw lands in a Korean War archive, in a city named for autonomous freedom, a city written into the day declaring U.S. freedom from colonial rule, a Louisiana Purchase city, a point of departure city for Manifest Destiny projects, I open folder after folder, sift through box after box. In one, I find mention of *The New Era*'s prison magazine articles on Korean War. In another, an author's correspondence with *Aztlán: A Journal of Chicano Studies* on the Korean War literature of Rolando Hinojosa. In another, the personal effects of a member of the U.S. Air Force "Mosquito" squad, which include sexually suggestive black-and-white photos of white veterans taken with Asian women, and the songbook *Songs My Mother Never Taught Me*. In another yet, newsletters of the United Daughters of the Confederacy (Independence Chapter 710), one from 2006 (volume 4, issue 4), soliciting for the center "pictures relating to service in the Navy during the Korean War." Unsurprisingly, when the center's materials were moved to the Truman Library, much of this did not make it into the transition. And there's much more, in physical ephemera and in memory, here and elsewhere, recorded and not, that was never collected by any archive. And I'm conflicted as I think of the genealogy of this book, of its tense relationship to this place, of the indebtedness of this project to compounding iterations of white supremacy—explicit white settler occupations, Korean War military occupations, the sourcing of materials through the United Daughters of the Confederacy. I want this to be a project of liberation, but tracing back to how I got here only compels a feeling of entrapment.

And I interrupt myself to remember. Genealogies aren't just followed back—as Octavia Butler imagines for us, in her novel *Kindred*, they are inextricably futurist, and in the queerest perception, no genealogy ends. And I owe more precious debts to those who struggled for this particular present and for what's yet to come. So I interrupt myself to remember. Even as we imagine otherwise, we are also embodying that which has been imagined otherwise. We are already someone's and somewhere's imagined otherwise.

NOTES

INTRODUCTION

1. Gandara, Ezekiel P. Gandara Collection (AFC/2001/001/92722).
2. *Handbook of the United Daughters of the Confederacy.*
3. Rivera, "Rebel Flags in Korea."
4. *The New Era*, 1950–1957, boxes 4–5, R6 129. U.S. Penitentiary Leavenworth, National Archives and Records Administration, Kansas City.
5. M. Kim, *Interrogation Rooms*, 35.
6. Yoneyama, *Cold War Ruins*, 23.
7. Fujitani, White, and Yoneyama, *Perilous Memories*, 3.
8. Hong, "Unending Korean War," 599.
9. A common refrain during the first months of the Korean War, with General Douglas MacArthur stating that "they are going to eat Christmas dinner at home," as quoted in Truman Library, Box, (45) MacArthur Dismissal, Box 1 of 1, Orange. 1–10, "Home by Christmas" by General Douglas MacArthur, November 28, 1950. See also Hinojosa, *Korean Love Songs*, 19.
10. See Crystal Baik, *Reencounters*; Bruce Cumings, *The Korean War*; Christine Hong, "Unending"; Daniel Kim, *Intimacies of Conflict*; Dong-choon Kim, *Unending Korean War*; Jodi Kim, *Ends of Empire*; Heonik Kwon, *After the Korean War*; Monica Kim, *Interrogation Rooms*; and Lisa Yoneyama, *Cold War Ruins*, among others.
11. See Melamed, *Represent and Destroy*.
12. Melamed, 7.
13. Ferguson, "Distributions of Whiteness," 1102.
14. Pash, *In the Shadow*, 92.
15. D. Kim, *Unending Korean War*, 188.
16. Pash, *In the Shadow*, 112.
17. Em, Hong, and Kim, "Coda," 841.

18. Kim, *Interrogation Rooms*, 25.

19. Lowe, *Intimacies of Four Continents*, 39.

20. Edwards, *Mistaken*, 86.

21. Edwards, 88.

22. Edwards, 88. He provides variations on one main reason, which is "the gap that currently separates the average American from the military" (88). The militarization of the police, normalizations of war, and aggressive recruitment into the armed forces, to name just a few examples, do not factor into Edwards's analysis.

23. James Kyung-Jin Lee argues that the political economy of the 1980s (a decade dramatically marked by urban racial realignment in the United States) determined the multiculturalist framework and cultural production's grappling with its economic, racial, and social contradictions. Here, I consider within a Cold War politics of knowledge his understanding of racial anxiety, "a response to the interracial constitution of American identity and culture in general . . . plac[ing] literary study in the circuitry of urban and ethnic studies." Ja. Lee, *Urban Triage* xx.

24. Gordon, *Ghostly Matters*, 3.

25. Gordon, 38.

26. Edwards, *Mistaken*, 81.

27. Hong, "Unending Korean War," 601.

28. Especially significant are analyses of Susan Choi's novel *The Foreign Student*, which has generated the following important critical work. J. Kim, *Ends of Empire*, 151; D. Kim, *Intimacies of Conflict*, 199; Ferguson, *Reorder of Things*, 153; and Parikh, *Writing Human Rights*, 132.

29. Muñoz, *Cruising Utopia*, 28.

30. Muñoz, "Ephemera as Evidence," 10.

31. Hong, *Violent Peace*, 199.

32. See Puar, *Terrorist Assemblages*; and Reddy, *Freedom with Violence*.

33. Pash, *In the Shadow*, 129.

34. Puar, *Terrorist Assemblages*, 4.

35. Reddy, *Freedom with Violence*, 46. While Reddy elaborates on the hate-crimes amendment to the 2010 NDAA and queer of color critique of it in relation to Western liberal epistemes' production of the autonomous subject, this analysis shapes my reading of Pash's attempt to include gays in Korean War historical narratives.

36. Hong, *Violent Peace*, 199; Atanasoski, *Humanitarian Violence*, 200–201.

37. R. Rodríguez, *Next of Kin*, 3.

38. Sandoval, *Methodology of the Oppressed*, 140.

39. "Korea: The 'Forgotten' War."

40. Yoneyama, *Cold War Ruins*, 192.

41. Cho, *Haunting*, 12; Kim, *Interrogation*, 359–360.

42. Pérez, *Decolonial*, 101.

43. See Kauanui, *Hawaiian Blood*; O'Brien, *Firsting and Lasting*; Barker, *Native Acts*; TallBear, *Native American DNA*; Hong, "Comparison and Coalition"; Nebolon, "Life Given Straight"; Day, Hu Pegues, Phung, Saranillio, and Medak-Saltzman, "Field Trip"; and Arvin, *Possessing Polynesians*.

44. Chang, "Transcending," 98.

45. hoʻomanawanui, "E Hoʻi ka Piko," 60; Suzuki, *Ocean Passages*, 8.

46. Yoneyama, "Toward a Decolonial Genealogy." Tracing the long intellectual discourses on the transpacific, Yoneyama poses the urgent question "What are the ways in which a transpacific framework can relate geohistorically distinct, ongoing critical engagements in ways that can expose the uneven yet intersecting and simultaneous workings of power?" (477).

47. Goldstein, *Formations*, 6.

48. Camacho, "Transoceanic Flows," xxvii.

49. Medak-Saltzman, "Empire's Haunted Logics," 18.

50. Lowe, "Metaphors of Globalization," 43.

51. For instance, see Freeman, "Queer Belongings"; R. Rodríguez, *Next of Kin*; Eng, *Feeling of Kinship*; Soto, *Reading Chican@*; Holland, *Erotic Life of Racism*; Mata, *Domestic Disturbances*; Heintz, "Crisis of Kinship"; and Cassinelli, "'It was Akiko 41.'" In a radically different yet interconnected context, Donna Haraway in *Staying With the Trouble* intends the notion of kin to "mean something other/more than entities tied by ancestry or genealogy" (102–103), with a rigor that is attentive against simple understandings of "*reconciliation*, which is used as a nation- and kin-making term. Intending to make kin while not seeing both past and ongoing colonial and other policies for extermination and/or assimilation augurs for very dysfunctional 'families,' to say the least" (207).

52. For an elaboration of metaphor and allegory in relation to neoliberalism, globalization, and critique of social science methods, see Lowe, "Metaphors of Globalization."

53. Pate, *From Orphan to Adoptee*, 155.

54. McKee, *Disrupting Kinship*, 6.

55. Hübinette, "From Orphan Trains," 147.

56. Baik, *Reencounters*, 6.

57. D. Kim, *Unending*; Kwon, *After the Korean War*; Liem, *Memory of Forgotten War*; and Han, *Seeing Like a Child*.

58. Rincón, *Bodies at War*, 47.

59. Rincón, 56.

60. Pérez, *Decolonial Imaginary*; and Ramírez, *Zoot Suit*, xiv.

61. Blackwell, *¡Chicana Power!*, 2–3.

62. Soto, *Reading Chican@*, 88.

63. Muñoz, *Cruising Utopia*, 28; Soto, 126.

64. Cho, *Haunting the Korean Diaspora*; Arce, "Nation in Uniform"; J. Kim, *Ends of Empire*; Park, *Cold War Friendships*; M. Kim, *Interrogation Rooms*; McKee, *Disrupting Kinship*; Baik, *Reencounters*; Hong, *A Violent Peace*; D. Kim, *Intimacies of Conflict*; and A. Lee, "Repairing Police Action."

65. Yoneyama, *Cold War Ruins*; Lowe, *Intimacies of Four Continents*

66. Benjamin, *Illuminations*, 262.

67. Park, *Cold War Friendships*, 9.

CHAPTER 1

1. McCain, "War Orphan Sponsorship," 10.

2. McCain, 10.

3. McCain, 9.

4. McCain, 9.

5. Espiritu, Lowe, and Yoneyama, "Transpacific Entanglements," 184.

6. Yoneyama, "Toward a Decolonial Genealogy," 472.

7. Jones, "To Whom It May," cover.

8. LaMaster, *U.S. Penitentiary Leavenworth*, 7.

9. Moreton-Robinson, *White Possessive*, xix.

10. Woo, "Imagining Kin," 29.

11. J. Kim, "Settler Modernity's Spatial Exceptions," 570.

12. Morris, *Jailhouse Journalism*, 81.

13. Morris, 81.

14. Earley, *Hot House*, 29.

15. Childs, *Slaves of the State*, 63.

16. Childs, 64.

17. Moreton-Robinson, *White Possessive*, xix.

18. James, *New Abolitionists*, xxviii, xxix.

19. Susan Gillman's argument for the stakes of comparative studies is especially useful for theorizing the space and time of empire in USP Leavenworth: "Comparability entails a theory of space (meaning geography and place) and time (meaning temporality and history) that would recognize the 'palimpsestuous' quality of the present, where multiple times exist simultaneously within and across the same places, or coexist as uneven temporalities." Gillman, "Otra Vez Caliban," 193. See also Heatherton, "University of Radicalism," for analysis on the USP Leavenworth as a space of radicalism from 1917 to 1922.

20. Rives, "Though We Are Prisoners," 127.

21. Rives, 128–129. *The New Era* "was founded in 1914 as a part of a larger wave of progressive penal reforms that offered inmates recreational and educational privileges in exchange for better behavior" (128–129). *The New Era* is a magazine with standard dimensions: 8 3/8 inches by 10 7/8 inches. Some issues were published in a smaller size: the common dimension of a "digest," or smaller issue, would have been 5 3/8 inches by 8 3/8 inches.

22. "Prison Magazine Now on Display: Leavenworth Staff Has Excellent One," *Southeast Missourian*, June 30, 1949.

23. C. Klein, *Cold War Orientalism*, 159.

24. The argument for prisoners to participate in the Korean War in place of "treacherous" Asian subjects in the U.S. military suggests that racialized others will never be trustworthy. The awkward spectrum of time and space articulated in *The New Era*, the tension and ambivalence, is a familiar story in U.S. history, in which various racialized groups are welcomed for their labor but pushed away from "belonging" in the national family.

25. *The New Era*, 20–21.

26. *The New Era* also reprinted news articles documenting USP Leavenworth's adoption efforts, including "Men behind Prison Walls Aid War Victims," by David L. Kirk, chief editorial writer of the *Spokane (Washington) Daily Chronicle*. Letters of appreciation from prison magazine editors, prison directors, and other subscribers from locations as varied as Ontario, Canada; Copenhagen, Denmark; and Oklahoma are documented in the winter 1954 issue.

27. *The New Era* changes tremendously during the next few decades. For instance, by the early 1970s, radical Chicano poet *raúlsalinas* published editorials in the prison magazine, in addition to starting another, *Aztlán de Leavenworth*. Rives suggests that dissent was "forbidden at Leavenworth. There was plenty of it behind walls, especially during World War One with inmates from the Industrial Workers of the World, the Green Corn Rebellion, and other antiwar groups incarcerated for criticizing the war and resisting the draft. But dissident views were censored completely. Surely there were antiwar prisoners during WWII, Korea, and Vietnam, but they too had no voice. Underground newspapers and manuscripts were forbidden so there is no written evidence of their activities." Rives, "Though We Are Prisoners," 132.

28. Agamben, *Homo Sacer*, 157–158.

29. Within the context of USP Leavenworth, given the hostility against "Asiatic" soldiers in the Korean War documented in *The New Era*, any Asian prisoner might have faced severe limitations in his capacity to "volunteer" in the war. While other nonwhite prisoners might also "volunteer," I suggest that they have restricted access to publishing pieces reflecting their racialized position within USP Leavenworth.

30. Harris, "Whiteness as Property," 1737.

31. Cacho, *Social Death*, 7.

32. Another letter from the inmates equates whiteness with Americanness and theorizes "freedom" as a condition they were capable of losing, given their access to whiteness as property. Indeed, the letter frames degrees of freedom and unfreedom in relationship to liberal democracy and capitalism, equating incarceration with popular perceptions of encroaching, "insidious" communism. Close to the time of the Korean War armistice in July 1953, *The New Era* published "An Open Letter to the President," which begins by congratulating Eisenhower, whom the prisoners commend for fighting the "insidious forces that are at continuous work to pull the props from under our country." The letter connects the articulation of "freedom" and national citizenship to the potential loss of liberal democratic, capitalist freedom. Even while designated as unfree by the capitalist state, the inmates would "resist the loss of it again." Furthermore, the letter's plea for "the continuing freedom of [the nation's] people" is utterly disconnected from the state's pervasive white supremacist practices, built into denying that very freedom in differential degrees to variously racialized groups. The assertion "by virtue of having lost our freedom and of knowing the degradation such a loss entails" posits a figure enjoying full possession of "freedom," with attendant possibilities of loss. Inmates of Leavenworth, "An Open Letter to the President."

33. Attributed to Rudyard Kipling's 1899 poem "The White Man's Burden."

34. D. Rodríguez, *Forced Passages*, 14.

35. Indeed, numerous contemporary agencies that advocate programs to "adopt a prisoner" suggest a similar distant benevolence toward inmates. Furthermore, as Klein argues, "The figure of the white parent to the non-white child has long worked as a trope for representing the ostensibly 'natural' relations of hierarchy and domination. The infantilization of racialized Others and marginalized social groups has been a standard rhetorical means of legitimating unequal power relations. . . . As a practice, trans-racial or trans-ethnic adoptions have also served as a means of social control." C. Klein, *Cold War Orientalism*, 175.

36. E. Kim, *Adopted Territory*, 20.

37. Linking the virulent anticommunism of the Korean War era to contemporary anxieties surrounding race, Angela Davis states, "The fear of crime has attained a status that bears a sinister similarity to the fear of communism as it came to restructure social perceptions during the fifties and sixties. . . . Racism is more deeply embedded in socioeconomic structures, and the vast populations of incarcerated people of color is dramatic evidence of the way racism systematically structures economic relations." Davis, *House*, 270.

38. Smith, *Prison and the American Imagination*, 22.

39. Dayan, *White Dog*, 44.

40. Within the domestic norms that continue to persist in the United States, marriage symbolizes a key stepping stone toward the idealized nuclear family. Until women gained the franchise in 1920, they forfeited their political and economic rights upon getting married and were also considered to be civilly dead. Ironically, women's roles in idealized domesticity and the "national family" also required their civil death.

41. Dayan, *White Dog*, 55.

42. D. Rodríguez, *Forced Passages*, 11.

43. Harris, "Whiteness as Property," 1721.

44. Foucault, *Society Must Be Defended*, 254.

45. Foucault, 255.

46. Letter written by Pete Jarman, March 10, 1945, cited in Love, *One Blood*, 194, quoted in Tucker, *Blood Work*, xxv.

47. Richards, *Maida Springer*, 74.

48. Ramírez, *Woman in the Zoot*, 46.

49. Singh, *Black Is a Country*, 101.

50. Baldwin, *Devil Finds Work*, 83–84.

51. May, *Homeward Bound*, 146.

52. Eng, *Feeling of Kinship*, 94; C. Klein *Cold War Orientalism*, 175; J. Kim, *Ends of Empire*, 171.

53. Cho, *Haunting the Korean Diaspora*, 8.

54. Butler, *Undoing Gender*, 103.

55. Eng, *Feeling of Kinship*, 10.

56. McKee, *Disrupting Kinship*, 2.

57. Davis, *Are Prisons Obsolete?*, 12, 84.

58. Gilmore, *Golden Gulag*, 13.

59. Gilmore, 14.

60. For the USP Leavenworth inmates, in addition to the possibilities of demonstrating belonging to the idealized national family by virtually adopting within the coercive carceral institution of the penitentiary, "prison professionalized people" into normative citizenship, similar to the way the U.S. military provided "professionalization" for those whose access to national belonging was otherwise curtailed. Foucault, *Power/Knowledge*, 24. Foucault, however, neglects to work his understanding of race into his formulation of prison's ostensible professionalism.

61. In the context of South Korea's lucrative relationship with the U.S. military during the Vietnam War, Jin-kyung Lee states, "South Korea operated as an offshore military-industrial complex for the United States during the Vietnam War years and beyond." Lee, *Service Economies*, 41.

62. K. Moon, *Sex among Allies*, 43.

63. J. Kim, *Ends of Empire*, 169. While the South Korean government has repeatedly made attempts to end transnational adoption, it did so primarily because of influence from other nation-states. Eleana Kim discusses one such moment "in the 1970s when South Korea announced the suspension of foreign adoptions due to censure by the North Korean government, which vilified South Korea's commodification of children as the logical end point of capitalism." E. Kim, *Adopted Territory*, 2.

64. E. Kim, 2–3.

65. E. Kim, 521.

66. J. Kim, *Ends of Empire*, 186. On the subject of social death, Jodi Kim states, "In using this term, I am not, of course, arguing that transracial adoptees and birth mothers are slaves. Rather, I am building on extensions of Patterson's work that take up 'social death' to index the persistence of gendered racial domination, violence, and the production of degrees of social nonpersonhood within the context of formal emancipation, freedom, or sovereignty. That is, I am pointing to the ways in which natal alienation and gendered racial governmentalities outside the space of formal slavery persist in creating a variety of 'social deaths' for subjugated groups" (281).

67. Cacho, *Social Death*, 6.

CHAPTER 2

1. Williams, *Marxism and Literature*, 134; Baik, *Reencounters*, 6.

2. J. Saldívar, *Rolando Hinojosa Reader*, 181.

3. Hinojosa, *Korean Love Songs*, 43.

4. Hinojosa, 43.

5. Hinojosa, 45.

6. Hinojosa, 43.

7. Muñoz, *Cruising Utopia* 28.

8. Soto, *Reading Chican@*, 126, 111.

9. Rodríguez, "X Marks the Spot," 203–204.

10. Orchard and Padilla, *Bridges, Borders, and Breaks*, 21.

11. Blackwell, *¡Chicana Power!*, 11.

12. R. Saldívar, *Chicano Narrative*, 136.

13. Yoneyama, *Cold War Ruins*, 5.

14. Limón, "Imagining the Imaginary," 595–603.

15. See Ja. Lee, *Urban Triage*; G. Hong, *Death Beyond Disavowal*; Ferguson, *Reorder of Things*; and Melamed *Represent and Destroy*, among others.

16. R. Saldívar, "Asian América," 584–594.

17. A. Lee, "Someone Else's War," 56.

18. D. Kim, *Intimacies of Conflict*, 231.

19. Imaginative interlude mine.

20. Hinojosa, *Useless Servants*, 91.

21. Hinojosa, 163.

22. Alonzo, *Badmen Bandits*, 16.

23. Valdez, *Zoot Suit*, 158.

24. Lowe, "International," 30.

25. Muñoz, *Sense of Brown*, 10.
26. Valdez, *Zoot Suit*, 195.
27. Valdez, 195.
28. Muñoz, *Sense of Brown*, 11.
29. Hinojosa, *Korean Love Songs*, 39.
30. Hinojosa, 67.
31. Soto, *Reading Chican@*, 124–125.
32. Soto, 125.
33. Vargas, *Dissonant Divas*, 65.
34. Hinojosa, *Korean Love Songs*, 31.
35. Korea is, like any place under the destructive siege of U.S. aerial warfare, a defoliated brown during war.
36. Muñoz, "Feeling Brown, Feeling Down," 680.
37. Muñoz, 687.
38. This image of the map constitutes part of the series of discursive and actual maps that appear through the Klail City Death Trip Series, which knit the Asia Pacific with South Texas, compelled to manifest themselves not only through the mechanisms of war, but also through intimate observations of actual terrains.
39. Calderón, *Narratives of Greater Mexico*, 148.
40. R. Saldívar, *Chicano Narrative*, 136.
41. Vargas, *Dissonant Divas*, xiv.
42. Militarized misogyny lurks furtively in songbooks circulated among members of the elite U.S. Air Force. Race, class, gender, sexuality, and nationalism interacted to cast a strange and substantive alchemy in the Korean War. I suggest that infiltrating the cultural texts of the elite corps of the U.S. military, such as unofficial songbooks, undresses the gendered, racialized, and sexualized logics informing U.S. imperial ventures in Asia.
43. *Songs My Mother Never Taught Me*, a mimeograph presented by the Mosquito Association, in the Center for the Study of the Korean War. Indeed, such eroticized misogyny characterizes the foundations of an institution like the U.S. military and therefore cannot be limited to "a particular generation": "Soldiers are purposely taught to *eroticize* violence—from a heterosexual, male-aggressor perspective. During the first U.S. Gulf War on Iraq in 1991, air force pilots watched pornographic movies before bombing missions to psyche themselves up. Internalizing a misogynist, violent sexuality becomes embedded in soldiers' training to function psychologically as killers. The widespread sexual abuse of female soldiers by male colleagues, with overwhelming impunity, is a symptom of this institution's modus operandi." Chew, "What's Left?" 80.
44. Starr, *Fighter Pilot's Hymn Book*, 40.
45. See Enloe, *Bananas, Beaches, and Bases*.
46. Randolph and Legman, *Roll Me*, 76.
47. Hinojosa, *Korean Love Songs*, 41.
48. Hinojosa, 41.
49. Soto, *Reading Chican@*, 124.
50. Hinojosa, *Useless Servants*, 163.
51. Valdez, *Zoot Suit*, 168.
52. Valdez, 200.

53. Valdez, 158.
54. Gordon, *Ghostly Matters*, 190.
55. Valdez, *Zoot Suit*, 194.
56. Valdez, 204.
57. Valdez, 204.
58. Hinojosa, *Korean Love Songs*, 50.
59. Hinojosa, 200.
60. Throughout the play, both Connie and Sonny express anxieties about the implicit connections between Buddy and Anita, calling attention to the legacies of hypersexualization of Asian women: "BUDDY: What the hell's going on? CONNIE: I don't know! Maybe he's head over heels in love? Like father, like son. BUDDY: What's that supposed to mean? CONNIE: Figure it out. BUDDY: I hope you're not talking about Korea? That was a long time ago—before I even met you!" Valdez, *Zoot Suit*, 185.
61. Cho, *Haunting the Korean Diaspora*, 14.
62. Hinojosa, *Korean Love Songs*, 43.
63. Hinojosa, 43.
64. Valdez, *Zoot Suit*, 94.
65. Sánchez, "One Morning," 193.
66. Sánchez, 193.
67. Manalansan, "Messy Mismeasures," 496.
68. Sánchez, "One Morning: 1952," 193.
69. Rivera, "The Portrait," 137.
70. Rivera, 136.
71. Rivera, 137. In this story, I'm struck by Belinda Rincón's observation that "the military's interest in fertility patterns and its market research on Latina/o parenting practices reveal its belief that to militarize (and recruit) Latina/o youth, one must first militarize the Latina mother." Rincón, *Bodies at War*, 39.
72. Rincón, 39.
73. Rincón, 39.

CHAPTER 3

1. Lie, *Han Unbound*, 86.
2. Limón's first novels were published by Bantam Books but are now exclusively published and reprinted by Soho Press. Limón's first novel, *Jade Lady Burning*, was a *New York Times* Notable Book in 1992. Limón's next novel, *Slicky Boys*, was reviewed in the *New York Times* on May 25, 1997. Limón's *G.I. Bones* was one of National Public Radio's best books in 2009, and NPR excerpted the novel on their website on December 11, 2009. Limón's series is critically acclaimed and continues to receive attention in mainstream media.
3. Ferguson, *Aberrations in Black*, 71.
4. N. Klein, *History of Forgetting*, 42.
5. Cho, *Haunting the Korean Diaspora*, 71.
6. Klein quoted in Villa, *Barrio-Logos*, 71.
7. Villa, 71.
8. Ji. Lee, *Service Economies*, 101.

9. M. Kim, "Human Rights," 32.

10. M. Kim, 33.

11. Gillem, *America Town*, 51.

12. Hurst, "It'aewon," 1.

13. Hurst, 2.

14. Hurst, 5.

15. Hurst, 6.

16. Hurst, 6.

17. Hurst, 6.

18. K. Moon, *Sex among Allies*, 10.

19. Mandel, *Delightful Murder*, 47–48.

20. R. Rodriguez, *Brown Gumshoes*, 8.

21. According to Mandel, "Raymond Chandler actually theorized the turn, and dated it as beginning with [Dashiell] Hammett's work [in the 1920s]. It was an abrupt break with the gentility of the classical detective story. . . . Social corruption, especially among the rich, now moves into the centre of the plots." Mandel, *Delightful Murder*, 35.

22. Oliver, Kelly, and Trigo, *Noir Anxiety*, 46.

23. N. Klein, *History of Forgetting*, 79.

24. On the genre's potential, Ralph Rodriguez states, "Aztlan offered a place of being for the alienated Chicana/o other. By contrast, the Chicana/o detective novel offers the alienated hero not a mythic homeland, but a discursive space from which to examine the world and its shaping discourses." R. Rodriguez, *Brown Gumshoes*, 7.

25. Limón, *Slicky Boys*, 16. The limitations of such racial conflation are called into sharp relief when we consider forms of anti-Black racisms in South Korea and in the United States. In other words, while the Korean policeman might not know or care to distinguish "Mexican or Anglo," the situation would be different if Sueño was racialized as Black.

26. Limón, 193.

27. Brady, *Extinct Lands, Temporal Geographies*, 78.

28. Limón, *Slicky Boys*, 22.

29. "The frequency of a term used in the Korean media, 'the Korean Dream,' referring to the desire of migrant workers from overseas to come to South Korea for work, seems at first puzzling. Echoing the more globally famous term 'the American Dream,' the South Korean counterpart implies a certain desire for equation between Korea and America as a destination for immigrants and migrants, as the term 'the Korean Dream' recognizes Korea's new place in the global hierarchy as a semiperipheral metropole." J. Lee, *Service Economies*, 214.

30. Limón, *Slicky Boys*, 22.

31. As Jorge Mariscal puts it, "Sustained by a constant flow of new immigrants and relatively limited career opportunities for the native-born working class of color, Latin@ military service has been a primary vehicle for assimilation, access to full rights of citizenship, and the construction of 'American' identities premised on traditional patriotism." Mariscal, "Latin@s in the U.S.," 37.

32. Limón, *Slicky Boys*, 25.

33. R. Rodriguez, *Brown Gumshoes*, 6.

34. In the series, the Vietnam War is staged as the "hot war" informing Ernie Bas-

com's more extreme views and is a significant occasion to historicize and examine the role of the war in U.S.-occupied South Korea.

35. George, *Burning Down the House*, 4–5.

36. Limón, *Slicky Boys*, 59, 57.

37. George, "Domestic."

38. Here, I extend José Esteban Muñoz's work on "disidentification": "Disidentification is about recycling and rethinking encoded meaning. The process of disidentification scrambles and reconstructs the encoded message of a cultural text in a fashion that both exposes the encoded message's universalizing and exclusionary machinations and recircuits its workings to account for, include, and empower minority identities and identifications. Thus, disidentification is a step further than cracking open the code of the majority; it proceeds to use this code as raw material for representing a disempowered politics or positionality that has been rendered unthinkable by the dominant culture." Muñoz, *Disidentifications*, 31.

39. Chandler, *Later Novels and Other Writings*, "Simple Art of Murder," 980.

40. Lye, *America's Asia*.

41. Lowe, *Intimacies of Four Continents*, 24; and Chang, *Chino*, 32.

42. Lye, *America's Asia*, 66.

43. Yoneyama, *Cold War Ruins*, 16.

44. Yoneyama, 16.

45. See also Dudziak, *War Time*.

46. Limón, *Wandering Ghost*, 2.

47. Limón, 4.

48. Limón, 62.

49. Ji. Lee, *Service Economies*, 84–85.

50. Kang et al., *Words of Farewell*, 17.

51. Kim and Choi, *Dangerous Women*, 109.

52. Limón, *Wandering Ghost*, 104.

53. Limón, 105.

54. Limón, 105.

55. Limón, 105.

56. Tadiar, *Things Fall Away*, 37–38.

57. Limón, *Wandering Ghost*, 226.

58. Limón, 3.

59. Limón, 12.

60. Such racialized, gendered, and sexualized violence turns on the axis of white supremacist acts of disciplining Black bodies throughout U.S. history, and Limón in this case locates Korean men as insidious threats to white women.

61. Limón, *Wandering Ghost*, 309.

62. Limón, 230.

63. Limón, 230.

CHAPTER 4

1. Choi, *Foreign Student*, 56.

2. Choi, 60.

3. Choi, 57.

4. J. Kim, "Settler Modernity's Spatial Exceptions," 570.

5. Yoneyama, "Toward a Decolonial Genealogy," 477.

6. Choi, *Foreign Student*, 56–57.

7. A phrase that is attributed to Griffis.

8. Griffis, *Corea, the Hermit Nation*, xiii.

9. Griffis, xv.

10. Griffis, 441.

11. Streeby, *American Sensations*, 10.

12. "In 1863 he served three months as color corporal in company A, 44th Pennsylvania militia, during Lee's invasion." Johnson and Brown, *Twentieth Century Biographical Dictionary*, 2303.

13. Streeby, *American Sensations*, 107.

14. Streeby, 57.

15. I use Jenny Edkins's notion of *encircling* trauma: Edkins proposes the concept of "trauma time" as a resistant temporality: "Trauma time is inherent in and destabilizes any production of linearity." Edkins, *Trauma*, 16. For witnessing and testimony (two acts I suggest are critical for the production of historical knowledge) to be part of politicized resistance to dominant history, they must not become written into linear narratives and therefore risk de-politicization or gentrification but should rather mark or encircle the moment of trauma (15).

16. As Nikhil Pal Singh notes, ideas of both individual and market "freedom"—in addition to "an antipathy to socially determined, collectively defined forms of ascription"—form the backbone to the definitions of liberalism. Singh, *Keywords*, 140. Critical understandings of liberalism must account for the "problems of political domination, exclusion, and inequality within liberalism . . . [in] the history of liberal-democratic nation-states founded in racial slavery and colonial expansion" (141).

17. Here, I also refer to U.S. discourses of delivering freedom and modernity to places governed by "repressed" and "fanatical" ideologies, justifying U.S. military action and occupation in the Persian Gulf War, the Iraq War, the war in Afghanistan, and other ongoing and unending wars. Chew, *Feminism and War*.

18. Cho, *Haunting the Korean Diaspora*, 67–68.

19. Cho, 69.

20. Maj. Gen. William Kean, Memo to commanding officers, July 27, 1950, Twenty-Fifth Infantry Division, Record Group 407, College Park, MD, U.S. National Archives.

21. Cumings, *Parallax Visions*, 184.

22. Cumings, 185.

23. "The feverish national concern over subversion, disloyalty, Communism, and milder threats to the American way of life that afflicted the country in the early fifties, affected the Ford Foundation but did not reduce its international activities. Indeed, it may have had the paradoxical effect of increasing them." Sutton, "The Ford Foundation," 84. Sutton's attention to "the American way of life" suggests, at once, the presumed objectivity of such disciplines as American studies and the occasion to consider American studies itself as intimately connected to area studies, and itself standing as an area study.

24. Cumings, *Parallax Visions*, 186. Sutton notes that "the Ford Foundation in the years after World War II shared proudly and worriedly in the common view that the U.S. had responsibilities in the world that it was ill-prepared to exercise. The country lacked international expertise and sophistication in government, private business, the media and indeed wherever our society touched others. The Ford Foundation set out to serve the national interest by training such people." Sutton, "The Ford Foundation and Columbia."

25. Cumings, *Parallax Visions*, 186.

26. Lowe, "International," 39.

27. Edkins, *Trauma and the Memory*, 46.

28. Choi, *Foreign Student*, 51.

29. *The Foreign Student* occupies a near-canonical position with American cultural studies scholars. The literary scholar Daniel Kim suggests that the novel's troubling of linear history as well as its ability to situate readers themselves as the "foreign students" of an unfamiliar Korean history "makes it a text tailor-made for an American Studies that has increasingly adopted a transnational orientation." D. Kim, "'Bled In, Letter by Letter,'" 551. Several scholars, including Daniel Kim, Jodi Kim, Crystal Parikh, and Roderick Ferguson, note the importance of translation in the novel, commenting on Chang's role as an interpreter for the U.S. military, as well as his role as an educator introducing Korea and the Korean War for church audiences, which he conducts in exchange for his tuition at the University of the South. Jodi Kim, in her significant book *Ends of Empire*, suggests that in addition to relegation as the "forgotten" war, the Korean War is also a war made unknowable or illegible, thus a project requiring translation. Her analysis of Choi's novel attends to Chang's multiple roles as translator and argues that both the character and the novel serve the critical function of "bad translators" of the war, calling attention to the "complex problem" of the Korean War and inaugurating understandings that critically lack fidelity to the dominant narrative of the war. J. Kim, *Ends of Empire*, 156.

30. Griffis, *Corea, the Hermit Nation*, xiii.

31. Yoneyama, *Cold War Ruins*, 49.

32. Yoneyama, 51.

33. J. Kim, *Ends of Empire*, 152. Ernst Oppert supplies such tropes in *A Forbidden Land: Voyages to the Corea*: "It is a somewhat difficult task to express an opinion on the origin and descent of the different races which people the peninsula. . . . The Coreans' reply to any question is, that they themselves do not know anything about it, and that they have altogether forgotten where they came from. This ignorance is easily accounted for by the deficiencies of their country's literature, which, as regards its own history, is very incomplete. . . . Of a taller and more powerful make than the natives of China and Japan, with a cast of features thoroughly pleasing, and endowed with a firm and energetic character, they remind us much more forcibly of the half-savage hordes and nomadic tribes of Mongolia." Oppert, *Forbidden Land*, 7.

34. Choi, *Foreign Student*, 52.

35. The Korean War scholar Dong-Choon Kim suggests both the unbroken genealogy of colonial and neocolonial occupation in Korea and Korean anticolonial resistance to Japanese colonialism in "The Long Road Toward Truth and Reconciliation": while "efforts by Koreans to face their dark past began on 15 August 1945 when the

nation broke free from Japanese occupation," the "U.S. policy of resurrecting Imperial Japan's governing architecture in South Korea reflected the ideological confrontation seen in the cold war era." D.-C. Kim, "Long Road," 525, 530.

36. Choi, *Foreign Student*, 39.

37. For a critical analysis of the state's paradoxical erasure of Native Alaskan subjects vis-à-vis Asian immigration to Alaska, see Juliana Hu Pegues's "Settler Orientalism" in *Verge: Studies in Global Asias*.

38. Choi, *Foreign Student*, 50.

39. Choi, 39.

40. Choi, 304. "Jejudo is an island located in the southern region of the Korean peninsula. In 1948, on Jejudo, hundreds of partisan forces, active in the mountainous areas, rebelled against the general election that was destined to legitimize national division. The South Korean military and police, supported by U.S. troops, were deployed to subdue the rebellious guerillas. Thirty thousand of the 150,000 residents were known to have been killed for serving the guerillas. This incident represented the prelude to the Korean War massacres." D.-C. Kim, "The Long Road," 534. While Chang's refuge on Cheju Island occurs during the war itself, Choi recalls the earlier violence authorized against the people resisting U.S.-backed rule.

41. Cho, *Haunting the Korean Diaspora*, 55.

42. Cho, 55.

43. Choi, *Foreign Student*, 308.

44. Choi, 308.

45. Choi, 51.

46. Choi, 52.

47. Edwards, *To Acknowledge a War*, 20.

48. Edwards, 20.

49. Edwards, 21.

50. Edwards, 23, 24.

51. McElya, *Clinging to Mammy*, 51.

52. *Handbook of the United Daughters of the Confederacy*, 9.

53. *Handbook of the United Daughters of the Confederacy*, 32.

54. Cox, *Dixie's Daughters*, 6.

55. In *Dixie's Daughters*, a study of the UDC, Karen Cox states, "Many members of the organization were, at the very least, social elites. Judging by the officers of the organization, the Daughters married well—to merchants, lawyers, judges, and members of state legislatures. Many were also descendants of planter families, whose fathers were Confederate officers. . . . Most received a formal education, at private female seminaries and women's colleges." Cox, 5.

56. *Handbook of the United Daughters of the Confederacy*, 30.

57. *Handbook of the United Daughters of the Confederacy*, 24.

58. *Handbook of the United Daughters of the Confederacy*, 32.

59. According to Cox, McCain "eventually became president of Mississippi Southern College (not the University of Southern Mississippi). He was also a national officer in the SCV [Sons of Confederate Veterans]." Cox, *Dixie's Daughters*, 193–194.

60. Cox, 159.

61. One flashpoint in the entwined anxiety of white supremacy and communism, as the people continue to dismantle Confederate memorials in the United States, and white supremacist memorials globally.

62. Cox, *Dixie's Daughters*, 16.

63. Cox, 95.

64. Choi, *The Foreign Student*, 54.

65. Choi, 48.

66. Choi, 48.

67. Choi, 48.

68. Cox, *Dixie's Daughters*, 49.

CODA

1. Maldonado-Torres, "Interrogating Systemic Racism."

2. Medak-Saltzman, "Empire's Haunted Logics," 18.

3. Choi, *Foreign Student*, 219.

4. Rosaura Sánchez and Beatrice Pita, email correspondence, July 15, 2020.

5. Morrison, "Home," 8.

6. Baldwin, *Devil Finds Work*, 83–84.

BIBLIOGRAPHY

Agamben, Giorgio. *Homo Sacer: Sovereign Power and Bare Life*. Stanford, CA: Stanford University Press, 1998.

Alonzo, Juan José. *Badmen, Bandits, and Folk Heroes: The Ambivalence of Mexican American Identity in Literature and Film*. Tucson: University of Arizona Press, 2009.

Arce, William. "Nation in Uniform: Chicano/Latino War Narratives and the Construction of Nation in the Korean War and Vietnam War." Ph.D. diss., University of Southern California, 2009. University of Southern California Digital Library (UC1126013). https://doi.org/10.25549/USCTHESES-M2036.

Arvin, Maile. *Possessing Polynesians: The Science of Settler Colonial Whiteness in Hawai'i and Oceania*. Durham, NC: Duke University Press, 2019.

Atanasoski, Neda. *Humanitarian Violence: The U.S. Deployment of Diversity*, 2013.

Baik, Crystal Mun-hye. *Reencounters: On the Korean War and Diasporic Memory Critique*. Asian American History and Culture. Philadelphia: Temple University Press, 2020.

Baldwin, James. *The Devil Finds Work*. Knopf Doubleday, 2013.

Barker, Joanne. *Native Acts: Law, Recognition, and Cultural Authenticity*. Durham, NC: Duke University Press, 2013.

Benjamin, Walter, Hannah Arendt, and Harry Zohn. *Illuminations*. New York: Schocken Books, 1986.

Blackwell, Maylei. *¡Chicana Power! Contested Histories of Feminism in the Chicano Movement*. 1st ed. Chicana Matters Series. Austin: University of Texas Press, 2011.

"Bok Nam Om." *New Era*, Winter 1954.

Brady, Mary Pat. *Extinct Lands, Temporal Geographies: Chicana Literature and the Urgency of Space*. Latin America Otherwise. Durham, NC: Duke University Press, 2002.

Butler, Judith. *Undoing Gender*. New York: Routledge, 2004.

Cacho, Lisa Marie. *Social Death: Racialized Rightlessness and the Criminalization of the Unprotected*. Nation of Newcomers: Immigrant History as American History. New York: New York University Press, 2012.

Calderón, Héctor. *Narratives of Greater Mexico: Essays on Chicano Literary History, Genre, and Borders*. 1st ed. CMAS History, Culture, and Society Series. Austin: University of Texas Press, 2004.

Camacho, Keith L. "Transoceanic Flows: Pacific Islander Interventions across the American Empire." *Amerasia Journal* 37, no. 3 (2011): ix–xxxiv. https://doi.org/10.17953/amer.37.3.m372lun15r8p420m.

Cassinelli, S. Moon. "'It Was Akiko 41; It Was Me': Queer Kinships in Nora Okja Keller's Mother-Daughter Narrative." *WSQ: Women's Studies Quarterly* 47, no. 1–2 (2019): 193–208. https://doi.org/10.1353/wsq.2019.0005.

Chandler, Raymond. *Later Novels and Other Writings*. New York: Library of America, 1995.

Chang, Jason Oliver. *Chino: Anti-Chinese Racism in Mexico, 1880–1940*. The Asian American Experience. Urbana: University of Illinois Press, 2017.

Chew, Huibin Amelia. "What's Left? After 'Imperial Feminist' Hijackings." In *Feminism and War: Confronting US Imperialism*, edited by Chandra Talpade Mohanty, Robin L. Riley, and Minnie Bruce Pratt. London: Zed Books, 2008.

Childs, Dennis. *Slaves of the State: Black Incarceration from the Chain Gang to the Penitentiary*. Minneapolis: University of Minnesota Press, 2015.

Cho, Grace M. *Haunting the Korean Diaspora: Shame, Secrecy, and the Forgotten War*. Minneapolis: University of Minnesota Press, 2008.

Choi, Susan. *The Foreign Student*. 1st ed. New York: HarperFlamingo, 1998.

Cox, Karen L. *Dixie's Daughters: The United Daughters of the Confederacy and the Preservation of Confederate Culture*. New Perspectives on the History of the South. Gainesville: University Press of Florida, 2003.

Cumings, Bruce. *The Korean War: A History*. New York: Modern Library, 2010.

———. *Parallax Visions: Making Sense of American–East Asian Relations at the End of the Century*. Durham, NC: Duke University Press, 1999.

Davis, Angela Y. *Are Prisons Obsolete?*, 2011.

Day, Iyko, Juliana Hu Pegues, Melissa Phung, Dean Saranillio, and Danika Medak-Saltzman. "Settler Colonial Studies, Asian Diasporic Questions." *Verge: Studies in Global Asias* 5, no. 1 (2019): 1. https://doi.org/10.5749/vergstudglobasia.5.1.0001.

Dayan, Colin. *The Law Is a White Dog: How Legal Rituals Make and Unmake Persons*. Princeton, NJ: Princeton University Press, 2011.

Dudziak, Mary. *War Time: An Idea, Its History, Its Consequences*. Cary: Oxford University Press, 2014.

Earley, Pete. *The Hot House: Life inside Leavenworth Prison*. New York: Bantam Books, 1992.

Edkins, Jenny. *Trauma and the Memory of Politics*. Cambridge: Cambridge University Press, 2003.

Edwards, Paul M. *The Mistaken History of the Korean War: What We Got Wrong Then and Now*. Jefferson, NC: McFarland, 2018.

———. *To Acknowledge a War: The Korean War in American Memory*. Contributions in Military Studies, no. 193. Westport, CT: Greenwood, 2000.

Em, Henry, Christine Hong, and Kim Dong-Choon. "Coda: A Conversation with Kim Dong-Choon." *Positions* 23, no. 4 (2015): 837–849. https://doi.org/10.1215/10679847-3148427.

Eng, David L. *The Feeling of Kinship: Queer Liberalism and the Racialization of Intimacy*, 2010.

Enloe, Cynthia H. *Bananas, Beaches and Bases: Making Feminist Sense of International Politics*. Berkeley: University of California Press, 1990.

Espiritu, Yên Lê, Lisa Lowe, and Lisa Yoneyama. "Transpacific Entanglements." In *Flashpoints for Asian American Studies*, edited by Cathy Schlund-Vials, 175–189. Fordham University Press, 2020.

Ferguson, Roderick A. *Aberrations in Black: Toward a Queer of Color Critique*. Critical American Studies Series. Minneapolis: University of Minnesota Press, 2004.

———. "The Distributions of Whiteness." *American Quarterly* 66, no. 4 (2014): 1101–1106. https://doi.org/10.1353/aq.2014.0064.

———. *The Reorder of Things: The University and Its Pedagogies of Minority Difference*. Difference Incorporated. Minneapolis: University of Minnesota Press, 2012.

Foucault, Michel. *Society Must Be Defended: Lectures at the Collège de France, 1975–76*. 1st ed. New York: Picador, 2003.

———. *The Archaeology of Knowledge*. World of Man. New York: Vintage Books, 2010.

———. *Power/Knowledge: Selected Interviews and Other Writings, 1972–1977*. 1st American ed. New York: Pantheon Books, 1980.

Freeman, Elizabeth. "Queer Belongings: Kinship Theory and Queer Theory." In *A Companion to Lesbian, Gay, Bisexual, Transgender, and Queer Studies*, edited by George E. Haggerty and Molly McGarry, 293–314. Oxford: Blackwell, 2008.

Fujitani, Takashi, Geoffrey M. White, and Lisa Yoneyama, eds. *Perilous Memories: The Asia-Pacific War(s)*. Durham, NC: Duke University Press, 2001.

Gandara, Ezekiel P., and Cody Thomas. Ezekiel P. Gandara Collection. Veterans History Project, American Folklife Center, Library of Congress, Washington, DC. Accessed September 18, 2021. https://memory.loc.gov/diglib/vhp/story/loc.natlib.afc2001001.92722/.

George, Rosemary Marangoly, ed. *Burning Down the House: Recycling Domesticity*. Boulder, CO: Westview, 1998.

———. "Domestic." In *Keywords for American Cultural Studies*, edited by Bruce Burgett and Glenn Hendler, 88–92. New York: New York University Press, 2007.

Gillem, Mark L. *America Town: Building the Outposts of Empire*. Minneapolis: University of Minnesota Press, 2007.

Gillman, S. "Otra Vez Caliban / Encore Caliban: Adaptation, Translation, Americas Studies." *American Literary History* 20, no. 1–2 (January 23, 2008): 187–209. https://doi.org/10.1093/alh/ajn010.

Gilmore, Ruth Wilson. *Golden Gulag: Prisons, Surplus, Crisis, and Opposition in Globalizing California*. American Crossroads 21. Berkeley: University of California Press, 2007.

Goldstein, Alyosha, ed. *Formations of United States Colonialism*. Durham, NC: Duke University Press, 2014.

Gordon, Avery. *Ghostly Matters: Haunting and the Sociological Imagination*. Minneapolis: University of Minnesota Press, 1997.

Griffis, William Elliot. *Corea the Hermit Nation*. New York: Charles Scribner's Sons, 1894.

Han, Clara. *Seeing Like a Child: Inheriting the Korean War*. New York: Fordham University Press, 2021.

Handbook of the United Daughters of the Confederacy. Richmond, VA: Memorial Building Headquarters, 1959.

Haraway, Donna Jeanne. *Staying with the Trouble: Making Kin in the Chthulucene.* Experimental Futures: Technological Lives, Scientific Arts, Anthropological Voices. Durham, NC: Duke University Press, 2016.

Harris, Cheryl I. "Whiteness as Property." *Harvard Law Review* 106, no. 8 (1993): 1707. https://doi.org/10.2307/1341787.

Heatherton, Christina. "University of Radicalism: Ricardo Flores Magón and Leavenworth Penitentiary." *American Quarterly* 66, no. 3 (2014): 557–581. https://doi.org/10.1353/aq.2014.0044.

Heintz, Lauren. "The Crisis of Kinship: Queer Affiliations in the Sexual Economy of Slavery." *GLQ: A Journal of Lesbian and Gay Studies* 23, no. 2 (2017): 221–246. https://doi.org/10.1215/10642684-3750437.

Hinojosa, Rolando. *From Klail City to Korea with Love: Two Master Works.* Klail City Death Trip Series. Houston: Arte Público, 2017.

———. *The Useless Servants.* Houston: Arte Público, 1993.

Holland, Sharon Patricia. *The Erotic Life of Racism.* Durham, NC: Duke University Press, 2012.

Hong, Christine. "The Unending Korean War." *Positions* 23, no. 4 (2015): 597–617. https://doi.org/10.1215/10679847-3148346.

———. *A Violent Peace: Race, U.S. Militarism, and Cultures of Democratization in Cold War Asia and the Pacific.* Post*45. Stanford, CA: Stanford University Press, 2020.

Hong, Grace Kyungwon. "Comparison and Coalition in the Age of Black Lives Matter." *Journal of Asian American Studies* 20, no. 2 (2017): 273–278. https://doi.org/10.1353/jaas.2017.0020.

———. *Death Beyond Disavowal: The Impossible Politics of Difference.* Minneapolis: University of Minnesota Press, 2015.

Hübinette, Tobias. "From Orphan Trains to Babylifts: Colonial Trafficking, Empire Building, and Social Engineering." In *Outsiders Within: Writing on Transracial Adoption,* edited by Jane Jeong Trenka, Julia Chinyere Oparah, and Sun Yung Shin. Cambridge, MA: Sound End, 2006.

Hurst, G. Cameron. "It'aewon: The Gentrification of a Boomtown." Hanover, NH: Universities Field Staff International, 1984.

Inmates of Leavenworth. "An Open Letter to the President." *The New Era,* 8, no. 3 (1953): np.

James, Joy, ed. *The New Abolitionists: (Neo) Slave Narratives and Contemporary Prison Writings.* SUNY Series, Philosophy and Race. Albany: State University of New York Press, 2005.

Johnson, R., and J. H. Brown. *The Twentieth Century Biographical Dictionary of Notable Americans.* Gale Research, 1968.

Jones. "To Whom It May Concern." *The New Era,* September 1950.

Kang, Sŏk-kyŏng, Chi-wŏn Kim, Chŏng-hŭi O, Bruce Fulton, and Ju-Chan Fulton. *Words of Farewell: Stories by Korean Women Writers.* Women in Translation. Seattle: Seal, 1989.

Kauanui, J. Kēhaulani. *Hawaiian Blood: Colonialism and the Politics of Sovereignty and Indigeneity.* Narrating Native Histories. Durham, NC: Duke University Press, 2008.

Kean, William. "Memo to Commanding Officers, 27 July." Twenty-Fifth Infantry Division, 1950. Record Group 407. U.S. National Archives.

Kim, Daniel Y. "'Bled In, Letter by Letter': Translation, Postmemory, and the Subject of Korean War; History in Susan Choi's *The Foreign Student*." *American Literary History* 21, no. 3 (September 1, 2009): 550–583. https://doi.org/10.1093/alh/ajp021.

———. *The Intimacies of Conflict: Cultural Memory and the Korean War*. New York: New York University Press, 2020.

Kim, Dong-Choon. "The Long Road toward Truth and Reconciliation: Unwavering Attempts to Achieve Justice in South Korea." *Critical Asian Studies* 42, no. 4 (2010): 525–552. https://doi.org/10.1080/14672715.2010.515387.

———. *The Unending Korean War: A Social History*. Larkspur, CA: Tamal Vista, 2008.

Kim, Elaine H., and Chungmoo Choi, eds. *Dangerous Women: Gender and Korean Nationalism*. New York: Routledge, 1998.

Kim, Eleana. "Our Adoptee, Our Alien: Transnational Adoptees as Specters of Foreignness and Family in South Korea." *Anthropological Quarterly* 80, no. 2 (2007): 497–531. https://doi.org/10.1353/anq.2007.0027.

———. *Adopted Territory: Transnational Korean Adoptees and the Politics of Belonging*. Durham, NC: Duke University Press, 2010.

Kim, Jodi. *Ends of Empire: Asian American Critique and the Cold War*. Minneapolis: University of Minnesota Press, 2010.

———. "Settler Modernity, Debt Imperialism, and the Necropolitics of the Promise." *Social Text* 36, no. 2 (June 1, 2018): 41–61. https://doi.org/10.1215/01642472-4362349.

———. "Settler Modernity's Spatial Exceptions: The US POW Camp, Metapolitical Authority, and Ha Jin's War Trash." *American Quarterly* 69, no. 3 (2017): 569–587. https://doi.org/10.1353/aq.2017.0051.

Kim, Min-Jung. "Human Rights and South Korea: U.S. Imperialism, State Ideologies, and Camptown Prostitution." In *The Subject(s) of Human Rights: Crises, Violations, and Asian/American Critique*, edited by Cathy Schlund-Vials, Guy Pierre Beauregard, Hsiu-chuan Lee, and Madeleine Thien. Asian American History and Culture. Philadelphia: Temple University Press, 2020.

Kim, Monica. *The Interrogation Rooms of the Korean War: The Untold History*. Princeton, NJ: Princeton University Press, 2019.

Kirk, David L. "Men behind Prison Walls Aid War Victims." *Spokane (Washington) Daily Chronicle*, n.d.

Klein, Christina. *Cold War Orientalism: Asia in the Middlebrow Imagination, 1945–1961*. Berkeley: University of California Press, 2003. http://site.ebrary.com/id/10048970.

Klein, Norman M. *The History of Forgetting: Los Angeles and the Erasure of Memory*. The Haymarket Series. London: Verso, 1998.

"Korea: The 'Forgotten' War." *US News and World Report*, October 1951.

Kwon, Heonik. *After the Korean War: An Intimate History*. Cambridge: Cambridge University Press, 2020.

LaMaster, Kenneth M. *U.S. Penitentiary Leavenworth*. Images of America. Charleston, SC: Arcadia, 2008.

Lee, A. J. Yumi. "Repairing Police Action after the Korean War in Toni Morrison's *Home*." *Radical History Review* 2020, no. 137 (May 1, 2020): 119–140. https://doi.org/10.1215/01636545-8092810.

———. "Someone Else's War: Korea and the Post-1945 U.S. Racial Order." Ph.D. diss., University of Pennsylvania, 2015. Publicly Accessible Penn Dissertations (1832). https://repository.upenn.edu/edissertations/1832.

Lee, James Kyung-Jin. *Urban Triage: Race and the Fictions of Multiculturalism.* Critical American Studies Series. Minneapolis: University of Minnesota Press, 2004.

Lee, Jin-kyung. *Service Economies: Militarism, Sex Work, and Migrant Labor in South Korea.* Minneapolis: University of Minnesota Press, 2010.

Lie, John. *Han Unbound: The Political Economy of South Korea.* Stanford, CA: Stanford University Press, 1998.

Liem, Deann Borshay, and Ramsay Liem. *Memory of Forgotten War.* San Francisco: Mu Films, 2013.

Limón, J. E. "Imagining the Imaginary: A Reply to Ramon Saldivar." *American Literary History* 21, no. 3 (September 1, 2009): 595–603. https://doi.org/10.1093/alh/ajp025.

Limón, Martin. *Slicky Boys.* New York: Bantam Books, 1997.

———. *The Wandering Ghost.* New York: Soho Crime, 2007.

Love, Spencie. *One Blood: The Death and Resurrection of Charles R. Drew.* Chapel Hill: The University of North Carolina Press, 1996.

Lowe, Lisa. "The International within the National: American Studies and Asian American Critique." *Cultural Critique,* no. 40 (1998): 29. https://doi.org/10.2307/1354466.

———. *The Intimacies of Four Continents.* Durham, NC: Duke University Press, 2015.

———. "Metaphors of Globalization." In *Interdisciplinarity and Social Justice: Revisioning Academic Accountability,* edited by Joe Parker, Ranu Samantrai, and Mary Romero. Albany: SUNY Press, 2010.

Lye, Colleen. *America's Asia: Racial Form and American Literature, 1893–1945.* Princeton, NJ: Princeton University Press, 2005.

MacArthur, Douglas. "Home by Christmas," November 28, 1950. Truman Library, Box, (45) MacArthur Dismissal, Box 1 of 1, Orange. 1–10.

Maldonado-Torres, Nelson. "Interrogating Systemic Racism and the White Academic Field." *fondation-frantz fanon* (blog), June 16, 2020. http://fondation-frantzfanon.com/interrogating-systemic-racism-and-the-white-academic-field/.

Manalansan, Martin F. "Messy Mismeasures." *South Atlantic Quarterly* 117, no. 3 (2018): 491–506. https://doi.org/10.1215/00382876-6942105.

Mandel, Ernest. *Delightful Murder: A Social History of the Crime Story.* London: Pluto, 1984.

Mariscal, Jorge. "Latin@s in the U.S. Military." In *Inside the Latin@ Experience: A Latin@ Studies Reader,* edited by Norma Cantú and Maria Fránquiz. New York: Palgrave Macmillan, 2010.

Mata, Irene. *Domestic Disturbances: Re-imagining Narratives of Gender, Labor, and Immigration.* Austin: University of Texas Press, 2014.

May, Elaine Tyler. *Homeward Bound: American Families in the Cold War Era.* New York: Basic Books, 1988.

McCain, John H. "War Orphan Sponsorship." *The New Era* 9, no. 4 (1954): 9.

McElya, Micki. *Clinging to Mammy: The Faithful Slave in Twentieth-Century America.* Cambridge, MA: Harvard University Press, 2009.

McKee, Kimberly. *Disrupting Kinship: Transnational Politics of Korean Adoption in the United States.* The Asian American Experience. Urbana: University of Illinois Press, 2019.

Medak-Saltzman, Danika. "Empire's Haunted Logics: Comparative Colonialisms and the Challenges of Incorporating Indigeneity." *Critical Ethnic Studies* 1, no. 2 (2015): 11. https://doi.org/10.5749/jcritethnstud.1.2.0011.

Melamed, Jodi. *Represent and Destroy: Rationalizing Violence in the New Racial Capitalism.* Difference Incorporated. Minneapolis: University of Minnesota Press, 2011.

Moon, Katharine H. S. *Sex among Allies: Military Prostitution in U.S.-Korea Relations.* New York: Columbia University Press, 1997.

Moreton-Robinson, Aileen. *The White Possessive: Property, Power, and Indigenous Sovereignty,* 2015.

Morris, James McGrath. *Jailhouse Journalism: The Fourth Estate behind Bars.* New Brunswick, NJ: Transaction, 2002.

Morrison, Toni. "Home." In *The House that Race Built,* edited by Wahneema Lubiano and Toni Morrison. New York: Vintage Books, 1998.

Muñoz, José Esteban. *Cruising Utopia: The Then and There of Queer Futurity.* Sexual Cultures. New York: New York University Press, 2009.

———. *Disidentifications: Queers of Color and the Performance of Politics.* Cultural Studies of the Americas, vol. 2. Minneapolis: University of Minnesota Press, 1999.

———. "Ephemera as Evidence: Introductory Notes to Queer Acts." *Women and Performance: A Journal of Feminist Theory* 8, no. 2 (1996): 5–16. https://doi.org/10.1080/07407709608571228.

———. "Feeling Brown, Feeling Down: Latina Affect, the Performativity of Race, and the Depressive Position." *Signs: Journal of Women in Culture and Society* 31, no. 3 (2006): 675–688. https://doi.org/10.1086/499080.

———. *The Sense of Brown.* Perverse Modernities. Durham, NC: Duke University Press, 2020.

Nebolon, Juliet. "'Life Given Straight from the Heart': Settler Militarism, Biopolitics, and Public Health in Hawai'i during World War II." *American Quarterly* 69, no. 1 (2017): 23–45. https://doi.org/10.1353/aq.2017.0002.

O'Brien, Jean M. *Firsting and Lasting: Writing Indians out of Existence in New England.* Minneapolis: University of Minnesota Press, 2010.

Oliver, Kelly, and Benigno Trigo. *Noir Anxiety.* Minneapolis: University of Minnesota Press, 2003.

Oppert, E. *A Forbidden Land: Voyages to the Corea; with an Account of Its Geography, History, Productions, and Commercial Capabilities, &c., &c.* London: S. Low, Marston, Searle, and Rivington, 1880.

Padilla, Yolanda, and William Orchard. *Bridges, Borders, Breaks: History, Narrative, and Nation in Twenty-First-Century Chicana/o Literary Criticism,* 2016.

Parikh, Crystal. *Writing Human Rights: The Political Imaginaries of Writers of Color,* 2017.

Park, Josephine Nock-Hee. *Cold War Friendships: Korea, Vietnam, and Asian American Literature.* New York: Oxford University Press, 2016.

Pash, Melinda L. *In the Shadow of the Greatest Generation: The Americans Who Fought the Korean War.* New York: New York University Press, 2012.

Pate, SooJin. *From Orphan to Adoptee: U.S. Empire and Genealogies of Korean Adoption.* Difference Incorporated. Minneapolis: University of Minnesota Press, 2014.

Pérez, Emma. *The Decolonial Imaginary: Writing Chicanas into History.* Theories of Representation and Difference. Bloomington: Indiana University Press, 1999.

"Prison Magazine Now on Display: Leavenworth Staff Has Excellent One." *Southeast Missourian*, June 30, 1949.

Puar, Jasbir K. *Terrorist Assemblages: Homonationalism in Queer Times*. Next Wave. Durham, NC: Duke University Press, 2007.

Ramírez, Catherine S. *The Woman in the Zoot Suit: Gender, Nationalism, and the Cultural Politics of Memory*. Durham, NC: Duke University Press, 2010.

Randolph, Vance, and G. Legman. *Unprintable Ozark Folksongs and Folklore*. Fayetteville: University of Arkansas Press, 1992.

Reddy, Chandan. *Freedom with Violence: Race, Sexuality, and the US State*, 2011.

Richards, Yevette. *Maida Springer: Pan-Africanist and International Labor Leader*. Pittsburgh: University of Pittsburgh Press, 2000.

Rincón, Belinda Linn. *Bodies at War: Genealogies of Militarism in Chicana Literature and Culture*. Tucson: University of Arizona Press, 2017.

Rivera, A. M., Jr. "Rebel Flags in Korea: Confederate Banners Fly Anywhere!!!" *Pittsburgh Courier*, September 29, 1951.

Rivera, Tomás, and Evangelina Vigil-Piñón. *Y No Se Lo Tragó La Tierra / And the Earth Did Not Devour Him*. Houston: Arte Público, 1992.

Rives, Tim. "'Though We Are Prisoners, We Are Still Americans': Leavenworth Prisoners and the Korean War." In *Center for the Study of the Korean War Proceedings*, June 2005.

Rodríguez, Dylan. *Forced Passages: Imprisoned Radical Intellectuals and the U.S. Prison Regime*. Minneapolis: University of Minnesota Press, 2006.

Rodriguez, Ralph E. *Brown Gumshoes: Detective Fiction and the Search for Chicana/o Identity*. Austin: University of Texas Press, 2005.

Rodríguez, Richard T. *Next of Kin: The Family in Chicano/a Cultural Politics*. Latin America Otherwise: Languages, Empires, Nations. Durham, NC: Duke University Press, 2009.

———. "X Marks the Spot." *Cultural Dynamics* 29, no. 3 (2017): 202–213. https://doi.org/10.1177/0921374017727880.

Saldívar, José David, ed. *The Rolando Hinojosa Reader: Essays Historical and Critical*. Houston: Arte Público, 1985.

Saldívar, Ramón. "Asian Americo: Paredes in Asia and the Borderlands; A Response to Jose E. Limon." *American Literary History* 21, no. 3 (September 1, 2009): 584–594. https://doi.org/10.1093/alh/ajp023.

———. *Chicano Narrative: The Dialectics of Difference*. The Wisconsin Project on American Writers. Madison: University of Wisconsin Press, 1990.

Sánchez, Rosaura, and Beatrice Pita. *He Walked In and Sat Down, and Other Stories*. Albuquerque: University of New Mexico Press, 2001.

Singh, Nikhil Pal. *Black Is a Country: Race and the Unfinished Struggle for Democracy*. Cambridge, MA: Harvard University Press, 2004.

Smith, Caleb. *The Prison and the American Imagination*. Yale Studies in English. New Haven, CT: Yale University Press, 2009.

"Songs My Mother Never Taught Me." Mosquito Association, n.d. Center for the Study of the Korean War.

Soto, Sandra K. *Reading Chican@ like a Queer: The De-mastery of Desire*. 1st ed. History, Culture, and Society Series, Center for Mexican American Studies. Austin: University of Texas Press, 2010.

Starr, William John. "The Fighter Pilot's Hymn Book," 1957.

Streeby, Shelley. *American Sensations: Class, Empire, and the Production of Popular Culture*. American Crossroads 9. Berkeley: University of California Press, 2002.

Sutton, Francis X. "The Ford Foundation and Columbia." Presented at the University Seminar on Columbia University, Columbia University, New York, November 16, 1999.

———. "The Ford Foundation: The Early Years." *Daedalus* 116, no. 1 (1987): 41–91.

Suzuki, Erin. *Ocean Passages: Navigating Pacific Islander and Asian American Literatures*. Philadelphia: Temple University Press, 2021.

Tadiar, Neferti Xina M. *Things Fall Away: Philippine Historical Experience and the Makings of Globalization*. Post-Contemporary Interventions. Durham, NC: Duke University Press, 2009.

TallBear, Kimberly. *Native American DNA: Tribal Belonging and the False Promise of Genetic Science*. Minneapolis: University of Minnesota Press, 2013.

Tucker, Holly. *Blood Work: A Tale of Medicine and Murder in the Scientific Revolution*. 1st ed. New York: W. W. Norton, 2011.

Valdez, Luis. *Zoot Suit and Other Plays*. Houston: Arte Público, 1992.

Vargas, Deborah R. *Dissonant Divas in Chicana Music the Limits of La Onda*. Minneapolis: University of Minnesota Press, 2012.

Villa, Raúl. *Barrio-Logos: Space and Place in Urban Chicano Literature and Culture*. 1st ed. History, Culture, and Society Series. Austin: University of Texas Press, 2000.

Wiegman, Robyn. "Whiteness Studies and the Paradox of Particularity." *boundary 2* 26, no. 3 (1999): 115–150. https://www.jstor.org/stable/303743.

Williams, Raymond. *Marxism and Literature*. Marxist Introductions. Oxford: Oxford University Press, 1977.

Woo, Susie. "Imagining Kin: Cold War Sentimentalism and the Korean Children's Choir." *American Quarterly* 67, no. 1 (2015): 25–53. https://doi.org/10.1353/aq.2015.0012.

Yoneyama, Lisa. *Cold War Ruins: Transpacific Critique of American Justice and Japanese War Crimes*. Durham, NC: Duke University Press, 2016.

———. "Toward a Decolonial Genealogy of the Transpacific." *American Quarterly* 69, no. 3 (2017): 471–482. https://doi.org/10.1353/aq.2017.0041.

INDEX

Joo Ok Kim is Assistant Professor of Literature at the University of California, San Diego.